Audio Systems Technology

LEVEL III

Handbook for Installers and Engineers

Other audio technology books from NSCA:

Audio Systems Technology, Level I

Audio Systems Technology, Level II

Audio Systems Technology

LEVEL III
Handbook for Installers and Engineers

Written by
Bob Bushnell and Melvin J. Wierenga

National Systems Contractors Association

PROMPT®
PUBLICATIONS

PROMPT© Publications is an imprint of Howard W. Sams & Company, 2647 Waterfront Parkway, E. Dr., Indianapolis, IN 46214-2041.

International Standard Book Number: 0-7906-1178-3
Library of Congress Catalog Card Number: 99-64939

Acquisitions Editor: Alice Tripp
Editor: Kim Heusel
Assistant Editor: Crickett Franklin
Typesetting: Kim Heusel
Cover Design: Christy Pierce
Graphics Conversion: Christy Pierce

PRINTED IN THE UNITED STATES OF AMERICA

9 8 7 6 5 4 3 2 1

Contents

Preface ix
Dedication and Acknowledgments xi
About the Authors xii

Chapter 1
Intermediate Audio
   Calculations & Acoustics, by Bob Bushnell **1**
The Speed of Sound 2
Sound Power Levels 3
Sound Intensity Levels 4
Sound Pressure Levels 5
Combining Decibel Measurements 6
Calculate Average Absorption Coefficient 7
Calculate/Measure Critical Distance 10
Calculate RT60 for a
   Simple Space Using Different Methods
   (e.g. Sabine & Fitzroy) 11
Calculate Needed Acoustic Gain (NAG)
   and Potential Acoustic Gain (PAG) 13
Identify Sources of, and Differences
   Between Flutter, Echo, and Reverberation 15
Questions 16

Chapter 2
Codes, Standards,
   & Safety, by Melvin J. Wierenga **19**
Overview: A Brief Description and Background of the
   National Electrical Code® and OSHA 20
National Electrical Code® 22
1993 Code Article 640 22
1999 Code Article 640 25
Ten Significant Changes to Article 640 25
1993 Code Article 820 35
OHSA 40

State / Federal Relationships 41
Enforcement Procedures 42
Postings Required.. 44
Penalties 46
Questions 55

Chapter 3
***Circuits, Switching,
  and Grounding,*** *by Bob Bushnell* **57**
Circuit Analysis 58
Current Calculations
  in a Closed-Loop Circuit 59
Analysis of Transistor Circuits 81
Ground References... 91
Identification of Ground Loops 92
Questions 99

Chapter 4
Systems Components, *by Bob Bushnell* **101**
Advanced Microphones 102
Power Amplifiers 110
Mixing Consoles.. 117
Audio Transformers 125
Questions 131

Chapter 5
Loudspeaker Systems, *by Bob Bushnell* **133**
Large Loudspeaker Arrays 134
Connection and Aiming of Large Loudspeaker Arrays 140
Questions 146
Testing of Large Loudspeaker Arrays 147
Questions 152

Chapter 6

Troubleshooting & Testing, *by Bob Bushnell* **157**
Troubleshooting Audio Systems Wiring 158
System Troubleshooting 163
Equipment Testing 170
Advanced Assembly 177
Questions 184

Chapter 7

System Design, *by Bob Bushnell* **187**
Architectural Mapping 188
Small Systems Layout 197
Questions 205

Chapter 8

System Equalization,
    Alignment, & Adjustment, *by Bob Bushnell* **207**
Basic Equalization 208
System Signal Alignment 215
Signal Processing Adjustment 220
Questions 224

Chapter 9

Project Management, *by Bob Bushnell* **227**
Interpersonal Communications 228
Project Analysis 232
As-Built Documentation 239
Questions 243

Appendix A
NICET Level III Work Elements
    NOT Covered in This Book 247
Level III Noncore General Work Elements 248
Level III Special Work Elements 250

Appendix B
Answers to Chapter Questions and Problems 255

Appendix C
The NICET Audio Certification Program 261
Levels, Work Elements, and Requirements 261
Applying and Preparing for Testing 263
A Personal Study/Review Program 263
Test-Taking Strategies 266
Moving Up: Strategies for the Subsequent Tests 267
Costs of Certification 267
Recertification 268
Being Certified: Promote It! 268

Appendix D
Selected Resources for Further Study 271

Index 275

Preface

How to Use This Book

This book is part of the NSCA *Audio Technology Handbook* series. The series consists of three books, each corresponding to a different level of NICET certification. Level I is essentially entry-level material best suited to the technician trainee or for use as a review by experienced technicians preparing for NICET. Level II is for the installer or design engineer who has a few years of experience and either an associate's degree or equivalent. Level III is for the more advanced technician who has several years of job experience and an associate's degree or equivalent. While each book in the series contains its own unique information, there is also some overlap from one level to the next. This intentional dovetailing provides repetition on the most important, fundamental points and allows the entire series to be used as a systematic, progressive course of study from the basics on up to the intermediate and advanced.

This book is meant to be used in a variety of ways:

- As a study and preparation guide for those seeking NICET certification in audio systems.
- As a training manual for installers and designers of audio systems.
- As an overview of the fundamental things a good audio technician should know.
- As a reference guide for installers and engineers needing a one-stop source of practical technical audio information.

The content of the chapters is organized loosely on "work elements," the subjects encountered on the NICET exams. All of the "core" elements and most of the "general" work elements are represented here, and each chapter begins by stating the NICET work element descriptions that apply to that chapter's content. Because many of NICET's "special" work elements deal with special systems or subjects that are not universal to the present-day audio industry, and because they are elective on NICET exams, we have chosen not to discuss them at length in this book. A list of work elements *not* discussed can be found in the appendix of this book. If you are not familiar with NICET's audio technician certification program you can read about it at the end of the book in the section entitled "The NICET Audio Certification Program."

Each chapter concludes with a Questions section, which encourages readers to test their understanding of the chapter content by attempting to answer a series of questions. Answers and solutions to all review questions can be found in the appendix at the back of this book. Trainers may want to use the Questions as homework or as an aid for live instruction. For those preparing for the NICET exams, the questions are an excellent way to get familiar with NICET-type exam questions.

Jay Johnson

Dedication and Acknowledgments

NSCA gratefully dedicates this book to Jay Johnson, longtime NSCA board member and audio industry leader. Jay's vision of a highly professional, certified technical audio workforce is being realized due to his leadership and dedication. This book is his legacy; it is both a culmination of his efforts to create an audio technician certification program and the beginning of new era of training and education that will raise the standard for all audio professionals.

We would also like to thank the following people who played a major role in making this book possible: Larry Garter, Brad Nelson, Katie McDonald, and Alice Tripp.

About the Authors

Bob Bushnell has an extensive background in electronics, serving in various capacities such as audio maintenance engineer, system designer, project coordinator, and chief engineer. Among other things, he organized and headed Bushnell Electronics Corporation, an early manufacturer of custom recording consoles. Later he was a system designer for Mitsubishi Pro Audio Group. He has participated in seminars at Brigham Young University in Provo, Utah, and has given several papers at AES conventions. Currently, he heads BL Associates, which provides writing, technical writing, and consulting services.

Bob Bushnell

Melvin Wierenga

Melvin J. Wierenga is a respected consultant to the systems contracting industry and has been a key developer of industry-related UL standards and NEC codes. Wierenga is a founding member of the NSCA and has held several offices on the NSCA board of directors, including president. He has also been president of Ascom, an electronic systems contracting company. Wierenga is one of the primary developers of the NICET Audio Technician Certification Program. He is owner of Wierenga & Associates, a consulting firm to the systems contracting industry.

Chapter 1

Intermediate Audio Calculations & Acoustics

by Bob Bushnell

- **NICET Work Element 15001, Intermediate Audio Calculations**
- **NICET's Description:** "*Perform electrical and acoustical calculations involving power, amplitude, the speed of sound, and sound pressure level.*"

- **NICET Work Element 16004, Acoustics**
- **NICET's Description:** "*Solve problems involving sound in various spaces. Define and use octaves and sabines. Consider such factors as boundaries, material absorption, diffraction, reverberation, critical distance, etc.*"

Note: The two work elements discussed in this section are similar to NICET work elements 13004, 13005, and 13006 (discussed in "Audio Systems Technology, Level II) but are more advanced.

The Speed of Sound

The term "speed" is a relatively casual term, whereas the term "velocity" is more specific; it indicates the direction of motion as well. You might be traveling at a speed of 60 miles per hour, or you might be traveling at a velocity of 60 miles per hour, northwesterly.

If you are at sea level on earth, with the temperature at 72°F, and tolerable humidity; the speed of sound is approximately 1130 feet per second (fps). As you go up in altitude, the speed decreases. The change can be disregarded except for unusual circumstances. For example, at sea level, the speed is 1130 fps; but at 10,000 feet above sea level, the speed is 980 fps. This is a decrease of approximately 15%. Changes in humidity affect sound velocity very slightly.

The speed of sound changes with ambient temperature. It increases at about 1.1 feet per second per degree rise. The equation is:

$$c = 49\sqrt{(459.4 + °F)}$$

where c is the speed of sound and °F is the temperature in degrees Fahrenheit. Since the speed of sound changes, the wavelength changes. If you are working with a system using narrow-band filters, you may experience a change in the system's frequency response simply due to the change in temperature.

The equation in metric units is this:

$$c = 20.6\sqrt{(273 + °C)}$$

If the air temperature is -40 °C, what is the speed of sound? Substituting in the above equation, we have:

$$c = 20.6\sqrt{(273 + -40)}$$

After calculating, your answer should be 314 m/s, or 314 meters per second.

The speed of sound through other media depends on the density of the medium in question. Through fresh water, the speed is approximately 4,856 fps; through soft wood it is approximately 10,990 fps; and through glass it is approximately 17,000 fps.

Humidity affects acoustical frequency response. At relatively low values of humidity (around 20%), the spreading loss at high frequencies (upwards of 5 kHz) is much greater than low- and midband frequencies.

Sound Power Levels

Sound power is measured in watts, but has no area relationship. The accepted reference for sound power is 1 pW, expressed as 1 picowatt. Sound power is equivalent to acoustic power, but must not be confused with amplifier power. The accepted term for sound power levels expressed in decibels is dB-PWL.

How many decibels above the reference level is 1 W? Here is an equation that should be familiar to you:

$$dB = 10\log (P_2 \div P_1)$$

We know that P_1 equals 1 pW, and P_2 equals 1 W. Substituting in the equation, we have:

$$dB = 10\log (1 \div 1 \times 10^{-9})$$

Therefore, your answer should be 90 dB-PWL. Do you agree? If not, why?

Aha! Yes, 1 picowatt equals 1×10^{-12} watts, not 1×10^{-9}. Before you go back to your calculator, note the relationship between the reference level and the value we're solving for. Since both the reference level and the given level use the number 1, can't we reduce the calculation to make use of scientific notation? Is it possible that the given level we're trying to find is 120 dB-PWL? Go ahead and solve the equation.

Sound Intensity Levels

Sound intensity is equal to sound power divided by the total spherical area over which the sound power is transmitted. Sound intensity is measured in watts per square centimeter. We quote: "The sound intensity in a specified direction at a point in a sound field is defined as the rate of flow of sound energy through a unit area at that point, the unit area being perpendicular to the specified direction." We are indebted to *Acoustical Designing in Architecture* by Dr. Vern Knudsen, 1950, published by John Wiley & Sons, Inc. for the quotation.

Two points of interest in that quotation are "the rate of flow," or how much sound, and "a unit area." If you consider the sound source essentially to be a point, then as the signal radiates, the area of radiation increases.

$$I = \frac{p^2}{10^7 \rho c}$$

where I is the intensity, p is the pressure in dynes per square centimeter, p is the density of air in grams per cubic centimeter, and c is the velocity of sound in centimeters per second.

Note that sound waves radiate from a point source outwards in a spherical direction. In the sound design and installation industry measuring sound intensity is very uncommon. We use instead sound pressure levels.

Sound Pressure Levels

Although sound energy is nothing more than compression and rarefaction of air molecules, measuring that energy on an absolute basis is a cumbersome and exacting task. It requires rather expensive equipment in skilled hands.

For convenience, sound pressure levels are measured on a relative basis, using the decibel. Since the decibel is a ratio, we must provide a reference. The accepted reference level is 20 µPa, expressed as 20 micropascals. The pascal is a unit of pressure, which is equal to 1 newton per square meter. The newton is the unit of force, which is equal to a force applied to a body having a mass of 1 kg (kilogram), accelerating that body to 1 m/s², or 1 meter per second per second. SPL is the accepted acronym for sound pressure level.

If the SPL is 120 dB, what is the pressure in pascals? We'll use an equation that you should recognize:

$$\frac{P_2}{P_1} = 10^{\left(\frac{db}{20}\right)}$$

therefore, P_2 is the unknown, P_1 is the reference pressure, and dB is equal to 120. Restating the equation, we have:

$$P_2 = P_1 \times 10^{\left(\frac{db}{20}\right)}$$

and calculating, you should have arrived at 20 pascals as your answer. Granted, you won't be using pascals over decibels, but you should be aware of the relationships.

Combining Decibel Measurements

A decibel number expresses a ratio, not a numeric quantity. In addition, decibels are a logarithmic expression. Therefore, they can't be added numerically without wrong answers. However, relative changes can be added. If a sound source is producing a level of 84 dB, and the operator increases the level by 3 dB, the new level is 87 dB.

Two levels can be added using logarithmic addition. If one sound source (**A**) is producing a level of 60 dB, and a second source (**B**) in the same room is producing a level of 63 dB, what is the resultant sound level? The equation looks like this:

$$\text{Total SPL} = 10\log (10^{\text{ SLP(A)/10}} + 10^{\text{ SLP(B)/10}})$$

Then substituting, we have:

$$\text{dB Total} = 10\log (10^{(60 \div 10)} + 10^{(63 \div 10)})$$

Then simplifying, we have:

$$\text{dB Total} = 10\log (10^6 + 10^{6.3})$$

Then solving, your answer should be 64.8 dB. When working with decibels, it is pointless to use more than one place to the right of the decimal point. If you calculate the voltage difference between +4 dBu and +4.1 dBu, you will find the difference very slight.

It is worthwhile to note that when combining two decibel numbers, if they are further apart than 10 dB, the larger value may be taken while ignoring the smaller value. This procedure is valid unless the acoustic spectra of the two values are quite different.

With SPL (Sound Pressure Level) measurements, if the two decibel values are the same, the combined level will be 3 dB higher. Combining decibel measurements must be done with an awareness of what you are combining. For example, if you are combining a

100 Hz sine wave tone with an SPL measurement of 100 dB, and a 2 kHz sine wave tone with an SPL measurement of 100 dB, the resultant number will not be 3 dB higher.

Combining equal voltages or currents expressed in decibel format will increase the level by 6 dB.

Calculate Average Absorption Coefficient

If sound is being transmitted through an area of 1 foot by 1 foot, that is an open window to the outdoors, the open window has an absorption coefficient of 1.0. That is, all the sound impressed on that 1-foot area is absorbed by the outdoors, and none is returned to the room. That absorption coefficient applies at 125, 250, 500, 1000, 2000, and 4000 Hz, each frequency being one octave higher than the previous. As well, that absorption coefficient applies throughout the audio spectrum.

If we simply express that as "1.0" or 1, we may have confusion. If we define that as one sabin, that will help resolve the confusion. Why a sabin? Wallace W. Sabine did some original work as to the absorption of sound by various materials, including air. He did this work between 1895 and 1900, barely 100 years ago. So far, we've stated that one sabin is equal to the absorption coefficient of 1 square foot of matter.

If we have a room with totally reflecting surfaces, no absorption at any frequency (impossible to achieve in reality), we might measure an absorption coefficient of zero. Even air itself has an absorption coefficient; as the humidity increases, so does the absorption coefficient.

Absorption coefficients have been measured for a multitude of materials, ranging from air to lead. The table on the next page shows a few of the more common materials in use, including humans.

Absorption Coefficients in Hz						
Material	**125**	**250**	**500**	**1000**	**2000**	**4000**
Brick, unglazed	0.03	0.03	0.03	0.04	0.05	0.07
Carpet, heavy on underlayment	0.08	0.27	0.39	0.34	0.48	0.63
Audience, on upholstered seats, per square foot of floor	0.60	0.74	0.88	0.96	0.93	0.85
Wood floor	0.15	0.11	0.10	0.07	0.06	0.07
Heavy velour fabric, 18 oz/yd², draped to half area	0.14	0.35	0.55	0.72	0.70	0.65
Acoustic ceiling tile, on firring strips	0.47	0.65	0.75	0.84	0.83	0.81
Acoustic ceiling tile, on hard material	0.08	0.44	0.79	0.83	0.74	0.65
Sheetrock, 1/2", nailed to 2 x 4, 16" oc	0.29	0.10	0.05	0.04	0.07	0.09
Air, sabins/100 ft³ @ 50% RH				0.90	2.30	7.20

In the United States, we still use feet and inches. If you wish to calculate absorption coefficients using the metric system, it's a simple task to perform the conversion. You'd probably refer to tables published in England or Europe, to determine what most of the world is using.

Let us assume that a given room has dimensions of 20 feet in length, 14 feet in width, and a ceiling height of 8 feet. The room has one door, 3'0" by 6'8", with no windows. Let us further assume that the floor is totally covered with heavy carpet over concrete, the walls are Sheetrock over studs, and the ceiling is acoustical tile, and there are no people in the room. Are the walls painted? It makes little difference.

	Area	Absorption coefficient	Total absorption coefficient
20 x 14 floor			
20 x 14 ceiling			
20 x 8 wall x 2			
14 x 8 wall x 2			
Totals:			

What is the average absorption coefficient of the room? You calculate the area of each different material, multiply that by the absorption coefficient for that material, add the results together, then divide by the total area of the room. One tip: in the table above, there are no figures for the door material. But the door has an area of approximately 18 square feet, a small proportion of the total area. We know that the door construction is similar to the wall, so we can consider the door area as part of the wall area.

You could do all the calculations using only your calculator, but let's do part of the calculations on paper.

Haven't we forgotten something? What frequency do we want? Let's calculate for all six frequencies. Did you get the same answers as we did?

> 125 Hz = 0.18 sabins
> 250 Hz = 0.23 sabins
> 500 Hz = 0.32 sabins
> 1 kHz = 0.32 sabins
> 2 kHz = 0.34 sabins
> 4 kHz = 0.38 sabins

Now that you've finished the calculations, you have six numbers which are the average absorption coefficients of the room in sabins for each of the primary frequencies. Reviewing our earlier discussions about open windows and totally reflecting rooms, we see that this room has fairly low numbers. The room might be described as "live," or "zingy," or as having "too much rever-beration." However, the room will be slightly "boomy," (have too much reverberation at low frequencies), but otherwise ac-ceptable. Later in this element, we will discuss the differences between flutter, echo, and reverberation.

Calculate/Measure Critical Distance

When sound is transmitted within a room, at some physical distance the reverberant sound within the room becomes equal to the direct sound. This distance is called the critical distance, and the accepted term is D_C. If the room is very live, with a long reverbera-tion time, the critical distance won't be very great. If the room is rather dead, with a short reverberation time, the critical distance could be equal to the maximum distance within the room.

The critical distance is directly related to the Q of the loud-speaker array. The basic equation is:

$$D_C = 0.141 \times \sqrt{(Q\,S\,\bar{a})}$$

where Q is the directivity of the sound source, S is the surface area of the room, and null-A is the room absorption. Q may either be measured, or more easily, obtained from the specifications for the desired loudspeaker or horn/driver combination.

The critical distance may be measured using a calibrated loudspeaker. From this measurement, you can calculate the room absorption. Then, from these measurements and calculations, you can measure the axial Q of a new device. Davis and Davis in *Sound System Engineering*, second edition, discuss this fascinating sub-ject in detail.

Calculate RT$_{60}$ for a Simple Space Using Different Methods (e.g. Sabine & Fitzroy)

RT$_{60}$ is the calculated or measured number for reverberation time in a room. RT stands for Reverberation Time, and the subscript $_{60}$ refers to the decay in decibels from the steady-state sound field. In practice, achieving a decay of 60 decibels may be difficult; requiring that the steady-state field of 110 dB SPL decaying to 50 dB SPL. In these cases, a 30 dB decay will be measured, then extrapolated downward to create the 60 dB slope.

Wallace W. Sabine's equation for calculating reverberation time is:

$$RT_{60} = 0.049 \ V/Sa$$

where **0.049** is a constant, **V** is the volume of the room in cubic feet, **S** is the surface area of the room in square feet, and **a** is the average absorption coefficient. We can expand the equation to show each of the surface area and absorption coefficients required. This equation is quite similar to the one above:

$$RT_{60} = 0.049 \ V/(S_1a_1 + S_2a_2 + S_3a_3 + \ldots)$$

where S_1 is the area of the first material, a_1 is the absorption coefficient of the first material, and so on until you have included all of the materials in the equation.

We'll use the room parameters on the preceding page, since the absorption coefficients have already been calculated. However, we'll add 20 upholstered theatre seats with a person in each of the seats. The people may be female or male, it doesn't matter. We'll even copy the table here and add the seats to the table.

	125 Hz TAC	250 Hz TAC	500 Hz TAC	1 kHz TAC	2 kHz TAC	4 kHz TAC
20 x 14 floor						
20 x 14 ceiling						
20 x 8 x 2 wall						
14 x 8 x 2 wall						
Seats with humans						
Totals:						

Ah, yes, how big are the seats with humans? After contacting a local theatre, we learned that an average seat and human occupy about 27 inches in width, and 31 inches in depth, which is an area of 5.8 ft². We've rounded it off to 6 ft².

Now that we know the reverberation time using Mr. Sabine's equation, let's look at a similar equation developed by Daniel Fitzroy. He realized that in rooms where the surfaces had rather different absorption coefficients, the reverberation time measured was longer than the calculated time. Accordingly, he modified Sabine's equation to read:

$$RT_{60} = 0.049V/S^2 \times ((2(XY)/TA_{XY}) + (2(XZ)/TA_{XZ}) + (2(YZ)/TA_{YZ}))$$

That's an eyeful, indeed. We shall clarify the terms. **V** is the volume of the room; **S** is the total surface area; **X**, **Y**, and **Z** refer to each of the room dimensions; and **TA** is the total absorption coefficient for each of those surfaces. It seems appropriate to consider the long dimension of our room as the **X** term, the short dimension as the **Y** term, and the height as the **Z** term.

As with all long equations, if you work from the inside out, it will be easier to calculate. That is, calculate each of the portions beginning with $2(XY)/TA_{XY}$, then add them together, then multiply by the first part. Even though you can't bring a computer to the

NICET exam, equations of this size are nicely solved using a spreadsheet and building the cells.

Our answers, using Fitzroy's equation are:

$$
\begin{array}{rcl}
125\ \text{Hz} &=& 13.9\ \text{sabins} \\
250\ \text{Hz} &=& 40.1\ \text{sabins} \\
500\ \text{Hz} &=& 80.1\ \text{sabins} \\
1\ \text{kHz} &=& 100.2\ \text{sabins} \\
2\ \text{kHz} &=& 57.3\ \text{sabins} \\
4\ \text{kHz} &=& 44.6\ \text{sabins}
\end{array}
$$

Calculate Needed Acoustic Gain (NAG) and Potential Acoustic Gain (PAG)

Don and Carolyn Davis started a new deal with their inauguration of the PAG/NAG concept. Potential Acoustic Gain and Needed Acoustical Gain are powerful tools when used with care. They are very useful for outdoor acoustical environments, and useful for indoor acoustical environments.

An outdoor acoustical environment is a free-field situation; the majority of sound waves from the loudspeakers or cluster travel outward, with little reflection. If the amphitheater is filled with people, so much the better, for the human body is an excellent sound absorber.

If you are working in an anechoic chamber, where all sound waves are direct and there are no reflective surfaces, you are in a nearly ideal free-field situation. In contrast, an indoor acoustical environment has various reflective surfaces, providing reverberation, possibly echo and flutter.

What is PAG? It is the increase in SPL (Sound Pressure Level) or the maximum acoustic gain that can be obtained from the sound reinforcement system before feedback occurs.

13

For an outdoor environment only, the equation for PAG is:

$$PAG = 20\log\frac{(D_1 \times D_0)}{(D_2 \times D_S)}$$

If we restate the equation on one line to make calculations easier, we have:

$$PAG = 20\log((D_1 \times D_0) \div (D_2 \times D_S))$$

What is NAG? It is the required SPL for the farthest listener to hear the amplified sound at the same level as the unamplified talker to the nearest listener.

The equation is:

$$NAG = 20\log D_0 - 20\log EAD$$

Defining the terms; D_1 is the distance from the microphone to the nearest loudspeaker, D_0 is the distance to the most distant listener, D_2 is the distance from the loudspeaker to the farthest listener, D_S is the distance from the talker to the microphone, **EAD** is the equivalent acoustic distance.

PAG/NAG Term Definitions

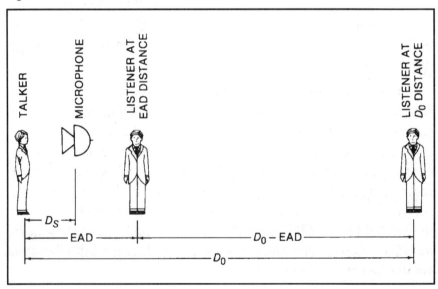

The PAG/NAG equations must accommodate the amount of absorptive material on the walls, floor, and ceiling; the volume of the room; and the directivity of the loudspeakers. Because of the various equations involved, and the amount of material that must be covered, we will not go into the discussion of PAG/NAG for indoor environments. We're not shrugging off an excellent topic, it would simply take too much time to study here. It is suggested that the books by Ballou and Davis (see the appendix "Selected Resources for Further Study" at the back of this book) be studied after this manual has been studied in detail.

Identify Sources of, and Differences Between Flutter, Echo, and Reverberation

An uneducated person is likely to use the terms "flutter," "echo," and "reverberation" interchangeably. But it is important to understand that the three terms do not mean the same thing.

Reverberation is one of the acoustic qualities of a room, indicating the decay of sound within that room caused by the various materials and the air itself. The reverberation time provides the "timbre" or "sound" of a room, and may be short (<0.5 seconds) or long (>2.0 seconds). For any room, the architect or acoustician should pay attention to the reverberation time.

Echo refers to a single reflection of a sound wave back to its source in sufficient strength and with a sufficient time lag to be separately identified by your ear. Shouting between two mountains may produce an echo, which is not reverberation. The recording industry uses "echo" chambers, which were originally rooms with a volume of approximately 1000 ft^3, hard plaster on all surfaces, equipped with a loudspeaker and a microphone. Truly, they should have been termed "reverberation" chambers, but the term has stuck since just after World War II. Digital devices have since taken their place.

It is difficult to create echo in a room, unless the room is badly designed. If the speed of sound in air is 1130 ft/second, and the Hääs effect states that the time interval between two sounds must be greater than 50 milliseconds to be perceived as two distinct sounds, how long must the hall be for this effect to occur indoors? This assumes that the hall has two highly reflective parallel surfaces. The envelope, please... The answer is 56 feet.

Flutter refers to continuous sound reflections between two parallel surfaces, limited in time only by the absorption coefficients of the surfaces, and the natural loss of energy. Yes, you're right, the example given above for echo also applies here. It is possible for a room to exhibit both echo and flutter. It will be a poor room, indeed.

Questions

1. If the ambient temperature is 110 °F, what is the speed of sound?

2. If the ambient temperature is -40 °F, what is the speed of sound?

3. If the ambient temperature is approximately -273 °F, and the volume is greater than 4 x 10^6 cubic feet, what is the speed of sound?

4. Achieving an absorption coefficient of 4.5 in a room isn't difficult for a good architect.
    a. Only if he's designing an anechoic chamber.
    b. No.
    c. Yes.
    d. Only if the OSHA inspector can verify it.

5. Wallace Sabine did his work on sound absorption by materials:
    a. In 1795.
    b. In his laboratory.
    c. In 1855.
    d. Between 1895 and 1900.

6. Air does not absorb sound.

        a. True.

        b. False.

        c. Only when heated.

        d. Only when it's raining.

7. What is the velocity of sound in a vacuum?

        a. The same as in air.

        b. Whatever the starship *Enterprise* measured.

        c. Zero.

        d. No velocity.

8. The absorption coefficient of a Sheetrock wall backed by studs is:

        a. Unmeasurable.

        b. 1.0 at 250 Hz.

        c. 0.10 at 250 Hz.

        d. 0.4 at 4 kHz.

9. The absorption coefficient of an outside window is 1.0.

        a. Only when it's open.

        b. True.

        c. False.

        d. At 4 kHz.

10. Critical distance is:

        a. When you're too far away from the restroom.

        b. The distance where the reverberant sound is equal to the direct sound.

        c. The distance where the direct sound is equal to the reverberant sound.

        d. Where the audience can comfortably hear.

11. The equation for calculating reverberation time was developed by:

        a. Morris Fitzroy.

        b. Martin Sabine.

        c. Wallace Sabine.

        d. NSCA.

12. The calculations for PAG and NAG were developed by Wallace Sabine.

   a. True.

   b. No, by Carolyn and Don Davis.

   c. No, by Daniel Fitzroy.

   d. False.

13. Flutter, echo, and reverberation are all characteristics of a room.

   a. False.

   b. True.

   c. True for reverberation only.

   d. True for echo only.

Chapter 2

Codes, Standards, & Safety

by Melvin J. Wierenga

NICET Work Element 15007, NEC® 640
NICET's Description: *"Understand the contents of NEC® Article 640"*

NICET Work Element 15008, NEC® 720
NICET's Description: *"Understand the contents of NEC® Article 720"*

NICET Work Element 16005, NEC® 820
NICET's Description: *"Understand the contents of NEC® Article 820"*

NICET's: Work Element 15009, OSHA
NICET's Description: *"Assure compliance with OSHA and state safety requirements. Correct and/or report violations."*

Overview: A Brief Description and Background of the National Electrical Code® and OSHA

We introduced both the NEC® and OSHA in *Audio Systems Technology, Level II*. In this chapter, we will move on to more detailed and specific information that you will be involved with in your work as a Lead or Senior Technician or possibly as a Systems Layout Person.

Once again, we would like to stress the importance of developing a good working relationship with the "Authority Having Jurisdiction"—the AHJ. This person more than likely has been an electrician for many years and has grown up with the Code®. As an AHJ, he is required to attend a number of training sessions conducted by experts who have either written or helped write significant segments of the Code®. In many instances, the experts have also served as a panel member on the specific code-making panel that has responsibility for the subject matter that they are teaching.

When talking to the AHJ you may find that while he has excellent knowledge of 120/240VAC power and light circuits and their installation, he may not have as much knowledge, or accurate knowledge, about audio circuits, their characteristics, how to measure audio power and voltages, etc. Be careful not to get into an argument with an AHJ. He may interpret the code differently than you do and *the AHJ is the final authority*. He can waive any irregularities, or he can make you modify your installation as he sees fit. AHJs are unlikely to be sympathetic when their decision generates a cost overrun on your job. After you have completed an installation is not the time to find out that you have installed the wrong wire in a plenum space, neglected to use riser-rated cable while running all those vertical runs between floors in the five-story office building project, or have the wrong wire in the instrumentation cable tray. If you are the lead technician on a large project, it is recommended that you set up a meeting with the AHJ and review your project with him before you start pulling your wire or installing your equipment. Make sure that he isn't going to make you replace all of the speaker back boxes or reinstall your wire, or install different wire ties in the plenum, etc.

As a Level III Technician, you should have ready access to, or own a copy of, whichever version of the National Electric Code® is in effect for your project. Many technicians are not interested in spending much time reading or studying the Code®, but there is no way that you can totally escape it. Sooner or later you will be brought face to face with it and if you wait until that fateful day, you will lose out.

If you work in an area where the local government has its own Electrical Code, you will need to take the time to review it and determine if there are any portions that are applicable. A local Code usually will mention the National Electric Code® as the basic reference and then identify modifications that apply to the local area. The modifications may or may not apply to audio systems wiring, but if you have not checked out the local Code, you could be generating a real problem job instead of one that is completed on time and within budget.

OSHA can affect your project when you are laying out a system, bidding a system, or if you are the Lead Technician on the installation of a project. For example:

■ When doing a system layout or bidding a project you should be able to envision how the equipment will be installed. Does it require the use of scaffolding, a lift, or ladders? If so, how does that affect the time required to install the equipment? Does our company have a copy of the appropriate OSHA documents for reference? Does our company own OSHA-approved equipment? If not, what is the rental cost for OSHA-approved equipment?

■ When working as the Lead Installation Technician for a project, do you have a working knowledge of the federal OSHA safety requirements? Are you aware of additional requirements that may be part of your state OSHA program? Is there any requirement that you or the technicians working on your project must complete a specific OSHA-certified training program before using a piece of equipment such as an aerial lift?

National Electrical Code®

Introduction

The Code® is updated every three years. The 1993 version of the Code® is the basis for the current articles included in the NICET certification program. The 1999 Code® has just recently been published and includes a complete rewrite of Article 640. It is expected that sometime during 1999, an industry advisory committee from NSCA will be appointed and, along with NICET, will review and update the associated work elements and questions as needed. Because of this new article, you will find two sections that deal with Article 640, the first based on the 1993 Code® and the second based on the 1999 Code®.

The NICET work element requirement for Article 720 will be deleted during the next review. Shortly after NICET published its Audio Technician Program Manual, it was decided to remove Article 720 from the list of work elements because it really did not apply to the audio installation industry. As a result of that decision, there are no questions written for that work element.

1993 Code Article 640

Sound-Recording and Similar Equipment (1993)

Article 640 can be traced back to 1935 (and was probably originated prior to 1935) and except for updating in 1956 to include 70- and 25-volt audio program signals, remained virtually unchanged until the 1999 Code®.

Par.1.   Scope. This describes the equipment and wiring that is included. The terminology is difficult to interpret because it mixes a broad general category as well as terms like centralized distribution of sound, public address, speech-input systems, and electronic organs. When you get into Article 640-2(b) you find included a category of systems called "amplifying equipment associated with radio receiving stations in centralized distribution systems."

Par.2.   Applications. The major concern in Article 640-2(b) is in the last few words "shall comply with Article 725." There you will find information that generates confusion when trying to apply rules for 60 Hz AC mains voltage to typical audio signals.

Par.3.   Number of Conductors. Article 640-3 directs you to Table 1, Chapter 9 that is immediately after Article 820 near the rear of the Code® book. There you will find Table 1, an FPN, 10 notes to the tables, and Table 4. These tables and notes provide the information that is used to determine the number of conductors that are allowed in conduits. You can find additional information in Chapter 5, page 154 of NCSA's *Audio Systems Technology, Level II* handbook.

Par.4.   Wireways and Gutters. When looking at Article 640-4, review the exceptions as well as the referred Articles 362 and 374. Some projects have a significant amount of wiring installed in wireways and gutters, and there are some requirements that need to be followed. As you read these two articles, you need to sort out the specific information that applies to the project you are working on.

Par.5.   Conductors. My guess is that for the audio technician, Article 640-5 and its FPN (Fine Print Note) has caused more struggles and disagreements with the AHJ than any other article in the code. The problem is that frequently AHJ's do not have a good grasp on the difference between 60 HZ AC mains voltages and a speaker level audio signal, and do not have a quick and easy way to measure an audio signal like they have for measuring the voltage at an AC wall outlet. *A typical pocket AC voltmeter does not do a good job of measuring an audio signal such as the spoken word or a music source because they are signals with widely varying intervals of peaks and valleys with random time intervals, and the meter normally has a movement that is highly damped.*

Paragraph 5 also mentions Class 2 and Class 3 wiring.

Remember:

■ Class 2 wiring presents neither a shock nor fire hazard.

■ Class 3 wiring presents a shock hazard but not a fire hazard.

Par.6, 7, 8,
9,10,11. These paragraphs are grouped together because they are technically outdated for all practical purposes. These paragraphs relate to power wiring that was generated to operate speakers (prior to permanent magnet speakers) and early tube amplifiers that were commonly used in the 1930s and '40s. Flexible cords and storage batteries were primarily used for the power supplies and batteries used with early amplifiers. The circuit overcurrent protection and amplifiers paragraphs apply only to obsolete tubes and amplifiers.

Par. 12. The most important thing to remember with this paragraph is that it guides you to the section of the Code® which defines the various classes and groups of hazards. If you are installing equipment in any of the following areas, you need to check Articles in Chapter 5:

a. paint manufacturing plants.

b. wood products manufacturing plants.

c. chemical manufacturing plants.

d. petroleum refineries.

e. propane storage areas.

f. areas which have combustible metal dust (such as aluminum or magnesium), and coal, carbon, flour, grain, or plastic dusts.

Par. 13. Protection against physical damage consists mainly of common sense. You don't want to install equipment racks in places where they will be run into by forklifts or other mobile equipment. You need to make sure that a paging horn is not going to be knocked down from the beam or truss on which it is installed because it was hit by a traveling crane.

1999 Code Article 640

Audio Signal Processing, Amplification,
and Reinforcement Equipment

This Article was rewritten by a small group of people from the NSCA Codes and Standards committee for a number of reasons:

1. to provide the installing contractor and the AHJ with an unambiguous and clear Article which would cover all issues of electrical safety regarding audio systems and their installations;
2. to utilize terminology that reflects current technology;
3. to include a wide variety of installation environments;
4. to clarify the use of temporary/rental systems;
5. reformat to agree with current Articles;
6. provide definitions that are unique to our industry;
7. to rename the Article so that it reflected the breadth and usage of contemporary audio systems.

The chairman of the NSCA Committee on the Revision of Article 640, Mr. Bill Keezer, developed a paper that was presented at NCSA's 1998 Codes & Standards Committee meeting. The paper presented 10 significant changes to Article 640 that gives a good overview of this article.

Ten Significant Changes to Article 640

A. General

Article 1: Scope—The title now indicates more specifically the installed systems that are everyday types of systems that are installed by the audio systems industry. In the past there was confusion among AHJs and sometimes they would attempt to use Article 800 instead of Article 640. Now the types of systems are indicated in this paragraph and the areas in which they are typically installed is included in FPN No.1. Additionally, FPN No.2 was added at the request of UL® to indicate what systems and devices that are *not* included in this article.

Article 2: Definitions—Definitions were added as part of the format upgrading which took place. The intent of the definitions is to help clarify terminology for the AHJ and should be useful to the installer when working with the AHJ. Not all of the terms that are used in conjunction with audio systems are used in the article, but what is included will certainly assist installers and AHJs in determining how this article is applied.

Article 3: Locations and Other Articles—This article spells out important information that in the past had been difficult to find because it was either not included in the earlier versions of Article 640, or was scattered in various locations throughout the entire article. Now subparagraphs (a) through (k) have consolidated references for specific articles to look up when working with or in the specific conditions, areas, circuits, or locations listed.

Article 4: Protection of Electrical Equipment—Environmental exposure has been added as a possible source of damage that might cause a risk of fire, shock, or personal hazard. This means that air- or liquid-borne hazards must be considered in locating equipment. Some of those hazards would be things such as dust, precipitation, splashing water, chemicals, etc. For example, don't install an equipment cabinet or rack in a janitor's closet where the equipment would be exposed to splashing from a faucet or where someone might hang a dust mop above or adjacent to the cabinet or rack. In other words, use good old-fashioned common sense.

Article 5: Access to Electrical Equipment Behind Panels Designed to Allow Access—Again, this is a matter of good common sense. Make sure your wiring is neat and well organized so that it allows removal of panels, including suspended ceiling panels. You cannot lay wire above the ceiling and allow it to lie on the ceiling panels.

Article 6: Mechanical Execution of Work—Very similar to what is used in Article 725 and 800 but not restricted to just Classes 1, 2, and 3 wiring. This allows you to use communications and power supply circuitry cabling as well as for audio systems installations.

Note the FPN. Don't take the time to find the references indicated. They are totally inadequate to define the industry practices for audio systems wiring. There is nothing in *ANSI/TIA/EIA 568A-1995* other than general statements saying that installations must be neat and well organized. *ANSI/TIA/EIA 569-A-1997* covers in detail the considerations and guidelines for selecting appropriate horizontal and vertical backbone pathways for telecommunications systems. The only installation techniques provided by *ANSI/TIA/EIA 569-91* deal with generalities about how to strip insulation from a telephone cord, how to install a wire under a screw head or a nut, etc. Code Making Panel 16 will have the opportunity to correct this matter during the next code cycle.

Article 7: Grounding—Grounding audio systems has been an area of conflict with some Authorities Having Jurisdiction for many years. Finally, we have an article that addresses appropriate audio systems grounding and bonding techniques allowed by the Code®. Section (a) General is a newly written paragraph that replaces *exception d* found in the previous version of the Code®.

The other two sections give clear references to sections that apply to separately derived systems with 60 volts to ground, and the use of isolated ground receptacles. See APPENDIX D for selected resources for further study. Be sure and look at both of the following reprints. The first is *Fundamentals of Grounding, Shielding, and Interconnection* by Kenneth R. Fause, an article which appeared in the AES *Journal of the Audio Engineering Society,* Volume 43, Number 6, June 1995. The other reprint is an article from *Sound and Video Contractor* (S&VC), September 20, 1995, Volume 13, Number 9 titled *Power and Ground Systems at the Hamilton Place Theatre* by Philip Giddings.

Article 8: Grouping of Conductors—This article now covers just the currently applicable parts of the original Article 640- 6. It clarifies what is meant by the term "grouped" by adding the words *or bundled so as to be in close physical contact with each other.*

To further clarify this article, the reference to Section 300-3(C)(1) was added.

Article 9: Wiring Methods—

(a) Wiring to and Between Audio Equipment. The words for Section (a)(1) are identical to the wording used in earlier versions of the Code® . Section (a)(2) was introduced in 1996 and remains unchanged. It allows a separately derived power system that works well in some types of audio systems. Notice that this unique power system is a 120V, single-phase, three-wire system with *60 volts on each of two ungrounded conductors to a grounded neutral connector*. If you have systems with interconnected audio equipment located in distant areas of a large building, and they share common audio signal lines, this power system will help you provide a system with the least possible amount of hum. It's absolutely necessary for you to coordinate with a consultant, electricians, and the electrical engineer in the design and use of this unique power system. You also need to look closely at and understand all the requirements indicated in Article 530-71 through 73. Section (a)(3) clarifies that all audio systems covered by Article 640 are subject to the wiring requirements in Article 725 except for separately derived systems or connections to the premise wiring system.

(b) Auxiliary Power Supply Wiring. Typically used with audio equipment for emergency paging or fire alarm systems. Auxiliary power supplies typically range between 12-48 volts DC and may be rack mounted, freestanding adjacent to a rack, or remotely located. You need to refer to Article 725 for correct wire size and installation requirements. If you are using a battery as your auxiliary power supply, then you need to look at Article 480 for installation and overcurrent protection requirements. You also should look at both FPNs for the exceptions that apply to UPS usage and when audio equipment used as fire alarm system.

(c) Amplifier Wiring and Listing of Amplifiers. This section now spells out three significant changes:

1-when to use Class 1, Class 2, or Class 3 wiring.

2-amplifiers must be listed – see FPN 1 and 2.

3-overcurrent protection must be provided and it is permitted to be inherent in the amplifier.

The newest proposed changes to ANSI/UL 813 and ANSI/UL 6500 provide that under prescribed test conditions, the open circuit output voltage may not exceed 120 volts when using Class 2 wiring as covered in Article 725. This new output replaces the previous maximum 70V output rating and sets up the following rules:

A. It is permissible to use Class 1 or Class 3 wiring methods with a Class 2-listed amplifier; however, it will not be cost efficient.

B. Class 3 wiring may be used for output voltages up to 300V providing the amplifier is listed for use with Class 3 wiring and you use wire that is Class 3 rated. The main difference between Class 2 and Class 3 amplifiers is that the output and speaker terminals of a Class 3 system must be touchproof because of the potential shock hazard. It is permissible to use Class 1 wiring methods with a Class 3-listed amplifier, but it will not be cost efficient.

C. Class 1 wiring must be used for Class 1-listed amplifiers. That means that the wiring must be in a conduit or cable tray system and use wire with insulation suitable for 600V. If your cable is going into a cable tray you need to look at Sections 318-9 through 11 and use tray-rated cable. Class 1 wiring is considered hazardous because it presents both a shock *and* a fire hazard.

To get some idea of what this means in term of wire size, length of run, and amount of power you can deliver with no more than 1/2dB signal loss, take a look at Figure 2-1.

(d) Use of Audio Transformers and Autotransformers   In previous versions of the Code, there was no mention made of audio transformers or autotransformers. An autotransformer consists of a single

LOSS DUE TO SPEAKER LINES

(IMPORTANT: The appendix contains information that should be understood before the table is used.)

The choice of wire size for loudspeaker lines is determined by an economic balance of the cost of copper against the cost of power lost in the line. The following table gives a considerable amount of information to help solve this problem. Examples are provided to illustrate the use of the tabulation, including the method for determination of cross-talk level when one wire is common to two circuits feeding separate zones.

LENGTH OF 2-WIRE 70v LINE DELIVERING VARIOUS VALUES OF POWER AT 0.5db (12-1/2%) LOSS

Wire Size AWG	Resistance per 1000' Wire pair	Max Safe Current	Max Safe Power	Nominal Power in the load									
	.8 ohms			10W	15W	20W	30W	40W	60W	100W	200W	400W	1000W
#6	.8 ohms	50 Amp.	3500W	(Length of Line)				9100	6200	3640	1820	910	360 ft.
#8	1.28	35	2450				7800	5700	3900	2280	1140	570	230 ft.
#10	2.0	25	1750			9900	7300	5000	3700	2500	1450	730	150 ft.
#12	3.2	20	1400	9100	6200	4600	3100	2300	1600	910	460	230	90 ft.
#14	5.2	15	1000	5600	3800	2800	1900	1400	950	560	280	140	56 ft.
#16	8.0	6	420	3600	2400	1800	1200	900	600	370	180	90 ft.	
#18	13.0	3	210	2300	1500	1100	750	560	370	230 ft.			
#20	20.6	1	70	1400	960	710	480	350	240	110 ft.			
#22	32.6	.5	35	900	600	450	300 ft.						
	Load Impedance (ohms)			490	327	245	163	122	81	49	24.5	12.2	4.9

For 1 db loss, double all Lengths. For 25-volt line: divide all Lengths by 8, divide Maximum Safe Power by 2.8, and divide Load Impedance by 8.

EXAMPLES:

1. A Line composed of two #14 wires 5600 ft. long can supply 10 watts to the load at 70 v with 0.5 db loss. For a line double this length or double this resistance per 1000 ft., the loss is 1 db.

2. A line composed of two #14 wires has a resistance of 5.2 ohms per 1000 ft. of line, and it is allowed to carry up to 15 amperes (N.E.C.) or, at 70 volts, a power of 1000 watts.

3. The impedance of a load drawing 10 watts from a 70 volt line is 490 ohms.

4. A 1000 foot, 70 volt line is required for a load of 30 watts. Use #16 wire for a loss slightly less than 0.5 db or #18 for approximately 0.6 db loss.

5. 100 watts is to be supplied to a load by a 100 foot line. #22 wire would have little loss, but the Code limits the current in #22 to 0.5 ampere or 35 watts.

6. A pair of #18 wires can supply 200 watts at 70 volts (impedance 24.5 ohms) a distance of 110 feet with 0.5 db loss. The same line at 25 volts (impedance 200 ohms) may be only 14 ft. long for 0.5 db loss, but on safe power basis, the conductors would be overloaded 2.8 times.

7. A 1000 ft., 70 volt line consisting of 3 #16 wires (1 common) supplies power to two 15 watt loads in different zones. The resistance of the common is 4 ohms and each load impedance is 327 ohms. The voltage drop in the common due to one load is 4/327 (roughly .01) of the load voltage. The resulting cross-talk voltage ratio is approximately .01 or -40 db (inaudible).

8. Note that the length of line for 0.5 db loss, in a given conductor size, is inversely proportional to the power. Thus, for #14 wire pair and 100 watts, read 560 ft. from the Table; for 150 watts, dividing this by 1.5 obtain 374 ft.

APPENDIX

The above tabulation shows the length of cable that causes a reduction of power in the load of 0.5 db (12-1/2%). Half of this reduction is actually a line loss. The other half is power not taken from the amplifier because the load at the amplifier is not, for example, 122 ohms (40 w for 70 v), but greater by the line resistance. As an example, consider a 4000 foot pair of #10's, with a total resistance of 8 ohms, and a load intended to be 40 w at 70 v (impedance 122 ohms). The power delivered by the amplifier into its load of 122 plus 8 ohms is 37.7 w, the drop in the line is 4.3 volts, the power lost in the line is 2.3 watts, the voltage at the speaker is 65.7 and the power taken by the speaker is 35 w which is 12-1/2% or .5 db less than intended. However, only half of this is actually lost; the rest is simply not taken from the amplifier. An additional load of 2.3 watts may therefore be connected to the amplifier. The following rules apply:

(a) The power in the final load will be 0.5 db (12-1/2%) less than the tabulated values for the lengths tabulated, 1 db or 20% less for double the lengths, 2 db or 37% less for quadruple the lengths, and 3 db or 50% less for 6 times the lengths or for conductors with 6 times the resistance.

(b) One half the above reduction is line loss; the other half is available for additional load. To recover the latter half by adding additional load to the far end of the line, proceed as follows:

No. of times tabulated length	Increase Load Watts nominally	Actual Power Delivered to Load
1	7%	94% or -.3 db
2	15	87 or -.6
3	25	81 -.9
4	35	74 -1.3
5	49	67 1.7
6	65	61 2.1
7	85	54 2.7
8	115	48 3.2

(c) For example, 4000 ft. #10 pair to supply a nominally 40-watt load: Increase the apparent load 7% to 43 watts; then 40 watts are drawn from the amplifier and 37.5 watts are delivered to the speaker. If the line is to be 4 times this length or if the wire is to be 6 sizes smaller (#16), in either case to have 4 times the resistance, increase the apparent load 35% to 54 watts. Then again 40 watts are taken from the amplifier and 30 watts (74%) actually delivered to the speaker, the remainder being lost in the line.

Fig. 2-1. Courtesy of Altec Lansing

winding with multiple taps and is used primarily on the output of an amplifier or on the input of a speaker. It is intended to provide impedance and voltage conversions without primary to secondary isolation. Be sure and check the manufacturer's instruction sheet when using autotransformers to be sure that you do not exceed the maximum permissible current draw. One other thing to consider if your amplifier output terminals are isolated from ground: do not ground the common terminal of the autotransformer because it possibly violates the manufacturer's instructions and therefore would probably invalidate the warranty of the amplifier.

Article 10: Audio Systems Near Bodies of Water—There are unique restrictions when installing audio systems near to bodies of either natural or artificial water. Notice the exception for systems intended for use on boats, yachts, etc., and the FPN for underwater equipment.

a. Equipment supplied by Branch Circuit Power. If you are plugging in equipment supplied by branch circuit power, be sure and follow the requirements listed. People have died when electrocuted in instances where these instructions have not been followed.

b. Equipment not Supplied by Branch Circuits. There are still some specific rules to follow even if you are using a low-voltage power supply to power audio system equipment. Also note the FPN; you need to take into consideration if there is *any* branch circuit voltage involved.

B. *Permanent Audio System Installation*

Sections B and C cover two fundamentally different categories of audio systems. Section B applies to systems that are installed in fixed locations such as auditoriums, gymnasiums, factories, hospitals, churches, etc. Equipment cabinets or racks are normally used to house amplifiers, equalizers, switching, and control equipment, etc. Wiring is installed from the rack to loudspeakers, microphone locations, remote control equipment, etc. Section C is applicable to portable systems and systems that are set up on a temporary basis.

Article 21: Use of Flexible Cords and Cables—This article allows flexible cordage and cable connections, which will facilitate equipment servicing and still retain the ability to maintain an isolated technical ground. It provides the choice to completely assemble and test a system in the shop and install it on site very quickly with loudspeaker wiring, input wiring, and AC power wiring all connecting via plugs and connectors. This whole section is straightforward and follows accepted installation practices that are commonly used. Articles 725 and 110-3(b) are the only two references to other sections of the Code. Each of the possible configurations of flexible cord usage is covered:

a. between equipment and primary power

b. between loudspeakers and amplifiers or between loudspeakers

c. between equipment

d. between equipment and power supplies other than primary circuit power

e. between equipment racks and premises wiring systems

Article 22: Wiring of Equipment Racks—Don't be confused by the first two sentences of this article. The first says that an equipment rack must be at ground potential. The second says that it can be accomplished either through bonding techniques or by connecting the rack to the ground of a technical power system. If you use the technical power system grounding technique, you must isolate the entire rack from any other possible ground source. For instance, you would need to make sure the rack was not setting on structural steel beams, was not sitting on the cover of a metallic floor trough, or was not connected to metallic conduit. If you are the project manager or the crew chief for this type of installation, you need to coordinate closely with the electrician, the electrical engineer, and certainly the AHJ, ahead of time so they understand what you are doing.

Article 22: Conduit or Tubing—

(a) Number of Conductors. This subsection has not changed from the previous version of the Code.

(b) Nonmetallic Conduit or Tubing and Insulated Bushings. This subsection tells you what you need to know when you are talking with an electrician, AHJ, or electrical engineer and explaining to him or her how you need to accomplish the ground isolation for your rack. It says very plainly that you are allowed to use nonmetallic conduit or tubing and insulated bushings when using a technical ground system.

Article 23: Wireways, Gutters, and Auxiliary Gutters—The scope of this section is for the usage of audio signal conductors only. Any wiring for power supply cables falls under the specific articles of Chapter 3 that apply to the type of wireway or gutter being used.

Article 24: Loudspeaker Installation in Fire Resistance-Rated Partitions, Walls, and Ceilings—This should clarify any questions anyone might have regarding what speaker enclosure is needed for adequate fire resistance when installed in rated partions, walls, and ceilings.

C. Portable and Temporary Audio System Installations

This section deals with systems that use equipment that is picked up and moved from one location to another from time to time. It may be located in one place for anywhere from a few minutes to several days. The equipment may be a small system, may be rented, used with or without an operator, or it may be several semitrailer loads with a large crew of people to install and operate the system. The equipment is normally in portable cases with handles and normally uses audio equipment similar in function to that used with fixed systems. There are three differences that define a permanent system from a portable system:

1. Character of use and ownership—a college performing arts facility could very well use its own portable equipment, which would be moved or relocated during a performance, but would not be used in any other building on campus.

2. Transitory nature of a performance—performers might use their own equalizer or special effects equipment in the same performing arts facility during a performance, and then would take that

equipment along with them when the performance is complete.

3. Temporary nature of an event—touring concerts, circuses, carnivals, local festivals, Grand Prix auto racing, fairs, etc.

Article 41: Multipole Branch Circuits Cable Connectors—This is a brand-new section for Article 640, which in part was taken from Section 520-67. Note that this section deals with *connectors*, not circuits. You probably are familiar with portable loudspeaker input connectors that have been modified to use a standard (ANSI/NEMA) locking multipole branch circuit cable connector. They are frequently used in high-power touring and rental systems because they are readily available, can handle large-gauge cables, and have a positive locking capability. The intent of this section is to limit the use of this type of connector to amplifier output and speaker wiring and to allow only those connector styles that are not commonly encountered as part of a facility branch circuit wiring system.

Article 42: Use of Flexible Cords and Cables—This is very similar to *Article 21* aside from three exceptions. The first is in *42(b)* and *(c)* that specifies the use of either hard or extra hard usage cords to improve reliability. The second is in *42(d)* and adds the reference to *Article 445* regarding portable generators. The third is you should also look at *Article 250-34* regarding the grounding requirements for either portable or vehicle-mounted generators.

Article 43: Wiring of Equipment Racks—This article allows the use of nonmetallic racks for portable systems providing they do not allow access to Class 1, Class 3, or primary AC power without the use of a tool or removal of a protective cover.

Article 44: Environmental Protection of Equipment—There are times when audio equipment and temporary systems are used in an outdoor environment and that the equipment is probably not listed for use outdoors. This article provides the AHJ with a guide for the use of appropriate environmental protection as an acceptable method of using audio equipment in a temporary outside setting. The intent of this Article is to allow the use of tents, tarps, erected canvas, or plastic shelters to provide adequate protection against adverse weather conditions.

Article 45: Protection of Wiring—Normally, a temporary system uses flexible cords and cables that can present a tripping hazard. This type of hazard is a life safety concern in crowded spaces in the event of an evacuation. A secondary concern for a system operator is always the concern about an attendee inadvertently kicking or tripping over a cable and rendering all or parts of the system inoperable.

Article 46: Equipment Access—This article provides protection for both an attendee and for the system operator. It requires the system operator to keep an attendee from an area where there is potential for an injury, and it provides the operator with the assurance that an attendee will not put the audio system out of operation.

Article 720: Requirement Deleted

1993 Code Article 820

*Community Antenna Television
and Radio Distribution Systems*

A. General

Article 1: Scope—This article covers what is commonly know as community antenna television (CATV) and master antenna television (MATV). The difference between the two distribution systems is that each MATV distribution system has a local, on-site antenna or antenna system as its signal source, and the system has one specific building or a local group of buildings with a common ownership. The CATV system has a common antenna and head-end processing/amplification system that services a large geographic area that may include an entire community or several communities.

*Article 2: Definitions—Simply provides a definition for the point of entrance that is unique to this article and therefore is not included in the general definitions found in Article 100.

*Article 3: Locations and Other Articles—Information is provided in subsections (a) through (g) regarding other Articles that have information common to installations covered in this article.

*Article 4: Energy Limitations—Provides rules for delivering low-energy power via coaxial cable for equipment required to operate the system. Note that voltage is restricted to 60V and must be provided by a power source that is energy limited for safety purposes.

Article 5: Access to Electrical Equipment Behind Panels Designed to Allow Access—Once again low-voltage equipment installers are reminded that when installing wiring in accessible places, accessibility must be maintained into the space. For example, you may not install cable in an accessible space such as above a suspended ceiling panel, and leave the cable piled up on top of the ceiling panels so that the ceiling panel cannot be removed.

Article 6: Mechanical Execution of Work—This article works together with the preceding article to accomplish a neat and workmanlike installation and is common to other low-voltage articles such as 640, 725, 760, 800, etc.

B. Cables Outside and Entering Buildings

Article 10: Outside Cables—Outside coaxial cables shall comply with subsections (a) through (f), which define installation requirements regarding:

a. Location on poles
  1. normally located below light and power and Class 1 or non-power-limited fire alarm.
  2. not on a cross arm that carries electric light or power conductors.
b. Lead-in clearances
  1. lead-in or aerial-drop cables shall be kept away from electric light, power, or non-power-limited fire alarm conductors.
  2. *Exception* allows for minimum of 12-inch (305mm) clearance in some specific cases.
c. Attachment points on masts — cable drops can be attached *providing* the mast does *not* contain or support electric light or power circuits.

d. Clearance above all points of roofs must be not less than 8 feet (2.44m) with three *exceptions*:

    1. Auxiliary buildings such as garages.

    2. A reduction to 18 inches (457mm) above the roof is permitted under certain conditions.

    3. A reduction to not less than 3 feet (914mm) above the roof is permitted under certain other conditions.

e. Between buildings, cables and associated hardware must be strong enough to support their loads. The *exception* is that it may be attached to a supporting messenger cable that is strong enough.

f. On buildings — separation from other conductors

    1. electric light, power, Class1, or non-power-limited fire alarm—4 inches (102mm) or a separation by a continuous and firmly fixed nonconductor.

    2. other communication systems—no unnecessary interference in the maintenance of the separate system and cause no abrasion to the conductors of any other system.

    3. lightning conductors—at least a 6-foot separation where practical.

Section 11: Entering Buildings—Subsection (a) provides the correct method of installing underground coaxial cables when electric light and power conductors are present in a duct, pedestal, manhole, or a handhole. Subsection (b) provides clearance information when direct buried cable is used. Please read the *exceptions*.

C. Protection

Section 33: Grounding of Outer Conductive Shield of a Coaxial Cable—This section covers the requirements for grounding the coaxial shield. It also refers you to the next section (820-40), which defines an acceptable grounding electrode. The FPN contains an explanation of the importance of using the shortest possible grounding conductor.

D. Grounding Methods

Section 40: Cable Grounding—Where cable grounding is required in Section 33, this section provides the specific methods that are acceptable.

a. The grounding conductor:
    1. must be insulated and listed as suitable for the purpose
    2. specifies the material and construction
    3. must not be smaller than No.14 and be able to carry at least as much current as the outer conductor of the coaxial cable
    4. must run in as straight a line as possible
    5. if subject to physical damage, it must be adequately protected

b. The grounding electrode:
    1. must be connected to one of seven mentioned nearest accessible locations; or
    2. if there is no grounding means as listed in the seven locations, you can use any one of the individual electrodes as described in Section 250-50; or
    3. if there is no grounding means as listed in either of the above subsection (b1 or b2), you may ground to an effectively grounded metal structure or to any one of the individual electrodes described in Section 250-52.

c. The electrode connection must comply with Section 250-70

d. Bonding of electrodes – you must use at least a No.6 copper or equivalent between the antenna systems grounding electrode and the power grounding electrode system when separate electrodes are used. An *exception* routes you to information dealing with a mobile home, and two FPNs have additional information. One regarding connecting to lightning rod cabling and the second provides the reason for bonding when involved with separate electrodes.

Section 41: Equipment Grounding—This section provides grounding for unpowered equipment, enclosures, or equipment powered by coaxial cable.

Section 42: Bonding and Grounding at Mobile Homes—This section has application if you install MATV systems in trailer parks, campgrounds, etc. You need to look at this section for guidance with both grounding and bonding.

E. Cables Within Buildings

Section 49: Fire Resistance of CATV Cables—Says that inside coaxial cable must be listed as fire resistant in accordance with the requirements of the next two Sections (50 and 51).

Section 50: Listing, Marking, and Installation of Coaxial Cables—This section says that coaxial cables must be marked in accordance with Table 820-50. There are three *exceptions* that you should note as well as an FPN.

Section 51: Additional Listing Requirements—This section explains the listing requirements and identifies the national standards that apply to four types of CATV coaxial cable.

Section 52: Installation of Cables and Equipment—Once you begin wiring beyond the point of grounding, there are five subsections that provide the rules for cable installation:

a.　Separation from other conductors

　　1.　In raceways and boxes,

　　　　(a)　Other circuits - CATV cables are permitted in the same raceway or enclosure with five other categories of low-voltage jacketed cables.

　　　　(b)　Coaxial cable is not permitted to be mixed with electric light, power, Class I, non-power- limited fire alarm, and medium-power network-powered broadband communications circuits. There are two *exceptions,* where barriers are provided, and where a minimum separation of 0.25 inches (6.35.mm) is maintained.

　　2.　Other applications — Coaxial cable must be separated by at least 2 inches from electric light, power, Class I, non-power-limited fire alarm, and medium-power network-powered broadband communications circuits.

There are two *exceptions* that deal with methods of separation that you should look at when you find yourself in this situation.

b. Spread of fire or products of combustion — requires use of approved methods of fire-stopping.

c. Equipment in other space used for environmental air — refers you to Section 300-22(c)

d. Hybrid power and coaxial cabling — refers you to Section 780-6.

e. Support of conductors — prohibits use of raceways as a means of support for coaxial cables.

Section 53: Applications of Listed CATV Cables—This cable-marking scheme is very similar to that for other cable and wire used in the audio industry. The suffixes P and R, following the cable definition code CATV, identify cable for plenum use or riser use. Any CATV cable without a suffix may be used for general use. A CATV cable with the suffix X is for limited use. Subsection (a), (b), and (c) provide specific information about the use of each type of cable. Each subsection also has one or more *exceptions* that are allowed. Subsection D provides the familiar cable usage and permitted substitution information in Table 850-3 and Figure 820-53.

OHSA

Introduction

Audio Systems Technology, Level II, introduced a few specific requirements that are part of the OSHA program. Aerial lift and boom operations were introduced and included OSHA requirements, the different types of lifts, preoperational checks, operational requirements, and hazard clearances. The Right to Know Law and information about the Material Safety Data Sheet (MSDS), which is enforced by OSHA, was also covered.

Level III moves on to another part of OSHA requirements. There are matters of state-federal relations that affect you every day, and there may be times when you work in a state that is not your home state. As a Level III technician, you may be the lead technician or a job foreperson who is considered your company's representative on the job site. If there is an OSHA site inspection, you will be the person the inspector comes looking for and that person will want to ask *you* questions about the project and will certainly review the inspection report with you.

State / Federal Relationships

Each state has the option of developing its own occupational safety and health program. There are two significant parts to the process of providing a state plan:

1. A state plan must develop and enforce state standards that are at least as effective as the federal plan in providing safe and healthful work conditions.

2. A state plan must be submitted to OSHA for approval. If it is not fully approved, the state may receive approval to use the plan immediately, but must submit a development plan to correct within three years, those items that are not in compliance with the federal program. If the corrections are not made within the three-year period, approval to use the state plan will be withdrawn and the state will revert back to the use of the federal OSHA program.

Once the state plan is in effect, you will be confronted with at least the same or perhaps more stringent regulations. You should contact the agency that administers workplace health and safety regulations in your state. Know what regulations affect you in your workplace. You should be able to locate either the closest state or U.S. government telephone number in your phone book. You might find it listed under a category such as Workers Compensation Commission, Worker's Hotline, Health & Safety, Consumer & Industry Services, Construction Codes, Occupational Health, or something similar. Experience has shown that the people in both state and federal OSHA offices have been very helpful and willing to provide information.

States with occupational safety and health programs

Alaska	Michigan	South Carolina
Arizona	Minnesota	Tennessee
California	Nevada	Utah
Connecticut	New Mexico	Vermont
Hawaii	New York	Virgin Islands
Indiana	North Carolina	Virginia
Iowa	Oregon	Washington
Kentucky	Puerto Rico	Wyoming
Maryland		

Table 2-1

There are currently 23 states and jurisdictions operating complete state plans (covering both the private sector and state and local government employees) and two states, Connecticut and New York, which cover public employees only (see Table 2-1). Eight other states were approved at one time but subsequently withdrew their programs.

Enforcement Procedures

Enforcement procedures begin when an inspection takes place or when a serious workplace accident happens. The inspector must present appropriate credentials to the owner, operator, or agent in charge. When he has presented his credentials, he is authorized to:

1. Enter the factory, plant, construction site, etc., where work is being performed by an employee; and

2. Inspect and investigate during regular working hours and at other reasonable times any and all pertinent areas, structures, apparati, devices, equipment, etc., and to privately question any employer, employee, operator, or agent.

The inspector has the authority to require attendance and testimony of witnesses under oath. If witnesses refuse to obey the order, they will come under the jurisdiction of their local U.S. District Court and be expected to comply with court orders or be declared in contempt of the court.

If the inspection or investigation uncovers unsafe workplace practices and/or conditions, one or more citations are issued. There are then three possible events that could take place:

1. Within a reasonable time after the inspection or investigation is completed, an employer will be notified by certified mail of the penalty, if any, that is assessed under OSHA Section 17 (Penalties). An employer then has 15 working days to notify OSHA that he wishes to contest the citation or the proposed assessment of penalty. If the employer does not contest the citation or proposed assessment of penalty within 15 working days *and* no notice is filed by employees or representatives of employees, *then* the citation and assessment as proposed is the final order and is not subject to review by any court or agency.

2. If OSHA has reason to believe that an employer has failed to correct a violation for which a citation has been issued within the period of time permitted for its correction, the employer will be notified by certified mail of the failure. An additional penalty is added for failure to correct the violation. In other words, if your company is told to fix a problem by a certain date and doesn't do it, you will get a notice that the cost just went up because now there is an additional penalty for not correcting the problem on time. You have the same 15 working-day window to appeal as in Step 1.

3. If an employer, any employee, or representative of employees, files a notice with OSHA that the period of time is unreasonable, he or she shall be afforded the opportunity of a hearing. Based on the findings of the hearing, there will be an affirmation, modification, or vacating of the original citation or proposed penalty. If an employer makes a good faith effort to comply with the abatement requirements of a citation, and the abatement has not been completed because of factors beyond his or her reasonable control, OSHA may, after a hearing, issue an order affirming or modifying the abatement requirements in the citation.

Postings Required

Here's good news for small employers. According to OSHA Standards – 29 CFR, Standard Number 1904.15: *"An employer who had no more than ten (10) employees at any time during the calendar year immediately preceding the current calendar year need not comply with any of the requirements of this part except the following:*

(a) *Obligation to report under §1904.8 concerning fatalities or multiple hospitalization accidents; and*

(b) *Obligation to maintain a log of occupational injuries and illnesses under §1904.2 and to make reports under §1904.21 upon being notified in writing by the Bureau of Labor & Statistics that the employer has been selected to participate in a statistical survey of occupational injuries and illnesses."*

For those employers that have more than 10 employees, the requirements for paperwork and a written program are more involved. There are four requirements that must be addressed:

1. You must post the OSHA notice (Form 1903) for employees. If an employer consistently disregards this posting, interviews show that employees are unaware of their rights under OSHA, or the employer has been previously cited or advised by OSHA of the posting requirement, then the employer is a candidate for a citation.

2. You must maintain Injury and Illness Records (Form 1904) for employees. There are two situations that might occur where there would be no citations issued for noncompliance. They are:

   a. when no records are maintained and there have been no injuries or illnesses.

   b. when the records have not been accurately recorded and the owner promises to correct the deficiencies, and is provided with additional information and then corrects the deficiencies.

When citations are issued, penalties are proposed only when OSHA can document that the employer was previously informed of the requirements to keep records or, where it can be documented that the employer deliberately deviated from record keeping requirements or demonstrated plain indifference to the requirements.

Here are some guidelines for record keeping and general concepts of recordability:

    a. an injury or illness is considered work-related if it results from an event of exposure in the work environment. The work environment is primarily the employer's premise and other locations where employees are engaged in work-related activities or present as a condition of their employment.

    b. all work-related fatalities are recordable.

    c. all recognized or diagnosed work-related illnesses are recordable

    d. all work-related injuries requiring medical treatment or involving loss of consciousness, restriction of work or motion, or transfer to another job.

Check the reference list for OSHA at the Web site listed at the end of this chapter.

3. Requirements for a Written Plan or Certification for Personal Protective Equipment Standards indicate that an employer must prepare a written plan to address a hazard. The written plan must provide for protective measures and practices that are required by the standard such as hard hats, protective footwear, fall protection, eye protection, hearing protection, etc. When protective measures are not provided or followed and employees are exposed to a risk of serious harm, a citation for a serious violation of the standard with a penalty normally is issued. There are several other scenarios that can generate citations and penalties.

If you think your business is too small and can't afford a customized safety and health audit, or you need guidance on OSHA standards, OSHA has released its newest on-line advisors covering hazard awareness and fire safety. These interactive software programs are designed to provide readily available safety and health information for both employers as well as employees. The Hazard Awareness Advisor helps you locate potential hazards in the workplace and then prepares a customized report detailing the pertinent OSHA standards that address those hazards. The Fire Safety Advisor addresses the general industry standards for fire safety and emergency evacuation as well as fire-fighting, fire-suppression, and fire-detection systems. It also helps you write a customized "Emergency Action Plan," and a "Fire Prevention Plan" for your workplace. Check the reference list for the OSHA Web site listed at the end of this chapter. For more detailed information review OSHA Directive CPL2.111. Check the reference list for OSHA Web site listed at the end of this chapter.

4. This requirement deals with exposure to hazardous chemicals in the workplace commonly know as the Right to Know Law and was included in *Audio Systems Technology, Level II* handbook, Chapter 4. For additional detail refer to OSHA Regulation 1910.1200, and 1926.59, which can be found on the OSHA web site listed in the reference at the end of this chapter.

Penalties

The OSH Act of 1970 Section 17 provides for penalties for violating the requirements of this act with civil penalties up to $70,000 for each violation.

If someone kills a person while that person is engaged in or on account of the performance of investigative, inspection, or law enforcement functions associated with the OSH Act, shall be punished by imprisonment for any term of years or for life.

If someone gives advance notice of any inspection to be conducted under this act without authority from the secretary or his designee, this person can be punished with a fine of not more than $1,000 or by imprisonment for more than six months or by both.

Penalties that are a result of citations are common and probably happen daily throughout the United States. These penalties are based on four factors:

1. Seriousness of the violation—Was it a serious violation where there was a substantial probability that death or serious physical harm could result? Was it a repeated violation? Was it an intentional disregard or plain indifference to OSHA regulations?

2. Size of the business—There are penalty considerations available to small business based on the number of employees.

Size	Possible Reduction
1-25	60%
26-100	40%
101-250	20%

3. Good faith can provide 25%, 15%, or no reduction depending on how well the employer has implemented an effective safety program in the workplace.

4. Employer's history: A 10% reduction is given to small businesses that had no serious, willful, or repeated OSHA violations in the past three years.

Here are three OSHA news releases that will give you some idea of the type of penalties that are assessed for violations.

Region 2 News Release

October 28, 1999

CONSTRUCTION FIRM CITED FOR ALLEGED REPEAT SAFETY VIOLATIONS AT MANHATTAN CONSTRUCTION SITES; $179,500 IN PENALTIES PROPOSED

The U.S. Labor Department's Occupational Safety and Health Administration has cited Laquila/Pinnacle JV, of 516 West Boston Post Road, Mamaroneck, New York, and proposed penalties of $179,500 against the firm for eight alleged repeat violations, seven alleged serious violations, and one alleged other-than-serious violation of OSHA standards. The company has until November 18 to contest the citations.

According to OSHA area director Robert D. Kulick, the action results from investigations conducted at three construction sites in New York City from April 27 through June 10 following complaints of employees being exposed to fall hazards. The contractor was engaged in concrete construction work on three condominium projects on Manhattan's East Side: 1356 Third Avenue, 400 East 90th Street, and 351 East 61st Street.

The firm was cited for eight alleged repeat violations carrying a total proposed penalty of $150,000, for not providing employees with fall protection, not ensuring that floor holes were covered, and not properly locating job ladders.

A repeat violation is one for which an employer has been previously cited for the same or a substantially similar condition and the citation has become a final order of the Occupational Safety and Health Review Commission. The firm was previously cited for these conditions at construction sites at 48-18 Fifth Street, Long Island City, New York, and 240 East 39th Street, Manhattan, in August, 1998.

The alleged serious violations for which the employer was cited included not providing eye protection, not providing hard hats, not providing fall-hazard recognition training, and not providing ladder-hazard recognition training, with a total proposed penalty of $29,500.

The firm was also cited for not providing enough toilets for the workers, an alleged other-than-serious violation.

A serious violation is defined as a condition which exists where there is a substantial possibility that death or serious physical harm can result. An other-than-serious violation is a hazardous condition that would probably not cause death or serious physical harm but would have a direct and immediate relationship to the safety and health of employees.

The investigation was conducted by OSHA's Manhattan area office, located at 6 World Trade Center, room 881, New York, New York, telephone (212) 466-2481.

Region 5 News Release V-121

June 15, 1999

U.S. LABOR DEPARTMENT FINES FIRM $37,750 FOR CHILD LABOR AND FEDERAL WORKPLACE SAFETY VIOLATIONS FOLLOWING INJURY OF 13-YEAR-OLD AT OHIO SITE

Two agencies of the U.S. Department of Labor have fined Pulte Homes of Ohio, Solon, Ohio, a total of $37,750 following injuries sustained on May 18 by a 13-year-old Middlefield youth who was working at a Twinsburg, Ohio, construction site, the department announced today.

The department's Wage and Hour Division issued civil money penalties to Pulte totaling $28,750 for child labor violations while the Occupational Safety and Health administration (OSHA) fined the firm an additional $9,000 for workplace safety violations. OSHA also issued a $1,800 penalty for safety violations to John Kuhns, doing business as J.K. Builders, a subcontractor at the job site.

The child labor violations alleged by the Labor Department include employment of a minor under 14 years of age, employment of two minors under 16 in a prohibited occupation, and employment of a minor in violation of hours during which children are permitted to work. OSHA alleged that Pulte violated worker safety protections by failing to regularly inspect for safety on the jobsite and for the lack of an effective safety and health program. Kuhns was cited by OSHA for failing to implement an effective safety and health program, unprotected floor holes, the lack of a safe means of access for employees to all work areas, and failing to have a competent person perform frequent and regular safety inspections.

The youth was working with a crew of carpenters on a residential construction project in Twinsburg when he fell approximately 10 feet onto a concrete basement floor. He had been stapling insulation to a wall section lying on the floor and stepped into an unseen window opening framed into the wall. The window opening was directly over a floor hole to the basement. The youth was carried on a helicopter to a nearby hospital where he was initially listed in critical condition with head injuries. He has since recovered from his injuries.

"It's clear that children should not be employed in areas which can pose serious safety threats," according to Wage and Hour District Director Barry Haber, Cleveland. "We are all fortunate that this child has apparently recovered from his injuries."

OSHA Area Director Rob Medlock, Cleveland, added, "An accident prevention program with site inspections to eliminate any safety hazards is the key to a safe construction site. Anything less is unacceptable."

Federal child labor laws allow minors under 16 years of age to work outside of school but restrict the hours and times they may work. They may work no later than 7 p.m. (9 p.m. June 1 through Labor Day). They may work no more than three hours on school days and eight hours on nonschool days and no more than 18 hours during school weeks and 40 hours during nonschool weeks.

Pulte Homes of Ohio may pay all the proposed penalties or file a letter of exception with the Wage and Hour Division regarding the child labor penalty assessments, appealing all or part of the fine. The firm and Kuhns may appeal the OSHA penalties to the independent Occupational Safety and Health Review Commission.

Region 1 News Release

Thursday, December 2, 1999

Need to Safeguard against Potentially Fatal Falls Stressed

OSHA CITES NEW HAMPSHIRE CONTRACTORS FOR AL-
LEGED FALL PROTECTION HAZARDS; NEARLY $40,000 IN
FINES PROPOSED

The U.S. Labor Department's Occupational Safety and Health
Administration (OSHA) has cited two Manchester, New Hampshire,
contractors—Exterior Designs, Inc., and Airtight, LLC—for alleged
violations of the Occupational Safety and Health Act at a Manchester work site and has proposed combined penalties against the two
companies totaling $39,900.

According to David May, OSHA area director for New Hampshire, the alleged violations were discovered during an inspection
conducted October 7, 1999, at a building renovation project located
at the corner of Kidder and Elm Streets in Manchester and chiefly
concern the lack of adequate fall protection for employees. Exterior
Designs was performing stucco work on the outside of the building
and had 13 employees working onsite at the time of the inspection;
Airtight, LLC, the renovation project's general contractor, had four
employees working onsite at the time.

"An OSHA compliance officer who was passing by this job
site observed employees working on the second and third floors of
this building without any visible fall protection, a situation which
exposed these workers to potentially fatal falls," said May. "In line
with OSHA's special emphasis program on fall protection, an inspection was opened immediately and these citations and fines are
the result of that inspection."

OSHA's inspection found employees of both contractors exposed to a variety of fall hazards; in particular, potential falls of up
to 50 feet through unguarded exterior wall openings on the second
through fifth floors of the building.

Workers for Exterior Designs, Inc. were also exposed to additional hazards involving the erection and use of scaffolding, including:

- employees erecting scaffolding without fall protection;
- an employee working in an aerial lift without fall protection;
- employees accessing the building's third floor by jumping from the scissors lift
- through a wall opening;
- improperly installed scaffolding support posts;
- employees not adequately trained nor knowledgeable about scaffold erection;
- scaffold erection not supervised by a competent person.

Noting that 28 New England workers fell to their deaths on the job in 1998, May explained that OSHA is seeking to reduce that number through a New England-wide special emphasis program that combines employer education with active enforcement. One element of that program includes unannounced spot inspections when OSHA inspectors observe employees working more than 10 feet above the next lower level without any apparent fall protection.

"So far this year, New Hampshire has been spared any fatal workplace falls but employer and worker alike cannot and should not be lulled into a false sense of security because of that," he said. "Fall prevention is not a product of good fortune. Rather, it's the result of knowing, providing, and utilizing clear, basic, and required worker safeguards."

Specifically, Exterior Designs, Inc. faces a total of $33,900 in proposed penalties for nine alleged Serious violations, accounting for $17,100 of the proposed penalties, for:

- scaffold erection not supervised by a competent person;
- employees accessed the third floor by jumping from an aerial lift through a wall opening;
- an employee operated an aerial lift without fall protection;
- scaffolding support posts not installed in a level and sound manner;

- scaffold support posts not installed plumb;
- an unguarded wall opening;
- an unguarded floor hole and an unguarded stairwell;
- a stairwell missing a handrail;
- a stairwell lacking guardrails.

Two alleged repeat violations, accounting for $16,800 of the penalties were proposed, for:

- employees erecting scaffolding without the use of fall protection;
- employees climbing cross braces to exit a welded frame scaffold. (Exterior Designs, Inc. had previously been cited by OSHA for substantially similar violations in citations issued April 6, 1998, following an inspection at a Portsmouth, New Hampshire, work site).

There was an alleged other-than-serious violation, with no proposed penalty, for inadequately supported scaffolding midrails and toprails.

Airtight LLC faces $6,000 in proposed penalties for four alleged serious violations for:

- an unguarded wall opening;
- an unguarded floor hole and an unguarded stairwell;
- stairwell missing a handrail;
- a stairwell lacking guardrails.

There were three alleged other-than-serious violations, with no penalties proposed, for inadequate training and exposure assessment for Class IV asbestos work.

May encouraged New Hampshire employers and employees with questions regarding workplace safety and health standards to contact the OSHA area office in Concord at 603-225-1629 and added that OSHA's toll-free, nationwide hotline—1-800-321-OSHA (1-800-321-6742)—may be used to report workplace accidents or fatalities or situations posing imminent danger to workers, especially if they occur outside of normal business hours.

A serious violation is defined by OSHA as one in which there is a substantial probability that death or serious physical harm could result, and the employer knew, or should have known, of the hazard. An other-than-serious violation is a condition which would probably not cause death or serious physical harm but would have a direct and immediate relationship to the safety and health of employees. A repeat citation is issued by OSHA when an employer has been cited for a substantially similar hazard in a previous OSHA inspection and that citation has become final.

OSHA is empowered by the Occupational Safety and Health Act of 1970 to issue standards and rules requiring employers to provide their employees with safe and healthful workplaces and job sites and to assure through workplace inspections that those standards are followed. The company has 15 working days from receipt of the citations and proposed penalties to either elect to comply with them, to request and participate in an informal conference with the OSHA area director, or to contest them before the independent Occupational Safety and Health Review Commission.

OSHA has a new Home Page that is very easy to use. It combined the content links of two different OSHA URLs, updated the graphics, provided an alphabetic index, provides a full-site search of both National Office and Technical Center contents, and provides an easy navigation scheme.

References

OSHA Web site—www.osha.gov

OSHA Regional News Releases—www.osha.gov/media/oshnews/

OSHA Interactive Software Advisories—www.osha.gov/dts/osta/oshasoft

OSHA Directives—CPL 2.111 Citation Policy for Paperwork and Written Program Requirement Violations

OSHA Regulations—Small employers: 1904.15; Log and summary of occupational injuries and illnesses: 1904.2; Hazard Communication: 1910.1200 and 1926.59

OSHA Guidelines—Chapter Number: SUMM; Chapter Title: Record Keeping Summary

Questions

1. As of January 1, 2000, the NICET work elements that cover Article 640 of the NEC® are still based on the 1993 NEC®. In 1999, NEC® updated Article 640. Which of the following is *NOT* one of the 10 significant changes made to the new version of Article 640?

    a. Definitions were added

    b. "Protection of Electrical Equipment" was added

    c. "Assistive Listening Priority" was added

    d. "Audio Systems Near Bodies of Water" was added

2. In the 1993 NEC® "Class 3" wiring is defined as wiring that…

    a. Presents a fire hazard but not a shock hazard

    b. Presents neither a shock hazard nor a fire hazard

    c. Presents a hazard to young children and the elderly

    d. Presents a shock hazard but not a fire hazard

3. Which section of Article 640 of the 1999 NEC® is applicable to portable audio systems?

    a. Section B

    b. Section IV

    c. Section C

    d. Section V

4. According to the 1993 NEC® Article 820, where cable grounding is required, the grounding conductor…

    a. must not be larger than No. 14

    b. must run in as straight a line as practicable

    c. must be insulated and listed as suitable for the purpose

    d. both B & C

5. With regard to OSHA, what do the states of Indiana, Virginia, and Oregon have in common?

　　a. All three states are OSHA exempt

　　b. All three states are under the supervision of the Mid-Atlantic Regional OSHA office

　　c. All three states have state occupational safety and health programs that cover public employees only

　　d. All three states have their own complete State occupational safety and health programs

6. If your employer has more than 10 employees he is required by law to…

　　a. Pay annual dues to OSHA at .1% per employee

　　b. Maintain confidential files on the personal habits of all employees

　　c. Maintain Injury and Illness records for employees

　　d. Employ an OSHA-certified Hazard Awareness Advisor

7. Which of the following is *NOT* one of the four factors that determine how severe a penalty resulting from an OSHA citation will be?

　　a. good faith

　　b. how serious the violation is

　　c. if the violation involved drugs and/or alcohol

　　d. employer's history

8. You are perusing the phone book to find an agency that can give you the most accurate information about occupational safety and health regulations in your local area. Which of the following entries is likely to lead you to what you want?

　　a. Worker's Hotline

　　b. Food and Drug Admin.

　　c. Workforce Development Center

　　d. Health & Safety

　　e. Both A and D

Chapter 3
Circuits, Switching, and Grounding

by Bob Bushnell

- **NICET Work Element 15003, Circuit Analysis**
- **NICET's Description:** *"Apply Kirchhoff's Laws to circuits with linear components. Calculate impedance and current in a circuit with resistive and reactive components."*

- **NICET Work Element 15004, Elements of Transistor Circuits**
- **NICET's Description:** *"Define the basic terminology associated with transistor circuits. Identify basic transistor types, pinouts, and configurations from markings or schematics."*

- **NICET Work Element 15005, Analysis of Transistor Circuits**
- **NICET's Description:** *"Determine signal phase and amplitude at various points in a transistor circuit. Interpret logic gates, tables, and diagrams."*

- **NICET Work Element 15011, System Grounding**
- **NICET's Description:** *"Identify possible ground loops. Use proper procedures for grounding connections between components within a system (balanced to balanced, balanced to unbalanced). Perform resistance to ground measurements. Recognize the different kinds of ground reference. (NEC Articles 200, 210, 250)."*

Circuit Analysis

Kirchhoff and his laws

In a scientific field such as electronics a physical *law* is a statement that cannot be disproved, or has been found to be consistent over time when verified under the same circumstances.

In 1845, Gustav Kirchhoff stated his laws of voltage and current. Now referred to as Kirchhoff's laws, they state that the sum of the branch voltages or currents in any closed loop is equal to zero, *at any time*. Rephrasing that law for current, the sum of the currents entering a point or node is equal to the currents leaving that node.

DC voltage calculation in a closed-loop circuit

Rephrasing that law for voltage, the sum of the voltage drops in a closed loop is equal to the sum of the voltage sources. In figure 3-1, we have a basic circuit that we'll use to discuss Kirchhoff's law.

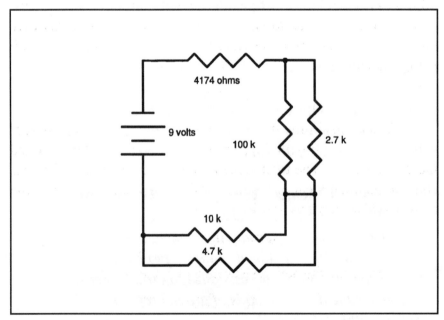

Figure 3-1. A basic circuit

Kirchhoff's law concerning currents states that the amount of current flowing to a point or a node must equal the amount of current flowing from that node. If we look at the junction or node of the 4174 ohm, 100k, and 2.7k resistors, the amount of current flowing from the 4174 ohm resistor is equal to the amount of current flowing to both the 100k and the 2.7k resistors. No exceptions!

How many nodes in Figure 3-1? If you said more than four, point them out and explain.

What do we know about the circuit? There are four elements — one active and three passive. The active element has a +9-volt point, and a 0-volt point. Therefore, the total voltage in the system must be 9 volts.

Current Calculations in a Closed-Loop Circuit

The three passive elements can be simplified to one equivalent resistor, or three equivalent resistors. One equivalent resistor allows us to calculate the current through the circuit. Three equivalent resistors allow us to calculate the voltage drop across each element. We must first calculate the current through the circuit using the equation:

$$I = E/R$$

We shall determine the equivalent value of the series/parallel combination. Begin with the parallel combination of the 100k and the 2.7k resistors. The total value of a group of parallel resistors is equal to the reciprocal of the sum of the reciprocal values of those resistors. If we have two resistors, the equation is:

$$1/R_t = 1/R_1 + 1/R_2$$

To calculate the new resistance value, the equation is:

$$R_t = 1/R_t$$

(The following short section explains how to solve this problem using a Sharp EL-531L calculator. [This is the calculator used in NSCA's CATTS™ — the prep course for NICET Audio Certification.] If you don't have this particular model of calculator you may want to skip this section, or try to translate it to the keystrokes on your calculator.)

Turn on the calculator by pressing the Red key, Row 1, Key 6. We'll use this method of key callout for the time being.

Besides division, another way of calculating a reciprocal is to state the number to the $^{-1}$ power.

1. Enter the 100k value by pressing "**1**," then **five zeros**.
2. Press the "**2ⁿᵈ F**" key, Row 1, Key 1, then the "x^{-1}" key, Row 3, Key 3.

Now you will see a neat feature of this calculator. Notice the display above the main number display. You should see "100000^{-1}." That is the equation you've entered so far. Whenever you enter a number and an operator, such as "+" or "–", you'll see what you've entered so far in the upper line.

3. To add the two values, press the "+" key, Row 7, Key 4.
4. Continue by entering the number "**2700**," which is the other resistor value.
5. Then press the "**2ⁿᵈ F**" key, Row 1, Key 1, then the "x^{-1}" key, Row 3, Key 3. Now the entire equation so far is in the upper line.
6. Then press the "=" key, lower right-hand corner. You'll see "0.00038037," which is the sum of the reciprocals of the two numbers. Don't clear anything. To complete the calculation, you want the reciprocal of that number. You see in the upper line part of the equation ending with "$0000^{-1}+2700^{-1}=$".
7. Press the "**2ⁿᵈ F**" key, Row 1, Key 1, then the "x^{-1}" key, Row 3, Key 3. You see "ANS^{-1}."
8. Press the "=" key, lower right-hand corner. Now you see the answer you've been waiting for, "2629.016553." Disregard all the digits to the right of the decimal point; they're overkill.

But here's a neat way to round off the number.

9. Press the "**2ⁿᵈ F**" key, then the "FSE" key, Row 8, Key 2. You'll see "**FIX**" at the top of the display.

10. Press the "**2ⁿᵈ F**" key, then the "**TAB**" key. Now enter the number of digits you want to the right of the decimal point. Since two digits is a reasonable start, press the number "**2**." Now you see the number "2629.02."

   Now you want the sum of the parallel combination and the resistor above it.

11. Add 2629.02 to 4174. You might note the result in Figure 3-1, just to remember it. Obviously, the answer is 6803.02 ohms. Let's calculate the equivalent value for the bottom two resistors.

12. Press the Red key to clear the display.

13. Enter "**10000**," then "**2ⁿᵈ F**," then "x^{-1}," then "+," then "**4700**," then "x^{-1}." You'll see the upper line ending with an "=," but the display shows "0.00." That's not a mistake on your part, simply that the reciprocal is too small a number to display.

14. Press "**2ⁿᵈ F**," then "x^{-1}," then "=." You'll see the answer, "3197.28."

15. Press "+", then "**6803.02**", then press the "=." That adds the two numbers together.

Your answer should be 10000.3 ohms, as that is the equivalent resistance of the series/parallel combination. For the rest of this problem, and other problems, we won't go through the keystrokes.

Restating the earlier equation:

$$I = E/R$$

We know the voltage, and we now know the resistance, therefore the current is 0.9 milliamperes. Is that your answer?

That is the amount of current flowing from the battery and the amount of current measured at any node in this circuit. Knowing this current, and knowing the individual and parallel resistances, we can calculate the voltage at any point in the circuit. And the equation is:

$$E = I \times R$$

Yes, that's the same equation, but restated. Now we can apply it to parts of the circuit, and obtain useful answers. Through the 4174 ohm resistor, 0.9 ma of current is flowing. What is the voltage across the resistor? Is your answer 3,756 volts? But the solution must be stated in amperes. Divide that answer by 1000 to calculate milliamperes.

Impedance is similar to resistance, but only in an AC (alternating current) circuit. DC has no frequency; it is a steady-state voltage or current. AC is a voltage or current varying from instant to instant. The AC line voltage from the wall receptacle in your home is approximately 120 volts in amplitude, but that number should be more correctly expressed as 120 V_{rms}, 60 Hz. The term "rms" means "root-mean-squared." This is also the effective value of the voltage. AC line voltage in the United States is varying from a positive peak value to a negative peak value, 120 times per second.

For a resistive load, the voltage and current peaks occur at the same instant. There are many cases where the voltage and current peaks do not occur at the same instant. In these cases, the AC resistance at a given frequency will not be the same as the DC resistance. This is due to inductive and/or capacitive reactance.

If we measure the impedance of a 1000-ohm resistor at 400 Hz, we will find the impedance to be very close to 1000 ohms. If we measure the impedance of an 8-ohm loudspeaker at 400 Hz, we will find the impedance to be close to 8 ohms. 400 Hz is the usual frequency at which loudspeaker impedance is measured. But if we measure the impedance of that loudspeaker at 800 Hz, the impedance probably won't be 8 ohms.

Impedance is a combination of AC resistance and reactance. The reactance can be either inductive or capacitive, or a combination of both.

Capacitive reactance is calculated by the equation:

$$X_c = \frac{1}{2\pi fC}$$

However, the capacitance is expressed in farads, just as inductance is expressed in henrys. Therefore, to express the number in microfarads, we either replace the "1" in the numerator with "1 x 10^6," or express the capacitance in farads. Since your calculator, like most calculators, has a reciprocal or "1 /" function, it's easier to express the capacitance in farads.

We have a 4 mFd capacitor. What is the reactance of that capacitor at 1000 Hz? Using the above equation, and plugging in the appropriate numbers, we have:

$$X_c = 1 \div 2\pi \times 1000 \times 4 \times 10^{-6}$$

Your answer should be 39.8 ohms. Do you agree?

One note: because of the math laws concerning the order in which multiplication, division, addition, and subtraction take place, you are better off entering the denominator first, than simply asking for the reciprocal of that number. Otherwise, you would need to enter the numerator first, then divide by, then precede and follow the denominator with parentheses.

What would be the capacitive reactance at 10,000 Hz? Can you supply the answer without using your calculator?

Study the schematic on the next page, Figure 3-2. What's the impedance at 1000 Hz? We know what the impedance of the 1000-ohm resistor is at 1 kHz, and we've just calculated the impedance of the 4 mFd capacitor at 1 kHz. Do we simply add them together? Unfortunately, it's not that easy. There are two methods for calculating series impedances. First, the square root of the sum of the squares, and a longer technique involving tangents and cosines. The first method is faster, but provides only the magnitude of the series combination, and not the phase angle of the impedance.

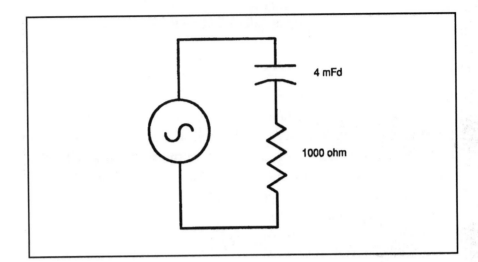

Figure 3-2

The equation for the square root calculation looks like this:

$$Z = \sqrt{(R^2 + Xc^2)}$$

Referring to Figure 3-2, let's plug in the numbers and calculate the circuit impedance:

$$Z = \sqrt{(1000^2 + 39.8^2)}$$

You should have calculated 1000.79 ohms as the answer. Do you understand how we got the answer?

When we're dealing with inductive reactances, the same equation is used.

That circuit (Fig. 3-3) is shown at the top of the next page, but with a 6.3 mH (milliHenry) inductance or choke in place of the capacitor. Inductive reactance is calculated by the equation:

$$X_L = 2\pi fL$$

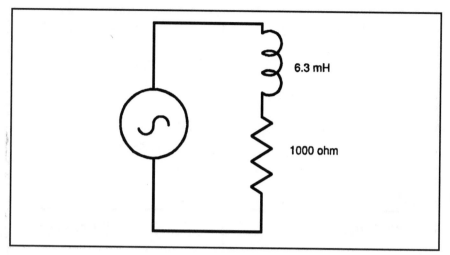

Figure 3-3

Calculating the value of the 6.3 mH inductance, our answer is 39.6 ohms, isn't it? Remember, the inductance value is in mH, not H. Let's calculate the series impedance, using the equation:

$$Z = \sqrt{(R^2 + X_L^2)}$$

Then plugging in the numbers, and calculating, your answer is 1000.78 ohms.

There is an important difference between the two impedances. That difference is the phase angle of each impedance. Capacitive reactance has a negative phase angle, meaning that the current lags the voltage. Inductive reactance has a positive phase angle, meaning that the voltage lags the current.

In reality, reactances without some quantity of resistance are impossible. Neither the perfect capacitor nor the perfect inductor can exist. A capacitor will always have some resistance, and an inductor will always have some resistance.

How do we calculate the phase angle? This equation shows an example:

$$\theta = \tan^{-1}(X_C \div R)$$

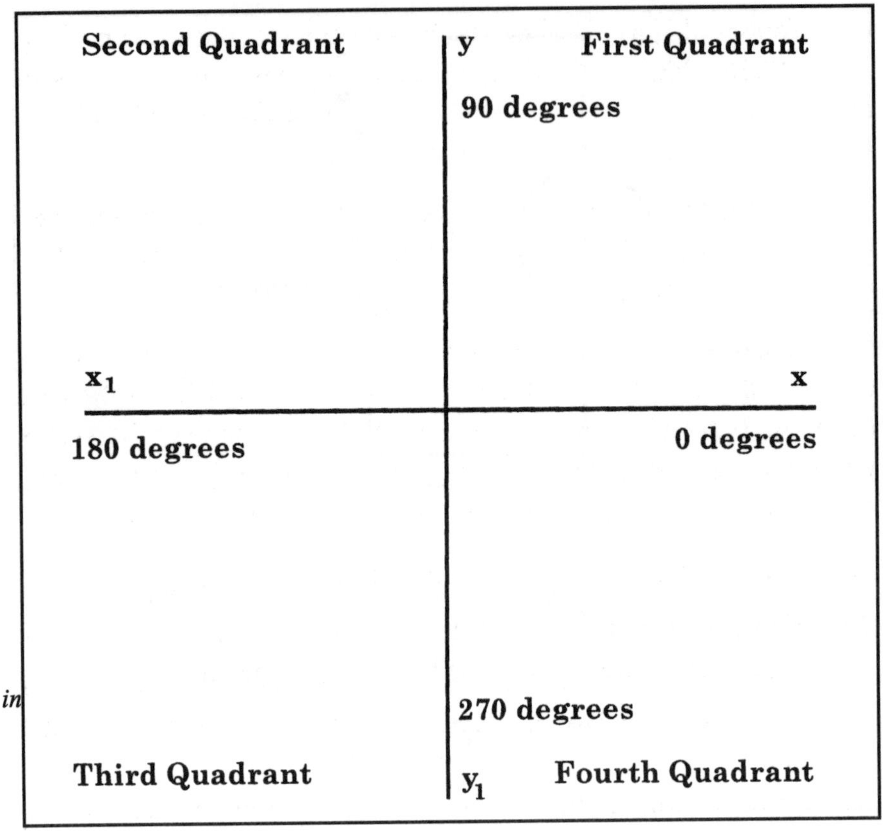

Figure 3-4. *The standard quadrants in electronics and electricity*

On the left side of the equation, the Greek letter, theta, is commonly used in electronics and electricity to express phase angle. That equation can be restated to include any reactive components, thus:

$$\theta = \tan^{-1} (X \div R)$$

The part of the equation, $\tan^{-1}$, is read as arctangent. You'll find all three of those trig functions on your calculator in the second row, second function keys. Let's take the result of the last inductive calculations, where we worked from Figure 3-3. The reactance is 6.3 mH, and the resistance is 1000 ohms. Putting those numbers into the equation, we have:

$$\theta = \tan^{-1} (6.3 \times 10^{-3}) \div 1000$$

You should have had no trouble in calculating the answer, which is +0.000361 degrees. To express that in degrees, minutes, and seconds; simply press the second "**F**" key, then the "**<> DEG**" key, Row 4, Key 3. That answer is +0°00′01.30.

To put this in perspective, see Figure 3-4 on the previous page, a diagram showing the standard quadrants used in electronics and electricity.

When we're considering resistance only, the vector or direction is 0 degrees. With inductances, the vector will lie in the first quadrant, between 0 and 90 degrees. With capacitances, the vector will lie in the fourth quadrant, between 270 and 360 (or 0) degrees. You'll note that the quadrants are in a counterclockwise direction.

Impedance calculations in a circuit having both resistive and reactive components

Here is a slightly more complex schematic. An inductor, a capacitor, and a resistor form a series circuit. Figure 3-5 is the example.

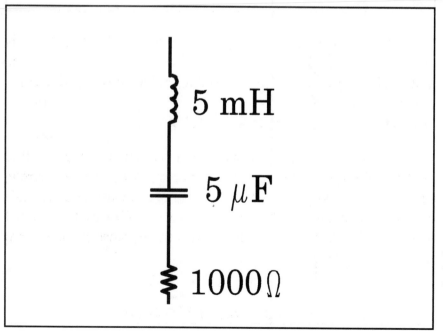

Figure 3-5. An example of a series circuit

This is called a series-resonant circuit. At 1 kHz, with the components selected, the two reactive components will have minimum impedances. This is the resonant frequency. The resistor in series with the combination provides a minimum resistance of 1000 ohms to the circuit.

Current calculations in a circuit having both resistive and reactive components

Here's a table that shows three major parameters concerning resistive and reactive components together.

Topology	Schematic	Impedance Equation	Current Equation
Series LR		$Z = \sqrt{(R^2 + X_L^2)}$	$I = \dfrac{E}{Z}$

Topology	Schematic	Impedance Equation	Current Equation
Series RC		$Z = \sqrt{R^2 + X_c^2}$	$I = \dfrac{E}{Z}$
Parallel RL		$\dfrac{1}{Z} = \dfrac{1}{R} + \dfrac{1}{X_L}$	$I = \dfrac{E}{Z}$
Parallel RC		$\dfrac{1}{Z} = \dfrac{1}{R} + \dfrac{1}{X_c}$	$I = \dfrac{E}{Z}$

Topology	Schematic	Impedance Equation	Current Equation
Series LC		$Z = \sqrt{(X_L{}^2 - X_C{}^2)}$	$I = \dfrac{E}{Z}$
Series RLC		$Z = \sqrt{(R^2 + (X_L{}^2 - X_C{}^2))}$	$I = \dfrac{E}{Z}$

Topology	Schematic	Impedance Equation	Current Equation
Parallel LC		$\dfrac{1}{Z} = \dfrac{1}{X_C} + \dfrac{1}{X_L}$	$I = \dfrac{E}{Z}$

You're familiar with the symbols I, E, and R. Here are some other definitions.

Z = impedance

X_L = inductive reactance = $X_L = 2\pi f L$

X_C = capacitive reactance = $X_C = \dfrac{1}{2\pi f C}$

Earlier, we referred to phase angles, impedance, and capacitive and inductive reactances. There is an important difference between capacitive and inductive reactances. That difference is the phase angle. Capacitive reactance has a negative phase angle, in that the current lags the voltage. Inductive reactance has a positive phase angle, in that the voltage lags the current, or as some references express the condition, the current leads the voltage. Nothing like being ahead in time.

In mathematics, a symbol that provides a specific change is called an operator. For example, the term "square root" is an operator. In working with phase angles, an operator is used, θ, the Greek character called theta. The impedance of a component is normally expressed as Z/θ, where Z is the magnitude of the impedance, and θ is the phase angle, or the amount of lead or lag between the voltage across the impedance and the current. Since we're not going into circuit design, we won't discuss this subject in any more detail.

Basic terminology of transistor circuits

Alpha—One measure of a transistor's performance. It is the current gain of a transistor in a common base circuit. Alpha is usually expressed by the Greek letter α. It is equal to the collector current divided by the emitter current, with the collector voltage held constant.

Base current—The amount of current flowing to the base.

Beta—One measure of a transistor's performance. It is the current gain of a transistor in a common emitter circuit. Beta is usually expressed by the Greek letter β. It is equal to the collector current divided by the base current, with the collector voltage held constant.

Base resistor—Same as a bias resistor, but identifies the location.

Bias resistor—A resistor which sets an operating voltage usually to a transistor base. No appreciable current flows through the bias resistor.

Bridge rectifier—Four diodes, usually in one package. They rectify a full-wave AC voltage to DC. Frequently found in audio electronic equipment as part of the power supply.

Bypass capacitor—A capacitor which is connected from a transistor element to ground. A low value of capacitance, serving to shunt unwanted high frequencies to ground.

Collector current—The amount of current flowing to the collector.

Collector load resistor—A resistor providing the operating voltage for the transistor. The output voltage from the transistor is developed across this resistor due to the current flow through the resistor.

Common collector circuit—A transistor stage where the collector is closest to ground potential. Also known as an emitter follower, providing a relatively low output impedance.

Common emitter circuit—A transistor stage where the emitter is closest to ground potential. The most common transistor circuit for audio.

Complementary pair—Two transistors working together, basically the same type of device, but NPN and PNP devices. Usually found in power amplifier output circuits.

Coupling capacitor—A capacitor which blocks the DC voltage present at the transistor from being passed to the following circuit elements.

Current gain—The measure of a transistor's gain. A transistor uses current rather than voltage for amplification.

Darlington pair—A pair of transistors cascaded. Available as a one package unit. Capable of high current gains.

Diode—A two-terminal semiconductor which will allow significant current to flow in one direction only. Higher current capacity diodes are usually called rectifiers.

Emitter current—The amount of current flowing to the emitter.

Field-Effect Transistor (FET)—A type of transistor which operates as a voltage, rather than current amplifier. They are usually not capable of handling any amount of power.

Heat sink—An aluminum fin fastened to the transistor, or an aluminum block to which one or more transistors are fastened. The heatsink helps dissipate heat developed in the transistor.

Heat sink compound—A thermally conductive compound smeared on either side of the heat sink insulator, so that heat from the transistor is passed to the heatsink.

Heat sink insulator—A mica sheet sized to fit a specific transistor. It is placed between the transistor and the heat sink to provide electrical insulation. The transistor collector is above ground potential, and the heat sink is usually at ground potential.

NPN transistor—A transistor that utilizes a positive voltage from the collector supply rail.

PNP transistor—A transistor that utilizes a negative voltage from the collector supply rail.

Power transistor—A transistor capable of handling large amounts of power, with little gain available. Frequently used in power amplifier output stages, connected in a parallel mode for greater power handling capacity.

Shunt capacitor—Large value electrolytic capacitor placed from positive or negative supply lines to ground to assist in reducing the effective supply line impedance.

Stage gain—The gain through one or more transistors which have specific input and output points.

Supply rails—The positive and negative DC supply lines to transistor circuitry. Other than for unique cases, they are not actual rails.

Thermal runaway—A condition in a transistor when the collector current increases beyond the safe limit causing heating of the junction, which causes the collector current to further increase. Usually the transistor will be destroyed.

Vcc—The term used to express the positive or negative supply voltage.

Pinout schemes for various types of transistors

The three general transistor types are germanium, silicon, and field-effect. Any transistor, whether germanium, silicon, or field-effect has at least three terminals. For germanium and silicon devices, the terminals are called collector, emitter, and base. Some specialized transistors have more than three terminals.

"FET" is a shortened version of the full name: field-effect transistor. However, the terminals for an FET have different names. These terminals are called source, gate, and drain.

The physical pinout depends on the transistor package, which is why we have shown the packages first. Here are some of the more common packages:

Figure 15004-1.
Common transistor packages

From left to right, the packages are: TO-220, TO-66, TO-92, and TO-39. We have not shown all packages available, just the more common packages. Some packages have been replaced by JEDEC with later numbers. However, many catalogs, schematics, and data sheets will show these earlier numbers.

For the packages shown, here are the common pinouts:

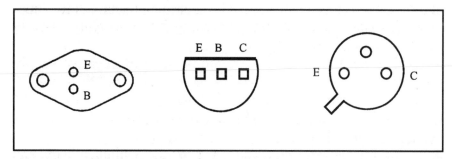

Figure 15004-3.
Common pinouts

We emphasize that these pinouts, particularly for the TO-66 and TO-92, change for different devices. Therefore, don't assume as to pinouts, but check the manufacturer's datasheet for the exact pinout.

The TO-92 package is common for FET devices used in audio, the common pinout from left to right is: drain, source, gate.

We have not shown the pinouts for surface-mounted devices; they are beyond the scope of this chapter. Probably you have seen surface-mounted devices. They are smaller than the conventional leaded devices, and the leads are connected to pads on the surface of the PCB, without going through a hole.

Small test lead points must be used when testing these devices. Replacing them should not be undertaken without adequate training, as a PCB can be quickly ruined if appropriate desoldering and soldering equipment is not used.

Various markings used on transistors

There are three marking system standards in use throughout the world. The American standard was created by the JEDEC (Joint Electron Device Engineering Council). JEDEC was created by EIA (Electronic Industries Alliance) in 1958 to provide for standardization of discrete semiconductor devices and later expanded in 1970 to include integrated circuits.

A transistor marked according to the JEDEC standard will show (for example): 2N4401. "2N" is a prefix to show that the device is a transistor, and "4401" indicates the specific device. In addition to the type number, you will find the manufacturer's logo, the country of manufacture, and a date code. The country of manufacture is provided to comply with U.S. import laws, and the date code provides some traceability for the device manufacturer.

JIS (Japanese Industry Standard) is type descriptive. Letter/number combinations that are used indicate the transistor type and specification. A transistor might be marked as "2SA1187," the first two letters indicating the device is a PNP-HF transistor, and the four digits are the specific device number. JIS is also used in the Far East. The manufacturer's logo, country of manufacture, and date code are printed on the device.

Pro-Electron, the European standard, is also type descriptive. Again, letter/number combinations are used. A transistor might be marked as "BC107," the first letter indicating the device is a silicon device, the second letter indicating the device is for small signal AF (audio frequency) usage. The three numbers are the specific device number. Pro-Electron is used throughout the United Kingdom and Europe. Again, manufacturer's logo, country of manufacture, and date code are printed on the device.

In addition to the three world standards, an equipment manufacturer will have transistors marked with numbers specific to that manufacturer. These numbers are assigned by the manufacturer. These are usually referred to as "house" numbers. The "house" number may be a combination of letters and numbers, having no relation to JEDEC, JIS, or Pro-Electron standards.

When confronted with a "house" number, there are several methods to find the equivalent JEDEC number. First, contact the manufacturer of the equipment and ask its tech support group for a JEDEC equivalent to the device in question. Second, through trial and error, supervised by a circuit design engineer, try similar devices to match the desired circuit configuration. Third, work with a circuit design engineer to determine the circuit parameters so that the engineer might suggest a JEDEC type. Lastly (and very time-consuming) measure a good unit, and display the operating curves of the device using a transistor curve tracer. Then, by matching against JEDEC specifications, a match might be made.

If you have a device marked to either JIS or Pro-Electron standards, and you want to substitute a JEDEC equivalent, there are various reference guides available. In addition, many distributors have devices in stock manufactured under JIS or Pro-Electron standards.

Identify various types of transistors

A transistor may be identified by recognizing the type number, measuring the device with a DVM to determine whether the transistor is NPN or PNP, or measuring the device with a curve tracer. The last technique is rather expensive. A skilled engineer may also identify the transistor by reviewing the circuit around the transistor.

The physical package is a definite clue. A power transistor will have a larger package than a signal transistor. In addition, the collector may have a mounting tab for connection to a heat sink. Packages having unusual shapes are apt to be high-frequency devices.

Three basic symbols are used to draw transistors and FETs on schematic drawings. An NPN transistor is shown by this symbol:

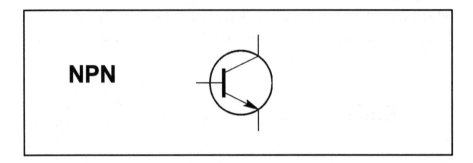

A PNP transistor is shown by this symbol:

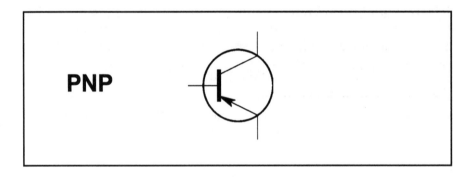

An FET is shown by this symbol:

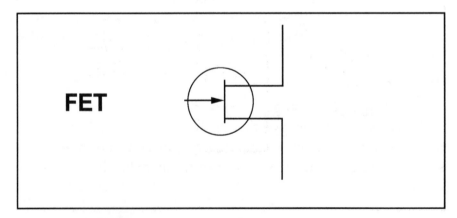

On a schematic, the letters NPN, PNP, or FET do not appear by the symbol. A semiconductor can be either a transistor or a diode. We're including diodes, even though they're not transistors, as diodes are used in many circuits. A diode is shown by this symbol:

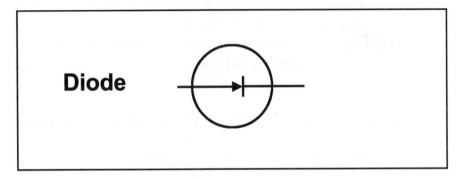

Identify basic transistor configurations

We have begun with a common emitter circuit, one of the most common circuits in audio. Figure 15004-8 is the diagram.

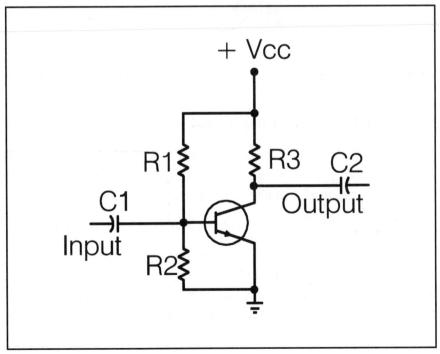

Figure 15004-8.
Common emitter circuit

The supply current from +Vcc flows through R1 and R2 to form a bias voltage-dividing network for the transistor base. R1 and R2 are bias resistors. The supply current also flows through R3, then through the collector to the emitter to ground or -Vcc. R3 is a collector load resistor. The output voltage is developed across R3. C1 is a coupling capacitor. It isolates the DC network around the transistor from affecting the previous circuit element. C2 is a coupling capacitor. It performs a similar function as C1, but as the output coupling capacitor.

Figure 15004-9 shows a common base circuit.

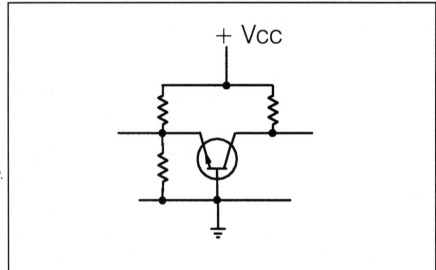

Figure 15004-9. A common base circuit.

Common base circuits aren't often used in audio, as the configuration isn't suited to audio. This circuit is more prone to oscillate, so they are useful in oscillator circuits.

On the next page, Figure 15004-10 shows a common collector circuit.

This circuit provides no gain, but provides a lower output impedance. As with the common base circuit, signal polarity doesn't change from input to output. This circuit is occasionally used as an output circuit.

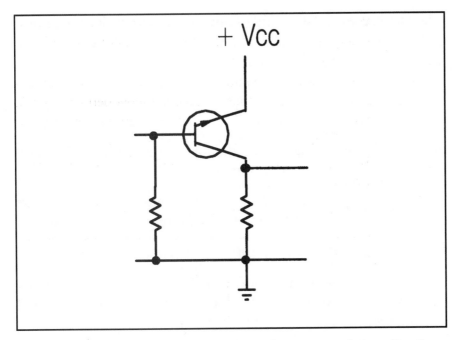

Figure 15004-10.
A common collec-
tor circuit.

Thousands of circuit designs have been created since Bardeen, Brattain, and Shockley developed the first transistor in the late 1940s. They received a Nobel Prize in 1956 for their work. These three basics are just the beginning. Totem pole, complementary pair, differential input; these are just a few of the recognized circuit configurations. As you study any transistor circuit diagram, review the transistor type, the supply voltage, and the basic configuration of each transistor. Determine where is the current flowing, where are the transistor inputs and outputs.

Understanding circuits requires studying them and using common sense. Designing circuits requires education and several years of study.

Analysis of Transistor Circuits

As you read in the description at the beginning of this chapter, the words 'signal phase' are used. A few years ago, the audio industry realized that the appropriate word is not phase, but polarity. Phase refers to the time relationship of any one frequency within a range of frequencies, using a stated frequency as the reference. In the technical specifications for an audio power amplifier, you might read: "Less than 5 degrees of phase shift from 20 Hz to 20 kHz."

Polarity refers to a signal at a point in a circuit with reference to the same signal at another point in the circuit. Polarity also refers to a signal at the input to an amplifier or other equipment with reference to the same signal at the output.

Therefore, we are using the correct terminology here, and are cautioning you as to the terminology used on the NICET exam.

Determine signal polarity (phase) in transistor circuits

The common emitter configuration is widely used in audio, which was also covered in Work Element 15004. The circuit is shown here:

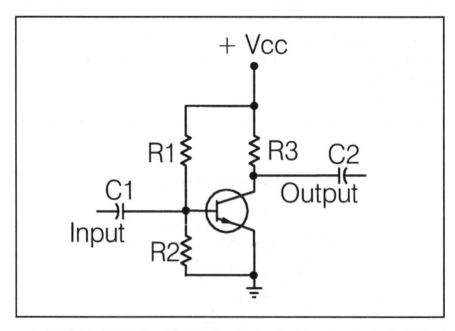

Figure 15005-1. Common emitter configuration

With both NPN and PNP transistors, the signal polarity is shifted 180 degrees between the base and the collector. The signal polarity isn't shifted between the emitter and the collector. Therefore, with a common emitter configuration, the output signal polarity will be shifted 180 degrees.

The reason is due, not to the manufacturing technique for transistors, but part of the inherent properties of the 'p' and 'n' carriers. We won't go into that, but those carriers are the reason for identifying transistors as NPN or PNP devices. If you study basic transistor theory, you will find more explanation.

Why is this of interest? If you are working with a monaural system (one loudspeaker channel, for example), the polarity is of little significance. If you are working with a stereo system of any sort, the polarity change is of great significance. If the polarity between two channels isn't the same, then one channel is 180 degrees out of polarity with the other.

As a result, your ear does not hear the stereo localization. Normally, any program material that is panned or appears on both channels will sound as though the program material is somewhere between the two loudspeakers. When the two signals are out of polarity, the sounds will not be perceived to lie between the loudspeakers, but will sound as though they are simultaneously at the left and right.

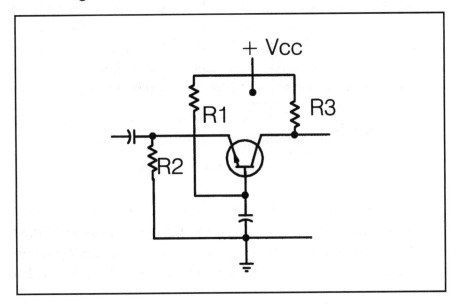

Figure 15005-2. Common base circuit

Audio equipment manufacturers design equipment so that the output signal polarity is the same as the input signal polarity. This simplifies system design, so you don't have to be concerned about system polarity. If two microphone cables are wired out of polarity, and the microphones connected to those cables are used near to each other, any sound picked up by both microphones will be greatly attenuated.

Restating what you earlier read, with both NPN and PNP transistors, the signal polarity is shifted 180 degrees between the base and the collector. The signal polarity isn't shifted between the emitter and the collector. Therefore, with both common base and common collector circuits, the signal polarity is not changed between input and output.

Determine signal amplitude in transistor circuits

You set an input signal, then calculate the gain for each stage, then calculate the signal amplitude at the output of each stage. If the stage gain is 10, and the input signal is 0.1 volts, then the output signal amplitude is 1 volt. If the stage gain is 10, and the input signal is 0.01 volts, then the output signal is 0.1 volts.

Determining signal amplitude is fairly straightforward. But you may need to be able to calculate gain in transistor circuits. (Expect this on the NICET test.) The technique for calculating transistor or stage gain is slightly more complicated. In 'Elements of Transistor Circuits,' we defined alpha and beta as applied to transistors.

Figure 15005-2 shows a common base circuit. This circuit is seldom found in audio designs, except for specific applications.

These are the equations for calculating gain:

$$R_{GAIN} = \frac{R_{OUT}}{R_{IN}}$$

$$E_{GAIN} = \alpha \times R_{GAIN}$$

This circuit will have a low input resistance, and a high output resistance. For emitter follower and common base circuits, the gain will always be less than 1. The output resistance is essentially equal to the value of R_3.

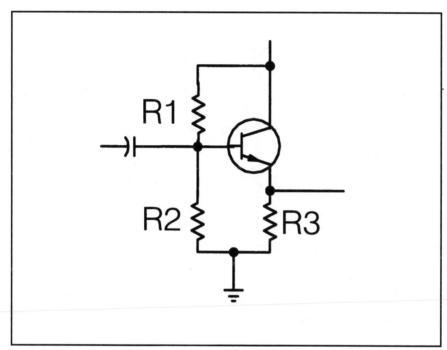

Figure 15005-3.
Common collector circuit

Figure 15005-3 shows a common collector circuit. This circuit is seldom found in audio designs.

These are the equations for calculating gain:

$$R_{GAIN} = \frac{R_{OUT}}{R_{IN}}$$

$$E_{GAIN} = R_{GAIN} \times [\alpha + 1]$$

This circuit will have a low input resistance and a high output resistance. For common collector and common base circuits, the gain will always be less than 1. The output resistance is essentially equal to the value of R_3.

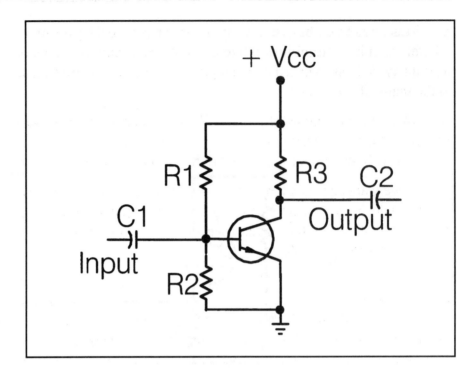

Figure 15005-4.
Common emitter
circuit

Figure 15005-4 shows a common emitter circuit.

These are the equations for calculating gain:

$$R_{GAIN} = \frac{R_{OUT}}{R_{IN}}$$

$$E_{GAIN} = \alpha \times R_{GAIN}$$

Identify various kinds of logic gates

Logic gates are basic decision makers, operating with two binary numbers, 0 and 1. If the lamp in your office is on, we represent that with an ON, or a 1. If the lamp is off, we represent that with an OFF, or a 0. If there are two lamps in your office, we use the same terms to indicate the condition of the lamps.

If there are two lamps in your office, and we want an indicator outside to show if both lamps are on, we use an AND gate. This gate provides a 1 as an output, *if, and only if,* both inputs to the gate are 1. Therefore, if both lamps are ON, both inputs are 1, and the output is 1. If only one lamp is on, only one input is a 1, the output will be a 0, since the AND condition hasn't been met.

If we want an indicator to show if either lamp is on, we use an OR gate. This gate provides a 1 as an output, *if either* input to the gate is 1. If both inputs to the gate are 1, the output is still a 1.

If we want an indicator to show if both lamps are off, we use a NAND gate. This is also called a negative AND gate. If we want an indicator to show if either lamp is off, we use a NOR gate. This is also called a negative OR gate.

If we have a lamp in a hallway, and a switch at either end to control the lamp, then we use an XOR gate, which is short for eXclusive OR. Both switches have two positions. If both switches are in the same position, regardless of the position, the lamp is OFF. If the switches are in opposing positions, regardless of the position, the lamp is ON.

It would seem that there might be an easier method of showing the conditions, and this is such a method. It's called a truth table, and for the 'AND' gate, it looks like this:

A	B	OUT
L	L	L
L	H	L
H	L	L
H	H	H

Each of the gates we've discussed are two input devices. They aren't limited to two inputs; three and four inputs are often used.

Just to keep yourself in shape, here are blank tables for you to construct truth tables for the balance of the logic gates.

A	B	Out

A	B	Out

A	B	Out

A	B	Out

Interpret logic gate symbols

Here are the various symbols. We've added the symbol types inside each symbol for your convenience. In schematics, you'll find only the symbol. In many cases, the pin number to the device will be shown next to the input or output connection. This helps considerably when troubleshooting.

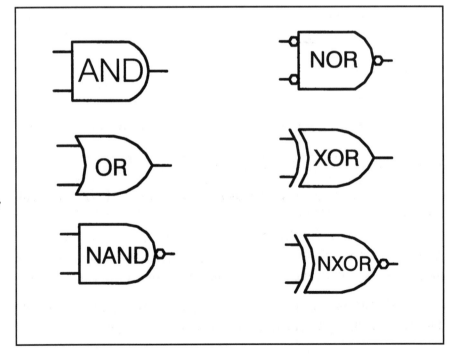

Figure 15005-5.
Logic gate symbols

Note the circle at some output pins. This is an indicator with logic gates to show that the output is inverted from the input. In each case, you'll note that the device type is preceded with an N.

In this discussion of logic gates, you may have noticed that we've made no distinction between discrete (transistor) and IC (Integrated Circuit) circuits. The same logic gate can be built very easily with discrete components, but the cost and size of IC components are such that discrete circuitry is confined to classroom or experimental use.

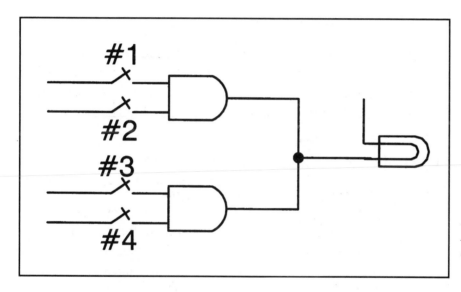

Figure 15005-6. An agreement device

Understand schematics/diagrams of logic gates

As you see by Figure 15005-6, all the gates are AND. Let's call this an Agreement Device. Each of the switches is controlled by one politician. In order for the lamp to go on, *all* of the politicians must turn on their switch. If only three of the politicians agree, then the lamp will stay dark, indicating disagreement.

Let's add to the system by adding a chairman's switch, which can override all of the politicians' selections.

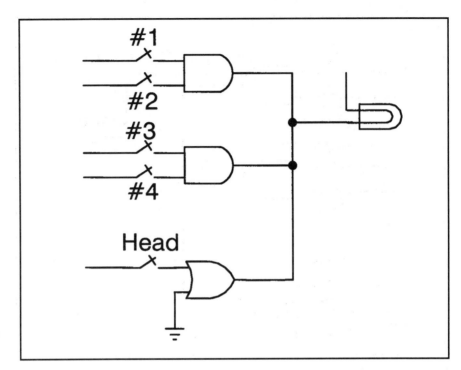

Figure 15005-7.
Agreement device
with addition of a
chairman's switch

You see an OR gate added in Figure 15005-7. The unused input is tied to ground to prevent noise and garbage from triggering the input. The majority of logic gates are 5-volt devices, although many other operating voltages are available.

Let's expand our Agreement Device one more step. Study Figure 15005-8 at the top of the next page. We replaced the OR gate with an XOR gate, one input controlled by the chairman, one input controlled by the voters. Other than our political comments, do you see the significance? If the chairman overrides the politicians, the people can operate the switch, changing the chairman's decision.

In the bibliography, you'll find references to books on transistors and digital logic circuits. Many of them are quite cheap. Also visit your local bookstore and browse the used-book section. If you have easy access to various databooks, make a point of doing that. Most of the major manufacturers—Motorola, National, Texas Instruments, among others—have some excellent basic information on digital logic circuits.

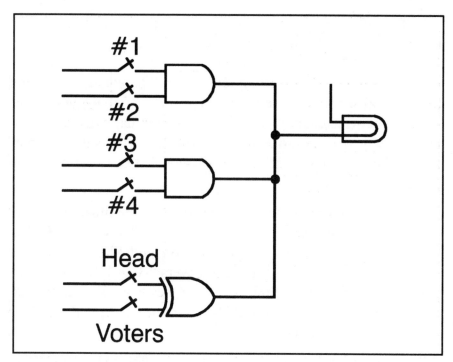

Figure 15005-8.

Ground References

There are two purposes for a ground system: safety and system noise. When a system is properly grounded, a person can touch two different conducting materials in an electrical system without receiving a lethal or annoying shock resulting from the potential difference, since both surfaces are at the same potential. System noise is reduced or eliminated in a grounded system because unwanted signals and noise are conducted to earth. Thus, the system is quieter electronically.

Relating to electronics, what is ground and what is earth? Even if you're standing on the earth, you don't necessarily have a low resistance path to earth. You may be standing on dry sand wearing heavy rubber-soled boots. In that case, the resistance between your body and earth is rather high. If you are working on 120-volt AC equipment, the probability of getting a lethal connection between you and earth is rather low.

The NEC definition of "grounded" refers to a connection to earth or some conducting path in place of the earth. Ground, therefore, is simply a reference, indicating either an actual connection to earth, or the part of a circuit at "ground" potential. You might have a total working system, with a ground reference within the system, yet no actual earth connection. This situation is very common. Any device operating from internal batteries, such as a portable radio or a personal stereo with no connection to earth, falls in this classification.

If a device is connected to AC power, then the situation is more complex. A review of Articles 200, 210, and 250 of the NEC® is recommended. Article 200 covers "Use and Identification of Grounded Conductors." Article 210 covers "Branch Circuits." Article 250 covers "Grounding." You may never work directly with electrical circuits, but you should be aware of the parts of the Code that deal with grounding.

In any residential location installed according to the NEC, from the service panel or breaker panel, a bonding wire of not less than #8 AWG must be connected to a made electrode of not less than 8 feet in length driven into the earth. For that residential location, the ground bar in the breaker panel is the ground reference. At that location, the neutral bus and the ground bus are connected together.

Commercial installations are more complex, but they are installed on the same basis—with a ground reference at the main power entrance to the installation. If separate power transformers are used for various parts of the installation, each transformer and breaker panel is considered a separate grounding location.

Identification of Ground Loops

The term is casually used, but sometimes not understood. Figure 3-6 shows an example of a ground loop. As you see, there are two paths to ground. There is a shielded cable between devices, with the shield connected at both ends. In addition, each device is con-

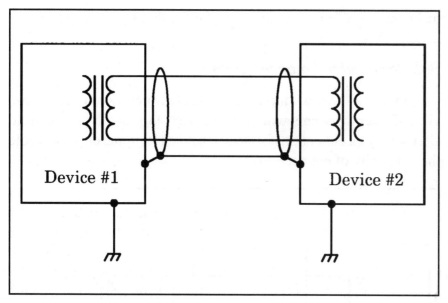

Figure 3-6. A ground loop

nected to earth. Since each path has a different resistance, any current flowing in those paths will create a potential difference between the two ground paths. There will always be voltage in a ground wire, but now we have a potential difference or a voltage between two ground wires.

In this case, the problem is solved by connecting the shield at one end only. The recommended convention is to connect shields at the source.

Measurement of resistance to ground

Using a VOM or DVM to measure the ground resistance is ineffective. Earth impedance measuring devices measure the earth's impedance in an area by sending a complex fixed potential current to earth via one reference rod, measuring the voltage at two or three variable rods, and calculating the resistance. If several locations are used, keeping the reference rod at one location, a better idea of the conductivity in an area may be obtained.

There are other techniques, which we won't go into. Regardless of the technique, the soil and moisture conditions in the earth make any set of measurements useful for that local area (approximately 20 ft. by 20 ft.) only.

Balanced and unbalanced connections

Figure 3-7 shows the connections between two balanced devices. The components within the devices, to provide the balanced circuit, may be either transformers or active electronic circuitry. Note the simplicity of connections.

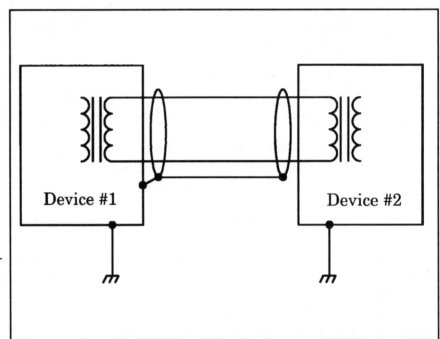

Figure 3-7. Connections between two balanced devices

We are showing transformer connections at both source and destination; however, the principle still applies for active electronic devices. In terms of ground isolation at all frequencies, a transformer will be more effective. Since there are components to ground in active electronic devices, isolation will not be as effective. However, the system requirements must be very strict for the effects to be noticeable. You may notice in the figures where two-conductor shielded cable is depicted, the cable is not twisted. This was done for drafting convenience, and isn't true in reality.

With unbalanced systems, the grounding system isn't so simple. However, if the same principles are followed, the system should operate satisfactorily. Figure 3-8 shows the connections between two unbalanced devices, the most difficult condition.

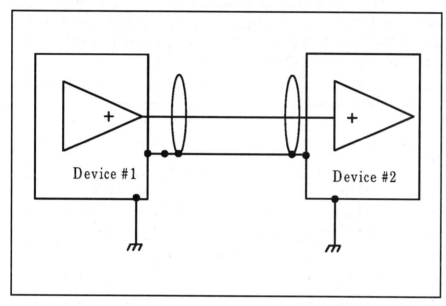

Figure 3-8. *Connections between two unbalanced devices*

In this case, you're between a rock and a hard place. If you remove the shield connection from Device No. 1, you're depending on the earth connection to carry the return signal. That may increase the system noise. On the other hand, if you disconnect the earth connection from Device No. 1, you may have an electrical hazard because the device now depends on the unbalanced connection for its electrical ground. First question: Does this connection scheme cause hum? If it doesn't, leave it alone. If it does, then experiment. Always remember that safety is paramount; do not use a ground-lifter or ground isolator.

Figure 3-9 shows an appropriate connection scheme for two unbalanced devices.

What is different? Notice the additional ground wire between devices. The recommended size might be AWG #10. Use of unbal-

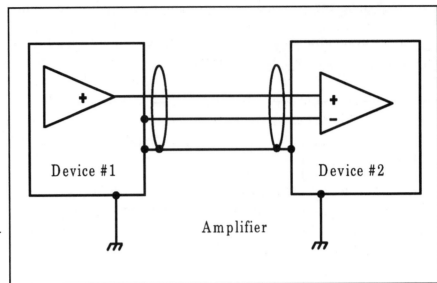

Figure 3-9. Connection scheme for two unbalanced devices

anced wiring should be confined to small systems, and short (less than 10 feet) cable lengths.

Connecting an unbalanced source to a balanced load is almost easy. Review Figure 3-10 to see the practice.

The ground reference for the balanced input doesn't care (within limits) where it is connected.

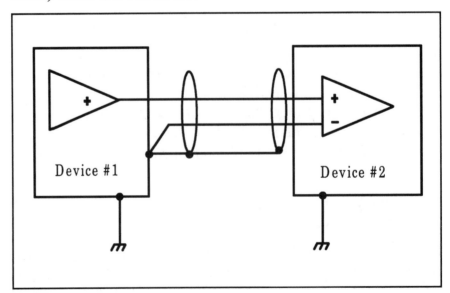

Figure 3-10. Connecting an unbalanced source to a balanced load

Grounding Systems: Isolated, unipoint, massive

Any grounding system, to be effective, requires attention to both power and audio circuits. Merely laying out and wiring the audio and audio ground system without paying equal attention to the AC power system may create problems requiring later solutions. If you're building a small boardroom sound reinforcement system with no A/V equipment, then you can probably consider the AC power system as a given.

But if you're installing a large system, requiring a week or more of on-site installation, then the AC power system should not be taken for granted. Even though you may not have any say in the installation of the AC power system, it is worth the time and effort to examine the system with the on-site electrical contractor.

An isolated ground system is also referred to as a unipoint, star, tree, or hub system. The beginning, or hub, of the ground system is physically close to the grounding location for the AC power system. Theoretically, the ground wire from each element or rack cabinet in the system is returned to that hub location. In reality, that's seldom achievable, so a system similar to Figure 3-11 is utilized.

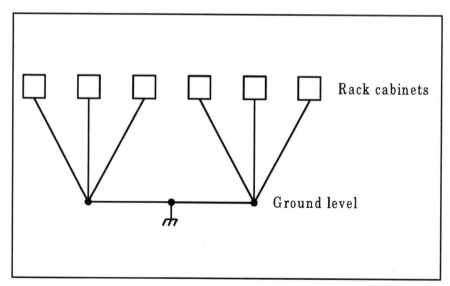

Rack cabinets

Ground level

Figure 3-11.

In this case the ground level is a bus bar near the rack locations, in a junction box of appropriate size. The wiring from each rack to the bus bar should be AWG #10 minimum, green insulation, in conduit. The bus bar must be electrically isolated from the junction box. From the bus bar to the grounding location, the wire size should be AWG #10 minimum, green insulation, in conduit.

With an installation of the size we're discussing, isolated ground AC receptacles are used. These are commonly referred to as "IG" receptacles. The receptacles are available in an orange color to differentiate them from conventional grounded receptacles. IG receptacles have a U-ground position, but the screw terminal for that position is isolated from the receptacle frame.

These are general practices only, and are not a reference to the NEC®. These are advisory to you, and must be discussed with a licensed electrician before being put into use. A separate insulated AWG #12 wire, green insulation, is run from the receptacle with the black and white wires to the panel board. All green wires from the IG receptacles are run through the panel board to a bus bar located in another junction box. Located in that junction box is a bus bar, similar to that used for the rack ground wires. From the bus bar to the grounding location, the wire size should be AWG #10 minimum, green insulation, in conduit. At the grounding location, the ground wire from the panel board, and the wires from the two bus bars are securely connected to the ground rod.

A wiring and grounding practice that is very common in large video installations and video postproduction houses is the use of a "massive ground" system. In this system, all shields, both video and audio, are connected to devices at both ends. An isolated ground system is provided for AC power. In addition, an AWG #8 cable connects the frame ground from each technical room or rack group to a central location.

This practice is necessary as almost all video cable within an installation is coaxial cable, with a center wire and shield. Therefore, the entire system is "unbalanced." Some equipment manufacturers may isolate the shell of the video connector (usually a BNC type) from the chassis.

The principle provides a massive ground plane, which has such low resistance because of the number of cables in the system that the IR drop is negligible.

With any grounding system, care must be taken that all connections are secure; they must be bonded. If dissimilar metals are fastened together, a galvanic reaction may set up over time, increasing the resistance of the connection. Any crimped connections must be gas-tight or made with ratchet-type crimping tools.

Questions

1. In Figure 3-1, if the battery voltage is 18 volts, what is the current through the top resistor? (Hint: Do you really need your calculator?)
2. In Figure 3-1, if all the resistors are 1k, what is the current flowing from the 9v battery?
3. When is impedance valid in a DC circuit?
4. Is the AC line frequency 60 Hz throughout the rest of the world?
5. What is the inductive reactance of a 4 mFd capacitor?
6. In Figure 3-2, if the resistor value is 2000 ohms, what is the impedance of the circuit at 2 kHz?
7. In Figure 3-3, if the resistor value is 1 ohm, what is the approximate impedance of the circuit at 1 kHz?
8. A complementary pair is:
    a. Two technicians who work well together.
    b. Two transistors working together, basically the same type of device, but NPN and PNP devices.
9. Heat sinks can only be used for transistors. True or false? Explain your answer.
10. JEDEC is a federal governmental department, similar to DOE. True or false? Explain your answer.

11. The basic transistor configurations shown are the only circuits that can be used in audio design. True or false? Explain your answer.

12. What type of logic gate is a turnstile at a football game?

13. How many inputs to that logic gate?

14. What is the difference between "ground" and "earth?"

15. The NEC® has jurisdiction concerning grounding systems. True or false? Explain your answer.

16. Are balanced connections valid only for transformers? True or false? Explain your answer.

Chapter 4

Systems Components

by Bob Bushnell

- **NICET Work Element 16009, Advanced Microphones**
- **NICET's Description:** "*Install and troubleshoot microphone systems. Perform repairs as needed. Lay out basic microphone systems considering such factors as loudspeaker location, NOM, ambient noise, working distances, etc. Use manufacturers' literature.*"
- **NICET Work Element 16014, Power Amplifiers**
- **NICET's Description:** "*Conduct performance testing of power amplifiers for power output, frequency response, signal-to-noise ratio, and gain. (Understand correct operation of) Interpret common power output indicators. Provide for proper load matching, and AC power requirements.*"
- **NICET Work Element 16015, Mixing Consoles**
- **NICET's Description:** "*Install and set up mixing consoles, considering gain structure, type of use, and connected devices. Identify the functions (e.g. output grouping, cue/solo, muting, mono/stereo, matrix mixing monitoring, etc.), applications, major components, and operational considerations of sound reinforcement, recording, and stage monitor mixing consoles.*"
- **NICET Work Element 15010, Audio Transformers and Autotransformers**
- **NICET's Description:** "*Identify the characteristics and applications of common loudspeaker transformers and autotransformers. Select appropriate taps.*"

Advanced Microphones

Choose the right microphone for a given application

Choosing the correct microphone is not simply a matter of selecting the most expensive unit, but narrowing the choices to find the appropriate unit or units for the given application. There are many types of microphones available on the market. You can narrow down the selection by asking the following questions:

1. What are the loudspeaker locations with respect to the microphone?
2. What polar pattern is needed?
3. Will an automatic microphone mixer be used?
4. Does your company concentrate on one microphone manufacturer?
5. Is quality or price more important?
6. What physical mounting is desired?

If the nearest loudspeaker is within 10 feet of the microphone, certainly a cardioid microphone is in order. If the nearest loudspeaker is 100 feet away, and the desired SPL (Sound Pressure Level) is no more than 100 dB, then the pickup pattern can be omnidirectional, if desired. These are general statements, and not to be considered as design guidelines.

There are several polar patterns to use. From the widest pattern to the narrowest, the patterns are omnidirectional, cardioid, supercardioid, hyper-cardioid. There is also a bidirectional pattern. A hyper-cardioid-pattern microphone is sometimes referred to as a shotgun microphone. If you study the manufacturer's literature, you will see graphs of the microphone's polar pattern.

If the system is a plantwide paging system, the selection is almost self-determining. We know that feedback isn't a problem, and that the microphone will be a desk-mount or gooseneck. Reasonable voice quality is required, but it must be a durable unit; definitely a dynamic unit, low-impedance, possibly with an XLR-type connector as the mounting device.

Automatic microphone mixers are a useful adjunct to a system. They are not perfect devices, as they don't control the level of the individual microphones. They are certainly effective in NOM situations, and in situations where an operator may be simply opening and closing microphone input channels.

Other than specialty microphones for recording or research applications, the primary microphone manufacturers have a wide choice of microphones available. In situations where you're free to select the microphone depending on the application, you should have no problems in searching through the manufacturer's catalog that you normally use.

Many microphones have optional mounting techniques, depending on the application. The most common mount is a 5/8-27 thread mount. Several manufacturers make a wide range of adapters working with that thread size.

Use PAG/NAG to place microphones relative to speakers

Don and Carolyn Davis started a new deal with their inauguration of the PAG/NAG concept. Potential Acoustic Gain and Needed Acoustical Gain are powerful tools when used with care. They are very useful for both outdoor and indoor acoustical environments.

An outdoor acoustical environment is a free-field situation; the majority of sound waves from the loudspeakers or cluster travel outward, with few reflections. If the amphitheater is filled with people, so much the better, for the human body is an excellent sound absorber.

If you happen to be working in an anechoic chamber, where all sound waves are direct and there are no reflective surfaces, that is a free-field situation. In contrast, an indoor acoustical environment has reflective surfaces, providing reverberation and possibly echo.

What is PAG? It is the increase in SPL (Sound Pressure Level) or the maximum acoustic gain that can be obtained from the sound reinforcement system before feedback occurs.

For an outdoor environment only, the equation for PAG is:

$$PAG = 20\log\frac{(D_1 \times D_0)}{(D_2 \times D_S)}$$

If we restate the equation on one line to make calculations easier, we have:

$$PAG = 20\log((D_1 \times D_0) / (D_2 \times D_S))$$

Defining the terms: D_1 is the distance from the microphone to the nearest loudspeaker, D_0 is the distance to the most distant listener, D_2 is the distance from the loudspeaker to the farthest listener, and D_S is the distance from the talker to the microphone.

An indoor acoustical environment has reflective surfaces, providing reverberation and probably echo. The PAG/NAG equations must accommodate the amount of absorptive material on the walls, floor, and ceiling; the volume of the room; and the directivity of the loudspeakers. Because of the various equations involved, and the amount of material that must be covered, we will not go into the discussion of PAG/NAG for indoor environments. It is suggested that the selected resources by Ballou and Davis be studied in detail in addition. (See *Selected Resources for Further Study* in the back of this book.)

Correct application of specialty microphones

Measurement microphones are omnidirectional devices, with flat response characteristics. They are usually part of the measuring device, such as a sound-level meter, or a 1/3-octave analyzer. A conventional microphone might be used in place of the measurement microphone, for example, when you might want to show the frequency response characteristics of the conventional microphone.

Low-cost magnetic microphones are available for telephone recording use. They utilize the magnetic field generated in the telephone receiver.

Musical instrument pickup microphones

Several manufacturers have made a specialty of providing contact microphones for almost all acoustic instruments. Use and installation of these microphones must be done in close coordination with the musicians involved in their playing. The musician will be well-acquainted with the sound of his or her instrument, and slight variations in the location of the pickup may drastically affect the sound quality of the instrument.

These microphones may be electret, magnetic, or piezoelectric depending on the instrument they will be used with. They may be mounted to the surface of the instrument, or for some wind instruments, built into the mouthpiece area. These units allow the musician to move about the stage or studio, while still providing good sound quality from the instrument.

Guitar pickups are still the most widely used devices. Magnetic devices have been popular. They depend on varying a magnetic field by the movement of a particular string. Since they are a magnetic pickup, external hum fields can degrade the instrument's sound quality. Hum bucking units may alleviate the hum pickup problem.

Boundary pickup

Another type of microphone that has received wide acceptance is the boundary microphone, also called a pressure zone microphone. The boundary microphone works on the simple principle that sound waves reflect from a point on a surface. If a microphone capsule is located very close (within 1 or 2 mm) of a surface, it will pick up sound waves reflecting from that surface, as well as the direct sound. The pickup pattern may be a hemisphere, or a narrower pattern.

A boundary microphone is an excellent choice for boardrooms and teleconferencing applications. It is unobtrusive, yet effective. If papers or books are placed on the microphone, they will affect the sound pickup. The microphone is also excellent for iive stage applications. Using a conventional microphone for live stage applications must be done with care. A conventional microphone located near to a surface will have an uneven frequency response due to comb effects. This is due to cancellations of specific frequencies because of the direct versus reflected sound paths at the microphone.

Selecting hanging microphones for audience or choir

Generally the first requirement for hanging microphones is unobtrusiveness, a blending into the background. This is particularly important in a church, where any element not in keeping with the architecture is disturbing. If the microphone(s) can be hung from the ceiling, with the cable in the attic, and the visible cable and microphone are colored to match the background, so much the better.

The microphone must be small in size, because of visibility and movement due to air currents. There should be no reflective surfaces on the microphone which will distract the congregation. If a microphone on a long cable is gently swaying, even on the order of parts of an inch, it will be very distracting. Light-gauge fishing line might be used to restrain the microphones. Again, the fishing line should not reflect light. If the gauge is small enough, the line may be invisible, depending on the distance.

A cardioid or even hyper-cardioid pickup pattern might be in order, depending on the main cluster location. Site inspection, as well as a study of the architectural drawings (if available), will help in determining acceptable microphone locations. Experimental microphone placements will be in order.

Audience microphones may be easier to locate, as applause or congregation responses tend to be more evenly spread among the congregation.

Troubleshooting microphone systems

Dynamic and ribbon microphones are generators; condenser and electret microphones are externally powered. In addition, the active element in a condenser microphone is simply the capacitive element in the microphone preamplifier.

Other than replacing the connector, repairing any microphone in the field is virtually impossible. The assembly is delicate, and the probability of getting magnetic particles into the voice coil gap of the dynamic microphone is high. The only tasks that can be performed on a condenser or electret microphone in the field is to replace the vacuum tube in the condenser microphone, or to replace batteries in either of those two microphone types.

Repairing a dynamic microphone in the shop may be performed, but under clean conditions. As previously stated, the probability of getting magnetic particles into the voice coil gap of the dynamic microphone is high. The voice coil is small, and the gap is on the order of thousandths of an inch.

As in any troubleshooting process, it must be logical and orderly. If you approach the process on a hit-or-miss basis, you are likely to waste time without finding the cause.

Troubleshooting a microphone is easily accomplished by substituting another microphone of the same general type, then verifying operation of the sound reinforcement system. The substitution should be first performed at the microphone location, then at the mixer with a known microphone cable. If the microphone has been physically damaged to the extent that sound quality is degraded, it should be returned to the manufacturer for repair or disposed of if the repair costs are prohibitive.

With condenser microphones, you should determine where the power supply is located for the microphone, or if the microphone is phantom-powered from the mixer. If there is a power supply, and substituting another supply of the same type cures the problem, you're done.

If the microphone is phantom-powered from the mixer, possibly the phantom power switch on the rear of the mixer was turned off. Be sure that the gain control for that input is at maximum attenuation before turning on the phantom power switch. Otherwise, a loud pop will be heard in the system, possibly damaging the high-frequency loudspeakers. It is a good idea to turn off phantom power or the power supply for condenser microphones before disconnecting or connecting the microphone.

Power amplifier output power and gain testing

When measuring any power amplifier under load, two conditions should be remembered. First, you're dealing with a heat-generating device. Skin burns aren't impossible. Second, use an adequate wire size, as the wire resistances should not be part of the measurements.

Even if you're measuring just one amplifier, try not to use a measurement technique suited for only that amplifier. Develop a standard technique, using either the same equipment each time, or note the equipment used. If you have access to a computer-based test system, use it. The minimum items you should have available are:

- Sine-wave generator
- Audio voltmeter
- Oscilloscope
- Dummy loads

If you're performing THD checks, the sine-wave generator should have low (<0.01%) THD. If you're simply performing power and gain testing, a function generator will be adequate. You're using the audio voltmeter to measure output voltage. You're viewing the amplifier output waveform on the oscilloscope. An oscilloscope is a fairly accurate method to verify waveform purity, without using a THD Analyzer.

A dummy load is nothing more than a resistor equal in resistance to the recommended output load for the amplifier, and a wattage rating equal or greater than the maximum output power from the amplifier. If you are checking a stereo power amplifier, the above requirements apply to each channel.

A good check for stereo power amplifiers is to drive only one channel and measure the maximum power output at the clip point.

Then drive both channels at the same time to the maximum output power level. Verify whether or not the maximum power output from the first channel has dropped in level. If it has, this is an indication that the power supply doesn't have sufficient power capacity for both channels when the amplifier is being driven to its maximum power output level.

Connect the oscillator to the power amplifier input, the dummy load, and the oscilloscope to the power amplifier output. Connect the AC cables for the power amplifier and the test equipment into the same power strip to assure a common source of AC power.

How do you determine the maximum power output? Set the oscillator to 1 kHz, and about 1 volt output level. While watching the oscilloscope trace, slowly increase the power amplifier gain until you see the positive or negative peak of the sine wave just begin to flatten. You may want to increase the oscilloscope gain and adjust the vertical position so you can see the positive peak of the sine wave in greater magnification. For any well-designed amplifier, both the positive and negative peaks should begin to flatten at the same output level.

Decrease, and then increase the amplifier gain until you are sure of the clip point. Then note the output level from the audio voltmeter. The power output of the amplifier is stated to be 100 watts, you are using a 16-ohm load, and you measured 41 volts at the clip point. Then by using Ohm's Law, you can calculate the power output according to the equation:

$$P = \frac{E^2}{R}$$

Therefore, your answer is 105.06 watts. Do you agree? Expressing power output to two places is overkill; why not round it off to 105 watts? Since the power amplifier was stated as a 100-watt device, the midband power output is about 1% above the stated level.

Now you check the gain of the power amplifier. Move the test leads from the audio voltmeter to the input of the power amplifier, and note the meter reading. You measure 0.5 volts at 1 kHz. Therefore, a voltage input of 0.5 volts is necessary to provide the maximum power output. Or, expressing that in dB, the equation:

$$dB = 20\log\frac{E_2}{E_1}$$

Then, replacing the known parts of the equation with numbers, we have:

$$dB = 20\log\frac{41}{0.5}$$

Solving, you get 38.2 dB. Any arguments? Why are you using "20log," rather than "10log"? Because you want the voltage gain of the power amplifier, not the power gain. You don't know how much power was fed to the amplifier, since you didn't perform any calculations using resistances. Later, when you use PAG/NAG equations, you can use voltage gain together with loudspeaker sensitivities to calculate SPL figures in a room.

Power Amplifiers

Frequency response of a power amplifier is normally referenced to 1 kHz and is usually measured at a low output level of about 1% or 10% of the maximum power output. If a reference frequency isn't stated, then the frequency response specification can be more liberally interpreted. If the frequency response is stated as: "61 dB from 20 Hz to 20 kHz, with reference to 1 kHz," the specification makes it clear as to the maximum deviation allowable for the specification.

The procedure is similar to that for determining maximum power output, but now you'll set the oscillator to various frequencies within the passband of the amplifier.

For most power amplifiers, the frequency ranges where the frequency response may depart from that measured at 1 kHz are usually 20 Hz to 100 Hz, and 12 kHz to 20 kHz. The usual practice for frequency checks:

- 20 Hz to 100 Hz in 10 Hz increments
- 200 Hz, 500 Hz, and 1 kHz
- 2 kHz, 5 kHz, and 10 kHz
- 12 kHz to 20 kHz in 1 kHz increments

It may be that for your company, the frequency ranges below 50 Hz and above 15 kHz aren't of interest. The frequency range of 20 Hz to 20 kHz is usually considered to be the maximum range of human hearing.

Conduct and measure power amplifier power response tests

Why should you measure power response of a power amplifier? To verify the manufacturer's claim; to provide measurements for in-house use; and to provide measurements stated in meaningful terms, if the manufacturer wasn't too exact with the specification.

Frequency response is not power response, and the two should not be confused. Power response is the frequency response measured near the maximum output level for the amplifier. At levels near maximum output, some power amplifiers will exhibit anomalies such as parasitic oscillations at high frequencies due to amplifier instabilities. The low frequency response may suffer, due to inability of the power supply to provide sustained DC power to the amplifier. If an output transformer is used, the transformer may have insufficient iron to provide adequate low frequency power output.

You'll see a similarity between frequency response and power response measurements, the difference being the output level from the power amplifier. Output power is normally referenced to 1 kHz; measured just below clip level, or at the manufacturer's stated maximum output level. If a reference frequency and power isn't stated, then the power response specification can be more liberally interpreted.

If the power response is stated as: "±1 dB from 20 Hz to 20 kHz, with reference to 1 kHz at 100 watts," the specification makes it clear as to the maximum deviation allowable for power response.

On the other hand, if the power response is stated as "±1 dB from 20 Hz to 20 kHz," then you might assume that the power response was measured at or near full power output. That is an unacceptable assumption. You don't know at what power level the manufacturer made those measurements.

The procedure is similar to that for determining maximum power output, but now you'll set the oscillator to various frequencies within the passband of the amplifier. As you make each measurement, you should check the oscilloscope to verify that the amplifier output waveform isn't distorted. If you see clipping on the oscilloscope, the oscillator level should be reduced to just below clip level, then you note the new output level.

For most power amplifiers, the frequency ranges where the power response may depart from that measured at 1 kHz is usually 20 Hz to 100 Hz, and 12 kHz to 20 kHz. The usual practice:

• 20 Hz to 100 Hz in 10 Hz increments
• 200 Hz, 500 Hz, and 1 kHz
• 2 kHz, 5 kHz, and 10 kHz
• 12 kHz to 20 kHz in 1 kHz increments

The 1 kHz measurement need not be noted, just checked to assure that no drastic changes have occurred. It may be that for your company, the frequency ranges below 50 Hz and above 15 kHz aren't of interest. The frequency range of 20 Hz to 20 kHz is usually considered to be the maximum range of human hearing.

Once the measurements have been taken, you should calculate the power response from the voltage measurements. We shall make use of the equation:

$$P = \frac{E^2}{R}$$

You'll use this equation for each measurement.

Frequency response and power response measurements are good, as far as they go. Real-world loudspeaker loads are a combination of resistances and reactances that are difficult to simulate as a collection of actual components. Various manufacturers have designed sophisticated output circuits to drive these complex loads successfully.

Procedures for signal-to-noise measurements in power amplifiers

Even if you're measuring just one amplifier, try not to use a measurement technique suited for only that amplifier. Develop a standard technique, using either the same equipment each time, or note the equipment used. If you have access to a computer-based test system, by all means use it.

The nominal noise level of most power amplifiers is about 100 dB below rated power output. Let's stop and do some calculations to see the expected noise level in voltage. There are two methods for calculating the noise level; one by voltage, and one by decibels. We'll start with the voltage technique. We'll assume we have 350 watts output from a power amplifier, with an 8-ohm resistive load on the output. Using the appropriate equation:

$$E = \sqrt{PR}$$

The power is 350 watts, and the resistance is 8 ohms. Therefore, you should have calculated 52.92 volts, or rounded off to 53 volts. Any questions? We want to calculate the expected noise level in voltage, therefore we'll use the equation:

$$\frac{E_2}{E_1} = 10^{(\frac{dB}{20})}$$

E_2 is the output voltage, and E_1 is the noise voltage. In this equation, the term dB is the noise level ratio. Substituting in the equation, we have:

$$\frac{53}{E_1} = 10^{(\frac{100}{20})}$$

Then rearranging and calculating the right side of the equation, we have:

113

$$E_1 = \frac{53}{10^{\frac{100}{20}}}$$

Any questions as to how we got here? Then when we solve, the answer will be 0.00053 volts. If you think about it, you don't need your calculator. Now, let's calculate that answer in decibels. The equation is:

$$dBu = 100 - 20\log (E_2 \div .775)$$

Your result should be -63 dB. Now, that's a nice number, but does it relate to power output? It doesn't, directly, but it does tell you the expected noise level in dBu. What is the noise output in watts? You know the nominal load impedance, 8 ohms, and the equation is:

$$P = \frac{E}{R}$$

Then you substitute and calculate. Your answer should be 0.035 microwatts, which is your first answer multiplied by 1×10^6. Not much power. In retrospect, the original specification is probably the most useful, 100 dB below maximum output power.

Now back to the workbench. The minimum items you should have available are:
- Sine-wave generator
- Audio voltmeter
- Oscilloscope
- Dummy loads

Set the oscillator to 1 kHz, and about 1 volt output level. Connect the oscilloscope and the dummy load to the power amplifier output. If the audio voltmeter has an output connector, connect the oscilloscope to that connector, otherwise connect the oscilloscope to the power amplifier output. The oscilloscope sensitivity should be set at about 1 V P-P. Connect the AC cables for the power amplifier and the test equipment into the same power strip, to assure a common source of AC power. While watching the oscilloscope trace, slowly increase the power amplifier gain until you see the positive or negative peak of the sine wave just begin to flatten.

Measure the output voltage, and note that number, together with the resistance of the dummy load. Then remove the oscillator input connection, terminate the amplifier input with a 620-ohm resistor to simulate field conditions, and turn the gain control down (maximum CCW). With the audio voltmeter connected to the power amplifier output, range down on the audio voltmeter until you see a reading on the voltmeter. Observe the oscilloscope display with a slow sweep setting so you see one trace. You'll be looking at what looks like random noise.

If you see any periodic waveforms, check the approximate frequency with the sweep control. If you see 120 Hz hum or 60 Hz in the display, check your measurement setup to be sure you haven't unintentionally introduced a ground loop. Nothing except the input termination resistor should be connected to the power amplifier input. While watching the oscilloscope, turn off the power amplifier. The periodic waveforms may reduce in amplitude as the power amplifier loses its operating voltage. If you still see periodic waveforms, thoroughly check your measurement setup for a loose connection or bad cable.

If you don't see any periodic waveforms, watch the audio voltmeter for about 15 seconds to get an idea of the average value of the noise.

Proper AC power requirements for power amplifiers

In working with power amplifiers of 100 watts or less, the AC power requirements and wiring are similar to any signal processing device. But when power amplifiers that provide more than 100 watts power output are used, the AC power and wiring requirements require close examination. If you're working with a 1 kW power amplifier, it may require 240 volts AC, rather than 120 volts AC.

Even if the amplifier requires only 120 volts AC, it may be necessary to provide a separate branch circuit just for the amplifier. Grounding should be in accordance with discussions elsewhere in this book and the NEC.

Amplifier load matching and operation of common output power indicators

When you are using 8- to 16-ohm output impedances and contemporary power amplifiers, the source and load impedances are not matched. The actual source impedance of the power amplifier is anywhere from 10% to 1% of the load impedance. This difference is usually termed "damping factor." The low source impedance presents a near short circuit to the loudspeaker. This helps in reducing unwanted excursions of the loudspeaker's voice coil.

In effect, a loudspeaker is bridging the amplifier output. If you attempted to match the amplifier's source impedance, you would be drawing a tremendous amount of power. It would be equivalent to attempting to match the source impedance of an AC circuit in your shop. The circuit breaker would instantaneously trip, shutting off the branch circuit. Even with 70-volt output power amplifiers, the output isn't matched.

Which is to say, avoid any attempt to match the load impedance to the amplifier source impedance. Simply note the minimum load impedance recommended by the manufacturer, and act accordingly.

Amplifier manufacturers have developed a myriad of schemes for showing power level and distortion levels. They range from LED indicators to show that a signal is present in that channel, to segmented LED indicators. Also, LED indicators to show distortion products of usually 1% or more. Some amplifiers have output protection relays which operate during overload or short-circuit conditions. An LED on the front panel will indicate relay operation.

There are no standards for these indicating devices. In addition to their obvious usefulness as indicators, some manufacturers have used them as a marketing tool.

Mixing Consoles

The smaller devices are usually referred to as mixers, and the larger devices, even table-top, are referred to as mixing consoles, or simply consoles. The United Kingdom refers to a mixing console as a mixing desk or simply a desk, which can be confusing to us colonials.

The usual description for the size of a mixing console refers to the number of inputs by the number of outputs. Thus, a device having eight inputs and two outputs is referred to as an "8 x 2" mixer. The demarcation between the two sizes is roughly 12 inputs and four outputs. Free-standing mixing consoles are usually found in recording studios and will cost more than $100,000.

With the smaller mixers, the power supply is integral. With larger mixers, hum fields generated by the power supply may deteriorate the performance specification of the mixer, unless design precautions are taken. The external power supply is a box, or a rack-mounted device with a fixed length of cable between the two parts.

The descriptions given here for each section are describing the controls from the front (closest to you as you're operating the mixer) to the back (where the meters are).

All mixers and mixing consoles utilize solid-state devices, using ICs (integrated circuits) over individual transistors by a large ratio. Individual transistors are used for specific functions where the use of an IC is unnecessary. The use of ICs allows for more compact and lower-priced mixers than would be possible using transistors.

Input section

The input section is duplicated for the number of inputs. If the mixer is a 12-input device, there are 12 input sections. Some manufacturers use one panel for the input section area, others provide the input section area as a group of plug-in modules. Some manufacturers include the input fader as a physical part of the input section, others install the faders as separate units.

We begin with the input fader, or simply the fader. The fader controls the gain of that input, either the microphone or line input. Almost all mixers use straight-line (as opposed to rotary) controls. Very small mixers for PA use, (4 x 1) units have rotary gain controls. The scale is marked in linear decibel increments, and the nominal operating position of the fader is marked at zero. The scale length is 10 dB up from zero, and down to infinity or off.

The next control is usually a pan pot, which moves the signal from left to right, or between two buses preselected by a pushbutton. When the pan pot is in the center, the signal on either channel will be either 3 dB down (equal loudness), or 6 dB down (equal level).

Somewhere in this area will be a solo switch. Normally, this mutes all other inputs, and either sends the signal to a solo loud-speaker, or the function may be an "in-place" solo. This mutes all other inputs and leaves the selected signal in place with any reverberation effects applied to the signal.

The next area up usually will be the equalizer. There are many varieties of equalizers, ranging from simple three-knob devices, to complex four- and five-knob devices that may include parametric equalization. Parametric equalization varies the Q of the equalizer frequency chosen.

Let's assume that a frequency of 3 kHz is selected, with a boost of 6 dB. In addition to the boost at 3 kHz, frequencies above and below will be boosted, but to a lesser amount as the frequency increases or decreases. If the response is viewed on an analyzer, a "haystack" curve will be seen. Whether the haystack curve has steep or broad skirts is dependent on the equalizer settings. If the curve has steep skirts, the Q is high. If the curve has broad skirts, the Q is low.

There are many choices for frequency selection, ranging from six to 12 frequencies per knob. Some manufacturers have sweepable frequency selection, the drawback being that frequency control is less exact. Older equalizers provided switch selection of frequencies. These are used where precise frequency control is desired.

Mixing control equalizers frequently use potentiometers for frequency selection. This is termed "sweepable," as the frequency choice is sweepable over a desired range.

The equalization either boosts or attenuates, usually in 2 dB steps. Some manufacturers graduate the positions, so that the last step is 3 dB. The limitations for frequency selection and equalization usually are cost and space availability.

Unfortunately, sundry abbreviations have crept into the lexicon or jargon of the recording and sound reinforcement industries such as *mic*, as an abbreviation for microphone, and *micing*, as an abbreviation for *miking*, which is a misnamed gerund. A gerund is a noun with the suffix *ing*. The word *mike* is an abbreviation, used as a noun or a verb. Such peculiar abbreviations will be used here, not from desire, but to avoid confusion on your part.

The next area is "AUX" sends. The word AUX is an abbreviation for auxiliary. The word AUX is used in the industry because of the physical size of the word when used on panels, and speaking the sentence, "I'm sending the signal to you on AUX 4," saves time. The word AUX is pronounced awks. AUX sends are additional outputs or buses available from the mixer. There may be from four to seven aux controls in each input section.

The majority of mixers and mixing consoles refer to the control of reverberation as echo. Some manufacturers may compromise and use the label reverb as a short-hand term. Echo is defined as a single reflection from a wall or other surface, whereas reverberation is defined as the total of all echoes within a room that give an acoustic flavor to the room. In a recording mixer console, the AUX sends frequently will be used as reverb sends.

Sometimes a pushbutton is available that switches the pickoff point of the signal to before the fader. In this case, the term normally used is "PFL," which is an abbreviation for Pre Fader Listen. The signal is sent to the AUX bus even when the normal signal through the fader is fully attenuated, or off.

The AUX sends are almost always rotary controls to save panel space and mixer cost. Some mixers may provide more switching functions for the AUX sends. These are usually in the more expensive mixing consoles.

In the next area up are usually trim pots. A trim pot provides for adjustment of the input level, so that the input faders may be set in an approximate straight line. Depending on the cost and complexity of the mixer, the trim pot may provide pads to avoid overload of the first amplifier section. The simpler mixers reduce the gain of the microphone/line amplifier.

If the mixer has more than four main output buses, bus assign pushbuttons will be at the top of the input section. These assign the input to one or more of the main output buses. With some mixers, these switches work with the pan pot as discussed earlier. The system should be designed so that assigning an input to several buses reduces the level to any one bus by only a fraction of a dB. The pushbuttons may be arranged in various ways, depending on the manufacturer.

Group and auxiliary bus section

This section, sometimes called the submaster section, contains the switching and level adjustments of the group or main bus outputs, the AUX buses, the echo (read reverberation) send masters, and possibly the talkback functions. The section is usually to the right, as most operators are right-handed. With larger consoles, this section may be in the middle of the panel area. This section to the right of 48 input sections would be a long physical reach.

Here will be found the group master faders, which control the level of each main output bus, possibly with pan pots to pan each output bus between the two "Main Mix" buses. The Main Mix bus fader will be found here as well. More discussion will be found under the section labeled **Group buses**.

The AUX send masters are located here, which allow the operator to control the overall level of each of the AUX buses. Ancillary controls may provide for introduction of an echo signal into the AUX buses. In an emergency, the AUX buses may be used as group buses, even though the maximum output capability of those buses may be lower than the group buses.

There may be a solo master level control, and it is normally placed in this section. A representative layout of a group and auxiliary bus section is shown below. No statement is being made by the author or NSCA as to the value of this manufacturer over any other manufacturer of similar equipment.

Cue/talkback section

Cue controls provide for overall level of a cue system, which is frequently the AUX send system. Talkback is providing communication from the operator/engineer to the talent in the studio. It is seldom used in sound reinforcement because of the danger of interrupting a church service with the operator's voice. If the mixer is equipped with a talkback system, the owner should be queried as to the desirability of disconnecting the system, or at least removing the talkback microphone.

Monitor section

If provided, the monitor section may be used in sound reinforcement. It provides a means by which the operator/engineer can monitor the recording in process. In a sound reinforcement system, where the mixer is in a separate room from the church or meeting room, it will allow the operator/engineer to monitor the service or meeting. In a mixer designed for sound reinforcement, a monitor section may not be provided, as the operator/engineer listens to the main system.

By definition, the monitor section does not interrupt or change the main sound reinforcement system, but independently monitors the mixer output to that system. A selector system allows for monitoring of various signals in addition to the main feed to the sound reinforcement power amplifiers. A monitor level control allows the operator/engineer to adjust the monitor level as desired.

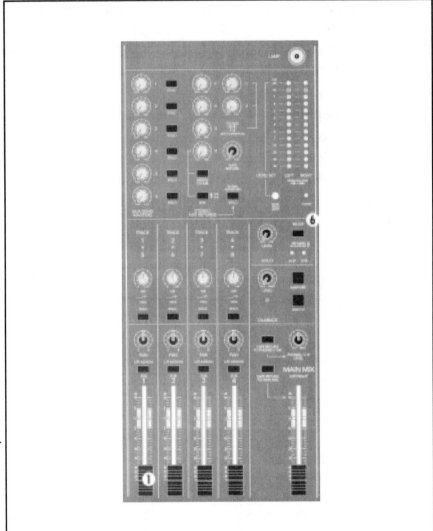

©*Mackie Design, Inc. 1997, used by permission*

Group buses

These are also referred to as output buses or main buses. The term *group* indicates the bus is a grouping of various inputs. In the segment titled *Group and auxiliary bus section* there was a discussion of the group master level controls. Above is a picture of a group and auxiliary bus section.

In a recording mixer, the group buses will feed the tape recorders. In a sound reinforcement system, a group bus will feed the main power amplifiers. As most sound reinforcement systems are monaural, the remaining buses are free for standby use or other functions.

The nominal output level of a group bus is +4 dBu, and the clip or overload level may be +20 to +28 dBu. The nominal source impedance will be approximately 40 to 60 ohms. This allows the sum total of loads to be as low as 5000 ohms without degrading performance or causing level shifts as smaller loads are added or removed.

Function of a matrix mix section

This refers to the summing circuits from the input sections to the group buses. The matrix refers directly to the number of inputs versus the number of outputs. If the mixer has 24 inputs and four outputs, then the matrix is 24 by 4. The matrix is mixing the individual inputs to the group outputs.

Technically, the operation is performed by summing amplifiers, one of the many applications of operational amplifiers, which are in the general class of integrated circuits.

Functions of metering section

The metering section provides the operator/engineer with a continual display of levels. It may be as simple as a two-channel bar graph displaying the two main outputs, or in the case of 24-channel recording mixer consoles, bar graphs and PPMs (peak program meter) displaying all 24 channels simultaneously.

The meters are normally calibrated to read zero when the output level is +4 dBu, or 1.228 volts. Calibration controls are usually provided internally so that the meters may be adjusted to read zero. Naturally, the frequency response of the metering circuit must be equal or greater than that of the mixer.

Gain structure and settings

Figure 4-1 is a sample gain structure of a sound reinforcement console. This is typical only, as each manufacturer has different design goals. Some levels are standard, such as high-level inputs, +4 dBu; group outputs, +4 dBu.

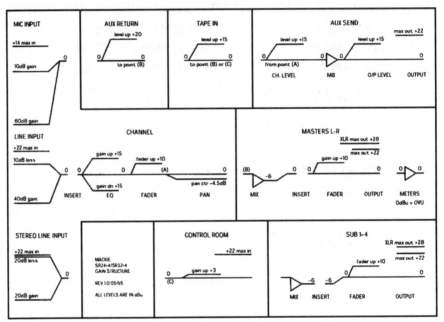

***Figure 4-1.** Sample gain structure of a sound reinforcement console (©Mackie Design, Inc. 1997, used by permission)*

Mixing and sound reinforcement

Within limits, a given mixing console may be used for sound reinforcement, recording, and stage monitor applications. There are specific features for each type that are unnecessary or redundant to other applications.

AUX and cue circuits are handy in a sound reinforcement mixer in a fixed location, but not vital. However, for live sound applications, as with recording mixer consoles, they are an essential part of the system. In live sound applications, they will be used as stage monitor feeds.

The quantity of group buses in a sound reinforcement mixer need not be greater than four or even two. However, for recording mixer consoles, 48 group buses are not unknown.

Metering in a sound reinforcement mixer is a support function, but not vital, as the operator/engineer is listening to the system and should hear distortion peaks. The operator/engineer is relying on their ears, rather than the metering.

Metering in a mixing or recording console is a vital function. The program material is being recorded, and will undergo much aural scrutiny before being finished. Any distortion that occurs in the recording process cannot be removed. The tape recorders being used, whether analog or digital, have definite recording level limits.

Console flow chart/ single line diagram

On the next page, Figure 4-2 is a representative single-line diagram of a sound reinforcement mixer. In the sound reinforcement field, the terms "block diagram" and "single-line diagram" are used more often than "flow chart."

Audio Transformers

These transformers are used for constant voltage distributed loudspeaker systems. The usual voltages encountered are 25-, 70-, and 140-volt systems. 25-volt systems are used where open wiring is desired. This low voltage is used for school and similar systems where conduit and associated costs required for 70-volt systems are prohibitive.

70 volts is the most widely used reference. Almost all manufacturers of sound reinforcement power amplifiers provide a 70-volt output capability. For applications requiring long cable lengths that would unduly increase wire sizes, 140-volt systems may be used. The reason for 140 volts as a reference is simply that the number is a multiple of 70, which simplifies transformer design and system design.

The particular advantage of 70-volt systems lies in the fairly high impedance presented to the power amplifier by the output transformer. If we assume that we are providing audio to 20 loudspeak-

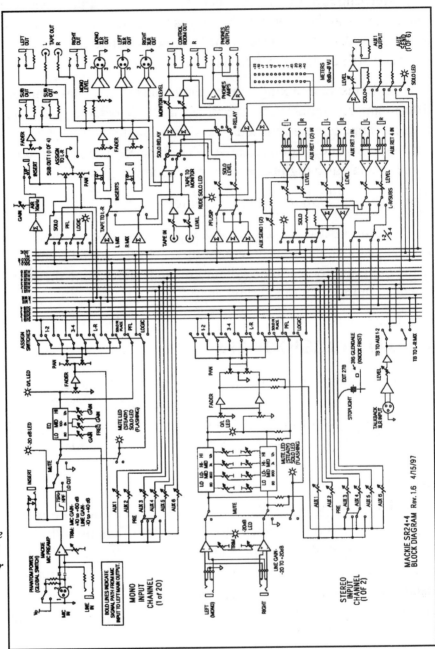

Figure 4-2. Representative single-line diagram of a sound reinforcement mixer (©Mackie Design, Inc. 1997, used by permission)

ers, and each loudspeaker has an impedance of 8 ohms, and all 20 loudspeakers are in parallel, then the load presented to the power amplifier is 0.4 ohm. This is close to a short circuit, and the power amplifier will certainly distort, if not shut down.

If we install a transformer at each loudspeaker, providing an impedance change from some relatively high value to the loudspeaker impedance, then the equivalent impedance of those 20 transformers and loudspeakers in parallel will be an acceptable value. If we further install at the power amplifier another transformer, providing an impedance change from the nominal output load of the power amplifier to some relatively high value, we will complement the design.

The question is, then, what value shall we use for that relatively high impedance? Since we're creating this system in the days of slide rules, and we know that the equation to determine resistance or impedance is:

$$R = \frac{E^2}{P}$$

We know the output power of the amplifier, and we want to calculate the impedance desired. Therefore, we must set some value for E. Our equation asks for E^2, so what number fits that requirement on the slide rule? We notice that 5000 is at a nice location on the slide rule, so we calculate the square root of 5000, and it turns out to be 70.7. We verify this on our mechanical calculator. Therefore, in our transformer design, we can use 70.7 as E, which squares to 5000, and that makes our transformer calculations much easier.

We think more about the situation and realize that if we use that value for E as a constant, we may use it for the output transformer secondary voltage and the loudspeaker transformer primary voltage. Then another thought occurs to us: why not refer to the loudspeaker transformer primary taps in watts rather than resistance? Why not disregard the impedance of the circuits and simply consider the watts involved in the system? Hence, we have a 70-volt system.

How do we do the calculations? We have a power amplifier with an output capability of 80 watts into a 70-volt system. We have 20 loudspeakers as above, but we set each loudspeaker primary tap at 4 watts. 20 loudspeakers times 4 watts per loudspeaker equals 80 watts, which is the output capability of the power amplifier. (We are indebted to an old friend for the above true story, which we have reworded.)

In the previous example, we showed the same wattage settings for all loudspeaker transformers. If required, each loudspeaker transformer might be set to a different wattage setting, with no harm to the system.

Using a distributed loudspeaker system, the sound pressure level requirements may differ from area to area. The ceiling height may differ, the expected ambient noise level may differ, you may be dealing with seated ear heights instead of standing ear heights; all of these may require different wattage settings. If one power amplifier is to be used for these separate areas, after the SPL requirements have been calculated the wattage settings may be adjusted as required.

Almost all line-to-voice-coil transformers provide wattage settings using 2 as the divisor, working from the maximum power setting. If the transformer's maximum power setting is 4 watts, then the lower power settings will be 2 watts, then 1 watt, and possibly 1/2 watt. Since you understand the use of decibels in power calculations, what will be the decibel difference for each wattage from the maximum setting? You shouldn't have to use your calculator for this.

Regardless of the number of loudspeakers, the output power of the amplifier, and the wattage settings, the maximum power output capability of the amplifier should never be exceeded. There may be a temptation to fudge on the calculations, and assume that the maximum power from the amplifier will never be required. This is a poor assumption, as that condition may well happen. If the maximum power output is exceeded, even for very short periods of time, distortion will be the result. The customer will be unhappy.

Characteristics of matching transformers

A transformer may provide an increase or decrease in impedance, voltage change, or current. Here we are primarily concerned with impedance and voltage changes. As with all transformers, the direction of the signal is immaterial, a matching transformer can be used in a step-up or a step-down application.

A line-to-voice-coil transformer is a general description. A description such as "4-watt, 70-volt to 8-ohm" provides specific details about the transformer. Such a transformer would match the voltage from the 70-volt line to the voice coil impedance of the loudspeaker.

The frequency response is usually from 50 Hz to 15 kHz, as is the power response. Wattage capabilities range from 4 to 32 watts for individual loudspeaker applications, and from 32 to 150 watts for distribution applications and installation on power amplifiers where 70-volt output is required.

Matching transformer applications

Transformers are used for power amplifier outputs, distribution in large systems, and to drive individual loudspeakers in distributed loudspeaker applications. Matching transformers can be used in loudspeaker clusters. There are disadvantages: insertion loss of the transformer, an additional component, and a restriction on low-frequency information. If the cluster is intended to provide extended low-frequency information below 60 Hz, matching transformers should not be used.

They may also be used where a long line is required between a power amplifier and one or two loudspeakers. A matching transformer is used at the power amplifier wired for 8 ohms to 70-volt; then the same transformer is used at the loudspeaker wired for 70-volt to 8 ohms. There will be two transformer losses involved, but that can be compensated for.

Insertion loss of matching transformers

An ideal transformer would have zero insertion loss, but that exists only on paper. A real transformer uses copper wire, which has resistance. The resistance contributes to the insertion loss. Other losses include less-than-perfect coupling between windings, and core loss. Insertion loss is the difference between power consumed by the primary and power available from the secondary.

In reality, insertion losses should be less than 1 to 1.5 dB from 60 Hz to 15 kHz. The insertion loss, which is a power loss, is either added to the primary load, or subtracted from the power delivered to the loudspeaker.

Insertion losses include low-frequency attenuation due to iron core sizing. A cheaper transformer will have less iron in the core. The basic specifications may not include the power response of the transformer, or the wide-band insertion losses. Regardless of the transformer quality, achieving low-frequency power response down to 20 Hz becomes quite expensive.

Characteristics of autotransformers

An autotransformer differs from a conventional transformer in that there is one winding, with various taps on that winding. Autotransformers are cheaper and simpler to manufacture than two-winding transformers. A conventional transformer has two electrically isolated windings on the same core. No similar electrical isolation exists in an autotransformer.

As with all transformers, the direction of the signal is immaterial. An autotransformer can be used in a step-up or a step-down application. The frequency response is usually from 50 Hz to 15 kHz, as is the power response.

Applications of autotransformers

Autotransformers are suggested in audio applications where the percent of voltage change is 25% or less. Two autotransformers may be used in series when a greater step-down ratio is desired.

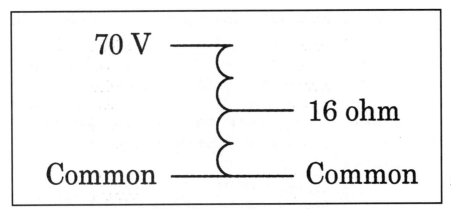

Figure 4-3.

There is a definite disadvantage in using autotransformers where a large voltage change is desired. As you see by the schematic in Figure 4-3, large amounts of current can flow in the winding common to the primary and secondary currents. That can degrade the power handling capability of the autotransformer.

We have drawn an extreme example to show the concern for the amount of current involved.

Questions

1. Selecting the correct microphone on the basis of cost is the most important requirement. True or false?
2. Who developed the PAG/NAG formulas?
    a. Electro-Voice.
    b. Carolyn and Don Davis.
    c. Ted Uzzle.
    d. Wallace Sabine.
3. Boundary microphones are frequently used instead of shotgun microphones. True or false?
4. Hanging microphones have the following pickup pattern.
    a. Omnidirectional.
    b. Cardioid.
    c. Shotgun.
    d. Any of the above.

5. If a microphone is found defective at the customer's location, it should be immediately repaired on the spot. True or false?

6. Any microphone must be used with and only with the cable that came with the microphone. True or false?

7. Measuring the power output of a power amplifier must be done only according to the manufacturer's instructions. True or false?

8. For testing the power output capability of power amplifiers, dummy loads should be used:

   a. In parallel with the loudspeaker load.

   b. In series with the loudspeaker load.

   c. In place of the loudspeaker load.

   d. When specified by the consultant.

9. A square wave is always useful for testing the power output capability of power amplifiers. True or false?

10. A good mixing console always uses vacuum tubes for better sound quality. True or false?

11. Pan pots on mixing consoles always have the center position at 6 dB down from either side. True or false?

12. Summing amplifiers are used to combine equalizer circuits with the main microphone channel when used in PFL circuits. True or false?

13. Where are summing amplifiers used?

   a. To combine echo feeds.

   b. To combine input channels.

   c. To combine L & R outputs.

   d. All of the above.

Chapter 5

Loudspeaker Systems

by Bob Bushnell

- **NICET Work Element 16006, Large Loudspeaker Arrays**
- **NICET's Description:** "*Assemble and install large loudspeaker arrays (those with three or more loudspeakers), including specified suspension, using appropriate safety precautions. Perform repairs as needed. (OSHA)*"

- **NICET Work Element 16007, Connection & Aiming of Large Loudspeaker Arrays**
- **NICET's Description:** "*Make a proper connection between the loudspeaker and the amplifier. Correctly implement mounting angles. Correctly position loudspeakers to achieve required signal alignment and coverage.*"

- **NICET Work Element 16008, Testing of Large Loudspeaker Arrays**
- **NICET's Description:** "*Conduct and perform initial evaluation of frequency response, loudness levels, and polarity tests of loudspeaker arrays. Make adjustments necessary to meet specifications. Provide accurate field as-built documentation.*"

Large Loudspeaker Arrays

Safety is the primary concern for installing (flying) loudspeaker arrays at any distance overhead. The cost of a single human life far outweighs any temporary advantage gained by omitting or disregarding safety considerations. Do you take on faith that the half-ton array you flew and now hanging over you will not drop on you or someone else? Have you verified all elements and know that the possibility of that array falling will not be due to human error?

OSHA provides a necessary service. It hosts a very useful and informative Web site, which should be consulted when you have questions. If necessary, a local office can be called.

These three work elements—16006, 16007, and 16008—are the nucleus topics for large loudspeaker arrays. We are reminded of earlier days of audio when you couldn't get the job without experience, and you couldn't get experience without having a job. Because of the safety aspect, designing strictly from specifications without a reality base may be disappointing or dangerous.

Mounting considerations (height, weight, size, etc.)

Array components are not designed and built for suspending above ground or aerial use (flying) without rigging hardware. Theoretically, there is no limit as to weight or size. If a 747 can support the Space Shuttle during flight, then any loudspeaker array can be flown. Not many commercial audio projects are funded by NASA, however.

The assembly shop must be equipped with appropriate frames and supports to simulate the field conditions. If you are working against plans and specs that do not specify the rigging hardware required, then you must use a mechanical or civil engineer or an individual skilled in rigging. You should verify that the plans and specs show some responsibility on the part of the consultant.

If you attempt unskilled estimates or design or fabrication of the system hardware required without a full knowledge of the materials involved, the mathematical relationship between components, and the hardware itself, your job probably will result in disaster.

A safety margin, safety factor, or design factor must be used, which is the ratio of the safe working load to the maximum load before breaking of the various materials. Some criteria use the term "working load limit." Various design factors have been recommended, 5:1 being the most common. This means that a cable supporting 1000 pounds has a breaking strength of 5000 lbs. In all cases, the load is static, not dynamic.

If the load is moving in any direction, it is a dynamic load. In that case, the vector forces on the cable must be analyzed and compensated for in the design. The process of lifting a load is dynamic. If the lift speed is sufficiently low, the dynamic forces probably can be disregarded.

Cabinets should be manufactured of Grade A-A plywood, with no interior knots. The joints between faces should be rabbeted, then glued. Screws are of help, but screws into plywood end grain are not as effective as screws in cross-grain material. The use of particle board, hardboard, or similar materials is not recommended, as the absence of grain in those materials causes them to be structurally unsound.

The rigging hardware should be structural steel, graded for the purpose. The loudspeaker cabinet usually will be the weakest link; first, usually because it is supporting other cabinets; second, steel has a greater strength per unit area than plywood; and third, the cabinet may not be capable of supporting itself. Shear strength of materials is almost always higher than the tensile strength.

A bolt fastened horizontally through the vertical side of a loudspeaker cabinet will provide a stronger support than the same bolt fastened vertically through the horizontal face of the same cabinet. In the first case, the shear strength of the bolt provides the main element of support. In the second case, the holding strength of the bolt is dependent on the tensile strength of the plywood, which is less than the bolt.

The solution may be to distribute the bolt head load over a larger area. The first impulse may be to use washers on the underside, without examining the design problem in full. There may be other cabinets below the first cabinet. How is the load distributed from cabinet to cabinet?

If two or more cabinets in line are suspended, particular attention should be paid to the suspension elements. Usually, loudspeaker cabinets will not be designed to allow other cabinets to be suspended from the top cabinet. In that case, suspension elements must provide for hanging all cabinets. The loudspeaker cabinet specifications must be inspected in detail to verify their suitability for flying.

There are several loudspeaker system manufacturers that have designed all or part of their systems for flying. Equal attention is paid to the physical and acoustical aspects of the cabinet. In spite of the fact that their design calculations shouldn't be taken for granted, these manufacturers provide a worthwhile group of systems from which to select.

As well, there are manufacturers of rigging hardware that specifically design for the sound reinforcement field. Although the hardware simplifies the design and construction phase, take nothing for granted. Even if the consultant has specified all elements of the array, yours is the final responsibility.

Even though concealing the array may not be under your purview, you should be aware of the negative and positive aspects of grille cloth. No matter how light it may be, conventional cloth will unfavorably attenuate higher frequencies. Grille cloth manufactured specifically for the purpose is woven of relatively large-diameter plastic strands. The weave is open, providing the least restriction possible for high-frequency material.

There are several manufacturers of grille cloth in various colors and patterns. Some of the materials are fire-resistant. The material in question should be measured to determine the degree of high-frequency attenuation.

Loudspeaker/driver pretesting

Wear ear protectors when doing audio measurements above 85 dB SPL (Sound Pressure Level), as hearing damage is cumulative and not reversible. Short exposure to high sound levels may be reversed by resting the eardrums, but each of these short exposures adds up over time, causing hearing loss. By that time, it's too late to repair the damage. You no longer have excellent hearing.

Examine and test the loudspeaker array on the ground before flying the array. Physical examination and load testing must be done to prevent injury or death, and to avoid physical damage to the area below. Individual component and array testing should be done so that time isn't wasted bringing the array back to ground for component replacement.

Examine each loudspeaker component, each cabinet, and each suspension element for physical defects. If the array is to be shipped with the wiring harness prebuilt, use that harness rather than makeshift wiring from the in-house scrap bin.

Perform the tests on each component, as well as the finished system. Perform system testing according to specifications, or to in-house standards. Run TEF performance tests. Perform rattle and buzz tests. Check the weight of the finished array using a dynamometer to verify the load on the on-site suspension system. Many dynamometers may be hung from the lifting device.

With more than one loudspeaker in an array, problems may appear that are a product of multielement arrays. Acoustical interaction between elements may appear in the form of comb filtering, so named because the response curve of the system may look like a rough comb. Lobing may also be an interaction between elements. The aural effects won't be pleasing to the ear. You will find more discussion of this problem in the next section, *Connection and Aiming of Large Loudspeaker Arrays.*

Test the array with the same type of power amplifier or power amplifiers as will be installed on-site. Include active or passive crossovers in the signal chain. This may uncover anomalies not predicted during the design phase. Drive the array to the same SPL as that stated in the specifications. This is one of the main reasons for all personnel in the area to wear ear protectors.

Rigging fixed arrays

Safety cannot be stressed too much when working overhead. Safety or body harnesses must be used when one or more individuals are working overhead. Other than the obvious advantage of staying alive, a safety harness provides the individual with two hands free. Even when working from a ladder, a safety harness is essential.

The normal practice is to build the array on the floor, then hoist it into place. In some cases, the array must be built overhead. In either case, individuals must be overhead at the array attachment location. A chain hoist or wire rope hoist may be used to lift the array. It should not be used as a permanent device to support the array.

The procedure should be planned in advance. Lifting devices, hardware, safety harnesses, safety lines, guide lines, and communication equipment should all be on hand, ready for use. If the final location for the array is some distance overhead, two-way radios may be of help. However, if the technician who is working overhead has a busy task, then a second person might be necessary.

Consider this: The array is overhead, in position, ready for securing. The technician overhead realizes a specific part was left at the shop. The array must be lowered to the ground while the part is retrieved from the shop, and this is assuming the job and the shop are in the same city.

You might consider using two lifting devices, even if one is adequate for the task. The second lift would share the load, or to provide a different direction of lift as required.

Rigging movable arrays

Movable arrays have all the hazards and difficulties of fixed arrays. In addition, add the requirement that the array be movable to accommodate variable acoustic conditions within the hall. Your conclusion: This is not an appropriate job for your first rigging assignment.

In addition to mechanical hazards, you may also encounter acoustical hazards. In the subsection titled *Loudspeaker/driver pre-testing*, you read about comb filtering and lobing. There is more on this topic in Work Element 16007, *Connection & Aiming of Large Loudspeaker Arrays*. Comb filtering caused by interaction between elements may be reduced by careful placement of elements with regard to their actual acoustical dispersion, not simply the polar graphs provided by the manufacturer.

If the array is only movable as a unit, the problem probably won't appear. But if the desire is for elements of the array to independently move, then the problem of comb filtering may result in atrocious sound from the array.

Methods of assembly

If you are working on a new construction site, you should have had prior approval from the general contractor and the architect before on-site assembly and installation was started. If the loudspeaker array design was performed by a registered professional engineer, the weight calculations and loading probably were approved by the architect. If you don't know if the procedure was followed, that must be checked—in advance.

If you are working on an existing building, the architect of record should be contacted, then have the calculations performed by a registered professional engineer. The building design may be unable to withstand the loading of a 1000-pound loudspeaker array. Not likely, but possible. That's the kind of information you should know before bidding the job.

The basic rigging hardware isn't complex. The basic tested and certified components include wire rope, welded chain, shackles, graded bolts, wire rope thimbles, and sleeves. Tested and certified hardware is available from recognized sources. If the local hardware store is used as a supply source, you have a problem. You have no certification, nor traceability, for that hardware.

Wire chain is not certified, and is not a substitute for welded chain. Shackles are a common item when an object needs to be lifted or suspended. If the shackle bolt in the shackle is damaged, don't use a conventional bolt, as it will bend. The shackle bolt is forged, while a conventional bolt is not. Graded bolts are manufactured from high-tensile steel, and are lightly tempered. They are marked on the heads to indicate grade. But they are not a substitute for shackle bolts.

Architects and engineers do not approve drilling through steel beams. Beam clamps are available for securing to I-beams or H-beams. Screw eyes in wood beams are totally unacceptable because they weaken the wood beam, and there is a high probability of the screw eye pulling out. Even if the screw eye is being used in a shear application, the angle of pull is 90 degrees. A steel eye is much weaker at that angle.

Connection and Aiming of Large Loudspeaker Arrays

To implement topics discussed within this work element on a practical level requires use of a TEF analyzer. The alternate is to perform lots of empirical measurements by listening—a time-consuming process.

Proper impedance matching

If a biamplified system is being driven from a two-channel power amplifier, the task is usually simple. The specifications should be checked to determine minimum load impedance. The majority of power amplifiers don't have output transformers to select load impedances; the manufacturer determines minimum load during design.

As you remember from Ohm's law, with a given voltage, as impedance decreases, current increases according to the equation:

$$I = \sqrt{\frac{P}{R}}$$

The limiting factor with most power amplifiers is output current capability, not voltage output, therefore impedance matching with these amplifiers isn't of concern.

If you are presented with four low-frequency loudspeakers to be driven from the same power amplifier, there are two options. First is the use of 70-volt transformers. Provide a 70-volt output transformer at the power amplifier, if the amplifier doesn't have 70-volt output provisions. Then provide 70-volt transformers for each loudspeaker.

The second option is wiring loudspeakers in a series/parallel combination. This may be done with an understanding of the drawbacks. Let's assume each loudspeaker to be an 8-ohm device, and the power amplifier has a minimum load impedance of 4 ohms.

Each pair of loudspeakers is wired in parallel, then two pairs are wired in series. Each loudspeaker pair has an impedance of 4 ohms, and the two pairs in series have an impedance of 8 ohms. Alternatively, each pair of loudspeakers is wired in series, resulting in 16 ohms impedance. Then two series pairs are wired in parallel, resulting in 8 ohms impedance.

If four loudspeakers are wired in parallel, the resulting impedance is 2 ohms (did you do the calculation in your head, or did you use the calculator?). That impedance is too low for two reasons. First, the load impedance is lower than that recommended by the manufacturer, and second, a heavy-gauge cable will be necessary to avoid unnecessary voltage drop.

The title of this subsection is a bit misleading, as impedance matching is not as common as in years before. If the power amplifier has several connections for output impedances, usually 4, 8, and 16 ohms, then impedance matching comes into use. If the power amplifier has only two output terminals, normally labeled high and ground, then the minimum impedance that the power amplifier will drive usually is the only concern.

If you are using passive crossovers, then the subject of impedance matching is of concern. Because of design parameters of passive crossovers, the load impedances for each section, usually low-frequency and high-frequency, must be followed.

We will discuss wire size, but only briefly. Two resistors, the first in series with the line, and the second across the line after the first resistor form a voltage divider. A potentiometer is an adjustable voltage divider. The power amplifier looking at cable and loudspeaker sees a voltage divider. The series element is the cable and the shunt element is the loudspeaker. If both cable and loudspeaker have the same impedance value, the level at the loudspeaker will be 6 dB less than at the power amplifier. This is a significant loss.

Coverage angles of typical loudspeaker devices

We shall not attempt to discuss individual loudspeakers; we don't want to be accused of favoritism. Loudspeaker types can be divided into two primary categories: cone and diaphragm. Planar units are a subset of diaphragm loudspeakers and are used in high-quality home stereo systems, not in sound reinforcement systems nor recording studios, as they cannot produce the required SPL.

Cone loudspeakers are used for the entire audio bandwidth, as well as for separate bandwidth groups. Coverage angles are primarily frequency dependent. The condition relates to the basic fact that as the frequency decreases, longer wavelengths result. However, the coverage angle changes within the audio bandwidth of the loudspeaker. And the coverage angle at a given frequency is not the same from one loudspeaker model to another.

Diaphragm loudspeakers include planar units, mid- and high-frequency devices. They are used upwards of approximately 500 Hz. The differing coverage angles relating to frequency and model numbers are more extreme than with cone loudspeakers. For both cone and diaphragm units, some of the coverage angle variations are deliberate. Diaphragm units primarily are drivers physically connected to horns and are ineffective without a horn. Because of directionality relating to mid- and high frequencies, a horn/driver combination may be selected to provide a desired coverage pattern.

Coverage angles are affected by the room's acoustic environment. If a horn/driver combination is located near a reflecting surface, that will immediately affect dispersion. If room acoustics affect critical distance, known as D_C, the loudspeaker coverage pattern might require reexamination. We suggest you review *Work Element 16004, Acoustics* for more information on this subject.

Coverage angles from polar patterns provide an excellent starting point, but calculated coverage angles should be tempered with TEF measurements, experience, and contact with other designers.

Adjusting the loudspeaker elements to cover specific horizontal, vertical, and rotational angles

Once calculated and empirical coverage angles have been determined, then elements may be adjusted as desired. However, aesthetic and architectural considerations may affect placement. Interaction between elements may cause combing effects, which are discussed later in this work element.

Unless the coverage angles are known and understood, and assuming specific details were not created as to aiming directions and angles, setting the coverage pattern is a trial-and-error procedure. This involves setting angles, then measuring and listening to assure even coverage and freedom from comb effects.

If the coverage angles are known, and specific details are available as to aiming directions and angles, then the process simply involves setting the various elements of the array.

Placing multiple loudspeakers
for signal alignment (acoustic origin)
and common center of coverage (apparent apex)

Dick Heyser, a gifted physicist with JPL (Jet Propulsion Labs), who originally turned his attention to the audio field as a side endeavor, did some very original research relating to loudspeakers. Before his untimely death in 1987, he patented the TDS (Time Delay Spectrometry) system, which caused a number of loudspeaker manufacturers to reanalyze their products.

His idea was simplicity itself. Conventional frequency response measurements ignore time aspects of a loudspeaker. He measured the response of the loudspeaker based on the arrival at the measuring microphone of a timed signal. (If you are curious about this we suggest that you read the patent issued to him, which is United States patent 3,466,652.)

Taking a clue from the advantages available from the TDS system, some loudspeaker manufacturers have redesigned their products so that they have a common acoustic origin relating to the physical structure. This can simplify your design procedure. If two loudspeakers mounted in the same plane do not have a common acoustic origin point, this intensifies the comb filter effect, as well as reducing the audio quality of the array. This effect would be considered phase distortion.

The common center of coverage or the apparent apex is an imaginary point somewhere behind the array. It represents the acoustic origin for each of the elements. The actual coverage angle or pattern is but slightly affected by the apparent apex, but the audio quality of the array is greatly affected by that parameter. If the acoustic origins aren't together, that leads to comb filter effects, and phase distortion.

Phase, interference, and comb filtering within loudspeaker arrays

These three forms of distortion are closely related; they are almost synonyms for one another. Phase distortion relates to two elements speaking the same frequency, but slightly out of time, therefore phase. Interference is a term defining acoustic interference between two elements. Comb filtering defines the bandwidth display of various phase distortions occurring between two elements.

Comb filtering caused by interaction between elements may be reduced by careful placement of elements with regard to their actual acoustical dispersion, not simply polar graphs provided by the manufacturer.

Crossover networks, whether active or passive, should be considered as polarity elements. If a two-channel crossover is being used to drive a low-frequency and a high-frequency element, which is the sum total of the array, whether the two channels are in or out of polarity is not as important as the condition at the crossover point, usually termed F_c.

In the crossover frequency region, the two elements are either in polarity or out of polarity. Therefore, when measuring or listening to the array, you will find either a rise or a dip in response in that frequency region, depending on the acoustic conditions of each element. This phenomenon is considered to be phase distortion.

Questions

1. You require a TEF analyzer:
    - a. Only if the array should sound good.
    - b. Only if your company owns one.
    - c. Only if the boss says so.
    - d. Only if the OSHA inspector is around.

2. Impedance matching is necessary:
    - a. Only if you're using transformers.
    - b. Only if you're using power transformers.
    - c. Only if the specifications require it.
    - d. Only if required by the NEC Code.

3. Loudspeakers should not be wired in series-parallel.
    - a. False.
    - b. Only if requested by the consultant.
    - c. Only if driven from a line amplifier.
    - d. Only if necessary.

4. Use cone loudspeakers only for high-frequency applications.
    - a. True.
    - b. When the design requires them.
    - c. False.
    - d. Unless otherwise specified by the consultant.

5. A room's acoustic makeup has no effect on a loudspeaker array's performance.
    - a. True.
    - b. Only if the array isn't energized.
    - c. Only if the room is the great outdoors.
    - d. False.

6. After the loudspeaker array is set, it should never be moved.
    - a. False.
    - b. Only if the measurements dictate it.
    - c. Only if the consultant requests it.
    - d. True.

7. Heisenberg discovered the uncertainty principle.
    a. Only for position and momentum of sound.
    b. True.
    c. When he was at JPL.
    d. False.

8. Comb filtering is what you do to your hair.
    a. True.
    b. False.
    c. Only when sound is passing through your hair.
    d. A phenomena unique to sound.

9. Crossover networks should never be used.
    a. When unnecessary.
    b. With one loudspeaker.
    c. When rejected by the consultant.
    d. In the Southern Hemisphere.

10. Low-frequency loudspeakers are very directional.
    a. Only when energized.
    b. True.
    c. Only if they're in a series-parallel arrangement.
    d. False.

Testing of Large Loudspeaker Arrays

Preinstallation checks

In Work Element 16006 you studied loudspeaker/driver pre-testing. After you've finished studying this chapter, we suggest that you review *Work Element 16006, Large Loudspeaker Arrays.*

Polarity checks will show wiring integrity. If there is any doubt as to the polarity of each element, a commercial polarity tester will allow acoustic checking. There is no common standard throughout the industry as to loudspeaker and driver polarity. Therefore, don't assume that all elements have the same polarity. Before the array is flown, it may be difficult to perform frequency response tests due to reflections from nearby surfaces, such as the floor or large cabinets. Using a TEF analyzer will ease the task. Nevertheless, these tests should be performed to verify that all elements are operating within their specifications.

Initial installed tests

Working from the floor and using a protractor, sight to the centerlines of the various elements to be sure the array is in reasonable alignment. Using pink noise at a reasonable level—about 75 dB—walk the floor to listen for any anomalies, or holes. Then repeat that test, but with an individual talking the system. You might know the term as a "sound check." In either case, an individual whose diction is reasonably clear is using the system for its intended purpose. A list of nonsense words might be used, or material might be read that the trained listeners are not acquainted with. In both cases, you're using your ear/brain combination with a minimum of test equipment.

Individual testing of elements should be performed to verify their coverage angles and patterns. The entire system and array should then be checked with pink noise to verify that no overlapping of coverage or comb effects are apparent. The array dispersion patterns should be checked against the specifications or consultant's parameters.

Frequency response testing

As we've said before, use of a TEF analyzer will speed the task. If you are not equipped with at least a pink noise generator and a 1/3-octave analyzer, you are guessing. Sine wave testing of a loudspeaker in any room, other than an anechoic chamber, is an exercise in futility. The only thing you will learn is the ever-present condition of standing waves in a hall or room.

After the array is installed, the raw frequency response should be tested and noted. Using 85 dB at seated ear level (4 feet) is a reasonable figure. This is far enough above the ambient noise of the room to provide an adequate signal to noise ratio, yet sufficiently within the power capabilities of the various elements before equalization.

Before equalization, the ambient noise level of the hall should be checked and noted. It is desirable to use the TEF system or a 1/3-octave analyzer to measure that parameter. During this test, all air handling equipment should be shut off and any ambient noises interrupted, if feasible. If the ambient noise level is above 40 dB, C scale, the source of noise should be tracked down, unless it is due to street noises. It may be worthwhile to perform these tests when street noises aren't a problem.

System equalization should then be performed. If the consultant has provided a desired response that will be used as the "house curve," so much the better. If not, a reasonable response should be set. The system should be talked with qualified listeners walking the hall. It may be desirable to adjust the system response to suit the listeners' ears. Music may be played through the system, but similar to that expected in actual use. The use of music alone is not an adequate substitute for pink noise and talking the system.

At each major step, response and level measurements should be noted, together with the date and time. Should any question later arise, temperature and humidity should also be checked and noted. As you're aware from earlier chapters, both temperature and humidity will affect the system response. Listeners' comments as to the sound quality of the system might also be noted. Obviously, names of individuals participating in the checkout should be noted.

Level testing

Ear protectors are again the rule. Either in-ear or earmuff devices may be used. When the SPL (Sound Pressure Level) is above 100 dB isn't the time to realize you left your ear protectors back at the shop. Pink noise is very pervasive, you don't realize just how loud it is until it's turned off.

OSHA's requirement for ear protectors begins at 85 dB SPL for octave band measurements. Quoting from 1910.95, Occupational Noise Exposure, *"Protection against the effects of noise exposure shall be provided when the sound levels exceed those shown in Table 5-1 when measured on the A scale of a standard sound level meter at slow response. . . ."*

Table 5-1

Permissible Noise Exposures (1)

Duration per day, hours	Sound level dBA slow response
8	90
6	92
4	95
3	97
2	100
1½	102
1	105
½	110
¼ or less	115

Notice that at 100 dB SPL, the maximum exposure *per day* is two hours. You may argue that OSHA is being extreme, but hearing loss is cumulative, and not usually noticeable until it's too late.

Why do we harp on the subject of ear and hearing protection? You have but one life, and you have but one pair of ears. If you never plan on listening acutely to the sound reinforcement system you've built, then good hearing is no problem. But if the client complains about noise in the system, which your coworkers hear, but you can't, it may be you who has the problem.

A typical specification for sound pressure level on a project might read: "The SPL (Sound Pressure Level) shall vary no more than plus or minus 3 dB from that measured at seat location E-24. The acceptable SPL shall be measured at any seat in the hall. The SPL at seat location E-24 shall be 95 dB, C scale, using a wideband pink noise generator fed into the high-level input of the mixer. All measurements shall be taken using a standard sound-level meter using the C scale, and set at slow response." A graph might be included, showing a further restriction of the specification. It might show the allowable variation measured using a 1/3-octave analyzer.

Incidentally, a 3 dB window measured using C scale at any seat in the hall is a tight specification, regardless of the seating capacity.

Documentation

Documentation of the finished array is important. It should include the following:

- Cluster as-built drawings
- Schematic drawing of the cluster
- Detailed component listing, including serial numbers
- Detailed listing of element-hanging hardware
- Photographs before and after the cluster is concealed
- Aiming angles for all elements
- Raw response curves
- Equalized response curves
- Measured SPL used for the curves
- Variations accepted by the consultant
- List of individuals involved in the testing and acceptance

Questions

1. If you are working more than 10 feet from the floor, safety harnesses are necessary:

    a. Only if you're afraid of heights.

    b. Only if the floor is hard.

    c. Only if you want to live after falling.

    d. Only if the OSHA inspector is around.

2. If the manufacturer of the rigging equipment shows a design factor of 5:1, you know you can set it to 3:1:

    a. If the array weight is less than 250 pounds.

    b. Never.

    c. If the consultant says so.

    d. If the array is installed inside where there is no wind.

3. It will save time if the array isn't tested and inspected until it's flown:

    a. Only if you have an unlimited budget.

    b. Only if you designed the array.

    c. Only if the consultant designed the array.

    d. Only if you have unwavering faith in the manufacturers.

4. Any power amplifier can be used to test the array.

    a. No.

    b. If the array will be tested on-site.

    c. Only if used for a short period of time.

    d. Why not?

5. Wire chain is acceptable for hanging an array:

    a. If for two weeks or less.

    b. No.

    c. If the array weighs less than 100 pounds.

    d. If three or more chains are used.

6. Brass screw eyes or hooks are acceptable.
   a. Yes, because they don't corrode.
   b. When they are visible.
   c. If selected by the designer.
   d. No.

7. Comb filtering is caused by:
   a. Improper system design.
   b. Improper adjustment of the 1/3-octave equalizer.
   c. Acoustical interaction between elements.
   d. Improper adjustment of the crossover network.

8. Loudspeaker arrays should never be installed below sea level.
   a. Yes.
   b. When required by the designer.
   c. No.
   d. Only if you're in Death Valley.

9. Movable arrays should be used in preference to fixed arrays.
   a. No.
   b. Yes.
   c. If the designer is competent.
   d. Only if the owner has an unlimited budget.

10. The local discount hardware store is a good source for rigging hardware.
    a. Yes.
    b. Only in an emergency.
    c. No.
    d. If the array weighs less than 100 pounds.

11. Polarity checks will show up phasing problems.
    a. Only if the array should sound good.
    b. No.
    c. Yes.
    d. Only if the OSHA inspector can verify it.

12. If your hearing loss is profound, doctors can perform surgery to correct the condition.

    a. True.

    b. False.

    c. Only if you're under 40 years old.

    d. Only if you can pay for it.

13. Talking and listening to the system is:

    a. A good idea.

    b. A good idea, if time is available.

    c. Mandatory.

    d. Not usually necessary.

14. Frequency response testing should be done with sine wave tones.

    a. No.

    b. A useless test.

    c. Usually OK.

    d. If performed with permission.

15. Sound levels above 85 dB SPL are:

    a. Good for the ears.

    b. Acceptable to OSHA under certain circumstances.

    c. Not recommended.

    d. Loud.

16. Signal-to-noise ratios apply only to electronic equipment, not rooms or halls.

    a. True.

    b. False.

    c. True when correctly measured.

    d. Only if the hall is used for music performance.

17. Ear protectors are necessary:

    a. When it is cold outside.

    b. When performing sound-level tests.

    c. When required by OSHA.

    d. False.

18. System equalization is a good idea:

    a. When the hall seats more than 10 persons.

    b. When requested by the consultant or designer.

    c. Only if the array is improperly designed.

    d. When the system doesn't sound good.

19. Level testing should be performed:

    a. With white noise.

    b. Only if requested by the owner.

    c. Before final adjustments to the array.

    d. With pink noise.

20. The wire size for the midfrequency and high-frequency elements can be smaller than the wire size for the low-frequency elements.

    a. True.

    b. False, all wire must be the same size.

    c. If found necessary by the NEC.

    d. Only if the loudspeaker impedances are 8 ohms or less.

Chapter 6

Troubleshooting & Testing

by Bob Bushnell

- **NICET Work Element 15012, Troubleshooting Audio Systems Wiring**
- **NICET's Description:** *"Identify, trace, and repair cable faults."*

- **NICET Work Element 15016, System Troubleshooting**
- **NICET's Description:** *"Verify problem. Analyze system configuration. Use the logical steps of troubleshooting to identity and locate faults and/or deficiencies. Report findings. Make recommendations regarding equipment and/ or cost estimates."*

- **NICET Work Element 15015, Equipment Testing**
- **NICET's Description:** *"Conduct tests of mixers, equalizers, and compressor/limiters for frequency response, output, total harmonic distortion, and signal-to-noise ratio. Test electronic crossovers for crossover point(s) and crossover slope."*

- **NICET Work Element 15014, Advanced Assembly**
- **NICET's Description:** *"Inspect and test completed rack systems for proper assembly and operation. Make internal modifications to the equipment as necessary. Prepare as-built documentation. Supervise and assist with on-site installation of completed assemblies."*

Troubleshooting Audio Systems Wiring

Measure wiring using impedance bridge

A VOM (Volt-Ohm-Milliammeter) or a DVM (Digital Voltmeter) will measure DC resistance, but it cannot directly measure impedance. An impedance bridge measures DC resistance, AC impedance, and inductance, usually at 1 kHz. Most bridges allow a test signal of other than 1 kHz to be sent to the bridge.

Using an impedance bridge with an oscillator will provide cable inductance measurements over the audio range 20 Hz to 20 kHz. Other than scientific curiosity, why measure cable inductance? For cable runs longer than 20 feet, measuring inductance may find cable faults. However, certain caveats do apply. The approximate inductance and capacitance per foot of shielded twisted-pair cable of the type that is usually used is 0.2 mH and 36 pF per foot. The minimum cable length should be approximately 10 times the inductance per foot, in order to make inductance measurements meaningful.

If a sample cable of 50 or 100 feet is measured, using 20 Hz, 1 kHz, and 20 kHz as reference frequencies, a useful table will be generated. Three measurements per frequency should be made: between wires, and between each wire and the shield. The cable should be laid out instead of being coiled up, as additional inductance is created by cable proximity on the reel.

If a fault on a long cable in a conduit is suspected, and not independently removable, there's not much choice except to abandon the cable. If the cable is accessible, then measuring with an impedance bridge will locate the fault to a reasonable location. At the source end, the inductance of the suspect cable is measured at 1 kHz, with the destination end disconnected. The fault in the cable, whether it is one wire that is broken or both, will provide a virtual cable length. Once the inductance is measured, the approximate length to the fault may be quickly calculated.

For example, if we assume that the test cable measured 20 mH for a 100-foot length and the suspect cable measured 35 mH, then the approximate length to the break is 175 feet. If the cable length overall is approximately 500 feet, then it may be worthwhile to remove the cable, measure to the approximate location, then either repair the cable, or splice in a new length.

As a further check, perform the same measurement from the destination end, then verify the accuracy of the measurements. Depending on circumstances, it may be worthwhile to measure the suspect cable using 20 Hz as the test frequency.

Identifying cable faults using a VOM

Basic cable faults can be identified using a VOM. The far end of the cable should be disconnected from the terminating equipment, and no electrical termination should be placed at that end. Low resistance shorts can be quickly identified and partial shorts can be estimated. Shorts between conductors, and between the shield and either conductor can be identified. These basic tests use the ohmmeter portion of the instrument.

Identifying cable problems based on equipment substitution

An audio cable from a mixer feeding a +4 dBu level to a 100-watt power amplifier is suspected of having a high-resistance fault. The cable is 200 feet long and is made up of two shielded AWG #22 wires. AWG #22 wire has an approximate resistance of 0.016 ohms per foot.

Disconnect the mixer output from the audio cable and temporarily wire a 16-ohm resistor across the black and white wires of the audio cable.

At the power amplifier, disconnect the output wires from the amplifier, and temporarily rewire the audio cable to the output terminals. Feed a 1000 Hz tone from an audio oscillator to the power amplifier, and adjust the power amplifier gain control so that 40.0 volts is measured across the power amplifier output.

At the mixer location, measure the voltage across the resistor. Allowing only for the voltage drop in the cable, you should have measured 28.6 volts across the resistor. How did we get that number? We used a little-known, but invaluable equation:

$$R_1 / R_2 + 1 = k$$

This provides the voltage ratio between any two resistors being used as a voltage divider. R_1 is the series resistor, and R_2 is the shunt resistor. "k" is the resultant voltage ratio. In this case, R_1 is the wire resistance value and R_2 is the load resistance. The wire resistance is 0.016 ohms/foot and the loop length is 400 feet. Substituting in the equation, we have:

$$((0.016 \times 400) \div 16) + 1 = k$$

Then k = 1.4. Dividing the voltage across the power amplifier output by that number, we get 28.57, which should be the voltage at the measuring end. As a side comment, here we see the need for adequate wire sizes.

If the voltage measured across the resistor is any less than 28.6 volts, there is a high-resistance fault in the cable. If the same audio cable has an apparent low-resistance fault, a check can be performed using a "D" cell from a flashlight and a DVM. Measure the battery voltage at the source end of the cable, then at the destination end.

Identifying shorts, opens, and high resistance splices

Shorts may be identified either with a VOM or a DVM. The cable destination end should be disconnected, then the resistance between wires and the resistance between either of the wires and the shield are measured. This technique will identify shorts or opens.

If the cable type is known, the resistance per foot is therefore known. All three wires at the cable destination end should be soldered together. Then measure the resistance between wires—red to black, red to shield, black to shield. The three loop resistances are compared. If they are not substantially equal, then the wire with the high resistance connection is known by process of elimination.

If the cable length is known, the process is simplified. The expected loop resistance may be calculated, then compared against the measured loop resistance.

Cable repair techniques

Cable repair should be undertaken only if the cable cannot be abandoned or replaced and as a last resort. Items required:

1. A normal complement of tools, as well as a heat gun for use on heat shrink tubing.
2. An assortment of heat shrink tubing suitable to match the various insulated wire and cable diameters.
3. A selection of tinned copper tubular braid to cover the inner conductors.

For this example, we will assume the broken cable is two-conductor AWG #22 with an aluminum/mylar shield, an AWG #22 drain wire, and a PVC jacket. We will further assume that the break had severed the black wire only, not the insulation around the wire. At the break or repair site:

1. Carefully cut back the overall jacket to about 2 inches on each side of the break.
2. Cut off the drain wire so that about 1 inch extends from the cut jacket on each side.
3. Cut back the shield so that about 1 inch extends from the cut jacket on each side.
4. Find the exact location of the break in the black wire and cut the wire.
5. Strip or cut back the insulation on both sides of the cut until you have located where the "good" wire begins.
6. The wire to be spliced in may be laid over the existing wire, or a small hook may be bent in each wire before soldering. For the wire to be spliced in, solder in a length of AWG #22 bare stranded wire to one end of the cut wire.

7. The piece of heat shrink you will use for the next step will replace the insulation at the cut location. It should slide over the black wire far enough so that the bare wire can be soldered at one or two locations. Depending on your dexterity and the working conditions, you may have to further cut back the overall jacket.

8. Prepare a length of heat shrink tubing of a diameter that will shrink down to the diameter of the repaired cable. Make the length about 2 inches longer than the distance from the cut jacket on the left to the cut jacket on the right.

9. Slide the tubing over either end of the cable so that it is out of the way.

10. Prepare a length of tinned copper tubular braid of a diameter that, when stretched, will shrink to the diameter of the two repaired wires, black and white.

11. Slide the tubular braid over the end of the cable opposite to where the heat shrink tubing is placed, and out of the way.

12. Prepare a length of heat shrink tubing sufficient to extend from 1/4 inch beyond the insulation of each cut wire piece.

13. Slide it over the unsoldered end of the black wire far enough so that you can solder the bare stranded wire to the black wire end.

14. Remember that once you have soldered the black wire to the bare wire, you have now established the finished length of the repaired cable. Do any other wires need repair? If not, then establish the finished length of the repaired cable.

15. After you have established the finished length, solder the black wire to the bare wire.

16. Slide the heat shrink tubing back so it is centered over the soldered connections.

17. Shrink the tubing, being careful not to burn any other wires, cables, or the cable bundle.

18. Slide the tubular braid over the repaired wires then stretch it so it is taut over those wires.

19. Cut the braid ends so they are even, then relax the tension and solder the drain wire to one end of the braid. Temporarily slide

a piece of wood or Teflon beneath the braid so that the soldering heat doesn't damage the insulation beneath.

20. Make the braid taut then carefully solder the other drain wire, being careful not to damage the insulation beneath.

21. Inspect the semifinished connection, and perform another measurement with an impedance bridge.

22. If the measurements are satisfactory, slide the overall heat shrink tubing in place, then shrink down to fit.

It is recommended that the above steps be practiced on scrap wires until you are familiar with the technique.

System Troubleshooting

Problem verification using proper test equipment

If you have access to a computer-based test system, without a doubt, use it. Use of such a system will not verify the problem for you, but it will give you immediate access to several measuring devices that can save you time.

You should begin, not with test equipment, but your ears, brain, and intelligence. Access to the best test equipment is useless without determining what equipment should be tested with what device. You can answer more questions with your intelligence, a logical approach to the problem, and a DVM (digital voltmeter), than with a shotgun approach and an expensive computer-based test system.

If you're in the field, you probably have access to the all the test equipment your company owns, but you must determine what equipment to bring. You must determine what is the problem. That is, what actually *is* the problem, not what somebody told you what he thought the problem was. If you trust the source of information, that's a good place to begin, but you're the individual who must solve the problem.

We'll assume you're working with a church sound reinforcement system. The church seats 700 people. There is one pulpit microphone, two choir microphones, and two microphone receptacles in the narthex. Your first rule of problem solving is: *don't assume anything.* If you make any kind of assumption without verifying the assumption, you may waste a lot of time. There are three items common to analyzing any problem: logic, common sense, and intuition, in that order.

The complaint from the church is: The system doesn't sound right. You were called to the church on Friday afternoon; Sunday, of course, will be the next service. You request the aid of one of the church staff to talk the system. You listen to her voice directly, then over the system through the pulpit microphone. You verify that the system has a problem. You move the pulpit microphone connector at the mixer to another input, but the problem remains. You substitute another microphone, yet the problem remains. You connect one of the microphones to a receptacle in the narthex, and her voice quality is excellent.

Therefore, you know that the problem is somewhere in the pulpit microphone cable, anywhere from the pulpit microphone connector to the connector at the mixer. You thank her for her efforts, advise her that the system will be ready for Sunday's service and begin looking for the source of the problem. You open up the box under the pulpit holding the microphone connector, and discover that the black wire had a poor solder connection at the connector. You get your toolbox, which always travels with you, then resolder the connection.

Then you ask the staff member to talk the system again, for two reasons. First, to verify for yourself that the problem is solved, and to show her that the problem is solved so that she may advise the minister. You talk the system, so that she may hear the system working. In this case, the proper test equipment was your two ears, brain, and intelligence. Not all problems are this easy. But any problem solving requires ears, brain, and intelligence.

You have a problem with a sound reinforcement system in a hall seating about 2000 people. The complaint is that the audience seated under the balcony is getting a "muffled" sound. You arrive with your toolbox, wits, and the service folder for the system, but knowing that you would be alone, with no one to talk the system, you brought along a cassette recorder with a powered loudspeaker. The recording on the tape is your voice, speaking sentences and nonsense words.

You power up the system, set your powered loudspeaker in front of a microphone on stage, and appropriately set the sound pressure level. You walk the hall from left to right, going back several rows at each pass. The system sounds excellent until you stand under the balcony. You listen and hear that the sound from the under-balcony loudspeakers is arriving earlier than the sound from the main cluster.

You check the electronics rack, which is not locked at the request of the owner, and discover that somebody has reset the controls on the under-balcony delay unit to zero delay. You refer to the service folder, and reset the delay to the 40 millisecond time originally measured. With the filled-out service order, you explain what had happened to the manager.

Utilize block diagrams/schematics to analyze system configuration and to determine location of problem

A good block diagram or schematic is your first reference source, even before checking the system. Studying a block diagram tells you a great deal about the system. It allows you to "walk" the system and see potential trouble spots. For example, the problem might be a piece of equipment with which your company has had repeated problems.

The block diagram provides the equipment installed, how the system is connected, where the cables are run, cable numbers for identification, and the connectors used. You might even find the AC circuit breakers identified.

Use correct troubleshooting techniques to solve problem

Here are "Robert's Rules" of orderly problem-solving:

- Don't assume anything.
- First, use logic.
- Next, use common sense.
- Then, use intuition.
- Don't make more than one change at a time.
- If two people are working on a problem, one must be the leader.

If you make any kind of assumption without verifying the assumption, you may waste a lot of time. If you begin a course of action by making an assumption, and remember that your logic is based on that assumption, that's acceptable. You should later be able to verify or reject that assumption.

Apply logical principles to the problem, mix that with common sense then use intuition. Using logic excludes the use of the word "maybe."

If you make two changes at the same time, you don't know which change corrected the problem. Do one change, then the other. If both people are trying different changes at the same time, the result isn't a corrected problem, but chaos.

We can't emphasize too much the importance of avoiding shotgun techniques or guesswork. If you have a device that has several low-priced ICs, and you feel certain about the technique, then replace all the ICs and see if the problem is solved. But if the problem isn't solved, then all you know is that (probably) the ICs aren't at fault. If you simply hope for the device to work, then change the ICs.

These next paragraphs are a combination of logic and an actual troubleshooting session to locate a source of oscillation either in, or associated with, a mixer. Use an audio voltmeter with a maximum sensitivity equal or more than -60 dBu. Use a 20 MHz oscilloscope, at a minimum. A 100 MHz oscilloscope is preferred. The electrical environment must be clean; no radio stations next door, no computers on the next bench, no stray magnetic or electrical fields. You want to find the source of the oscillation, not how quiet the environment is.

Connect the AC cables for the mixer and the test equipment into the same power strip to assure a common source of AC power and common ground reference. Connect an audio oscillator to microphone input #1 (by convention) of the mixer together with the audio voltmeter. Set the audio oscillator's output level to - 50 dBu at 1 kHz. Then connect the audio voltmeter to the mixer's left output bus.

Set the audio oscillator output level, and the mixer's output level to +4 dBu. Disconnect the audio oscillator from the mixer, and move the connector away from the mixer to prevent signal leakage. Don't change any settings on the mixer. Solder a 150-ohm resistor across a male plug that matches the microphone input connector. Plug that into microphone input #1. Be sure that all other input faders are down or at the infinity setting.

If the audio voltmeter has an output connector, connect the oscilloscope to that connector. If the audio voltmeter doesn't have an output connector, parallel the oscilloscope across the output bus with the audio voltmeter. Range down on the audio voltmeter until you see a fixed reading of the meter needle, which is indicating the oscillation.

Experiment with the oscilloscope timebase until you see one or two cycles of the unwanted waveform. This will give you a clue as to the frequency. Is it low-frequency? If it is, then most likely it's either 60 or 120 Hz. You may have unintentionally created a ground loop, which is causing the 60 Hz signal. If it is 120 Hz, it may be coming from the mixer. Almost all mixer power supplies are full-wave devices; therefore, the power supply is using both the positive and negative peaks of the AC line, and the resultant product is 120 Hz.

If the unwanted waveform is high frequency, there are many other areas to search. The unwanted waveform or oscillation may be external to the mixer. In this case, comparison with other devices may provide a clue as to the source. If the oscillation is internal to the mixer, careful analysis and searching is required. HF oscillation tends to be pervasive and elusive to track down.

1. If you shut off the power to the mixer, does the unwanted signal either disappear or decrease in level?

If yes, this input channel or another input channel is oscillating.

If no, the oscillation is external to the mixer.

2. If you adjust the input trim control, does it change the amplitude of the unwanted signal?

If yes, this input channel is oscillating in one or more of the amplifier sections before the input fader.

If no, the oscillation may be later in the mixer or in another input channel.

3. If you shut off the input fader, does the unwanted signal disappear?

If yes, this input channel is oscillating in one or more of the amplifier sections before the input fader.

If no, this input channel or another input channel is oscillating.

4. If you adjust the high-frequency equalizer control on the mixer, does it change the amplitude of the unwanted signal?

If yes, this input channel or another input channel is oscillating.

If no, the oscillation may be later in the mixer.

5. If you shut off the submaster control, does the unwanted signal disappear?

If yes, this input channel or another input channel is oscillating.

If no, the oscillation may be later in the mixer.

If you touch either of the leads of the termination resistor connected to the input, does it change the amplitude of the unwanted signal? You will introduce hum into the mixer, but that is a low-frequency, not a high-frequency signal. This discussion is not meant to lead you to an answer, but to show you areas to explore, and techniques to use.

Document and report findings

You diagnosed and repaired the problem, but you're not done. If you're in the field, the owner or the contact individual should be notified. If you're in the shop, the individual requesting the work should be notified.

The field service order should be filled out in sufficient detail for someone else to understand the problem and the diagnosis. The service order becomes part of the system history, helping you or someone else to later diagnosis other problems. If your company doesn't use such systems, it will be beneficial if it starts doing so.

The usual practice for tracking problems with equipment is word of mouth, from one tech to another. Start a set of files, with a separate folder for each device. A simple hand-written and dated sheet is added by a tech that works on the device. This will show the types of problems encountered and provide a history for specific devices. Does Model XYZ usually have problems with the input connectors? In this case, the manufacturer should be contacted, or an alternate manufacturer should be used.

Correct problem by repairing vs. replacing defective item

Here's logic at work again. A few ideas:
1. If the defective item is expensive, can it be repaired?
2. Can the defective item be quickly replaced?
3. Is there a similar item that can be modified or will fit?
4. Will it take longer to fix the defective item or to wait for a replacement?
5. Can an alternate item be substituted until the defective item is repaired?
6. Will the system operate with diminished capacity until the defective item is repaired?

7. Must the defective item be repaired on the spot?

8. Does the manufacturer's warranty program allow for an immediate no-charge replacement?

9. Is the manufacturer still in business or must the item be repaired?

10. If the defective item is an electronic component, will a field repair affect the warranty?

11. Is it cheaper to replace the item and perform the repair in the shop?

12. If the manufacturer is out of business, is it cheaper to substitute an alternate item, and repair the defective item in the shop?

These are some suggestions, and the choice between repairing versus replacing oftentimes is a judgment call tempered by your company's policies. As you see by the suggestions, there is no clear-cut answer. If a beginning tech is available for the field call, it might be cheaper to replace the item, then perform an in-shop repair, than the expense of a more qualified technician involved with travel time.

Equipment Testing

To perform all of the following tests, the equipment required is a low-distortion audio oscillator capable of +24 dBu output level with a balanced output, an audio voltmeter that has a maximum sensitivity of at least -60 dBm, an oscilloscope, a THD (Total Harmonic Distortion) analyzer, terminating resistors, and semilog graph paper or your workbook. If a computer-based test system is available, use it, as it will simplify moving cables, provide faster testing, and provide very meaningful figures.

How to conduct frequency response tests
on mixers and signal processors

Connect the AC cables for the mixer and the test equipment into the same power strip to assure a common source of AC power and common ground reference. Connect the oscillator to microphone input #1 (by convention) of the mixer together with the audio voltmeter. Set the audio oscillator's output level to - 50 dBu at 1 kHz. Then connect the audio voltmeter to the mixer's left output bus.

Set the input fader at the zero setting on the dial and the submaster or master at its zero setting. Adjust the input trim so that the output level of the mixer is +4 dBu. Depending on the mixer's gain parameters, you may have to change the audio oscillator's output level so that the trim control is in the middle of its range.

Frequency response of an electronic device is normally referenced to 1 kHz and measured at its nominal output level, which is usually +4 dBu. If a reference frequency isn't stated, then the frequency response specification can be more liberally interpreted. If the frequency response is stated as "plus or minus 1 dB from 20 Hz to 20 kHz, with reference to 1 kHz," the specification makes it clear as to the maximum deviation allowable for the specification.

For most electronic devices, the frequency ranges where the frequency response may depart from that measured at 1 kHz are usually 20 Hz to 100 Hz, and 12 kHz to 20 kHz. The usual practice for frequency checks:
• 20 Hz to 100 Hz in 10 Hz increments
• 200 Hz, 500 Hz, and 1 kHz
• 2 kHz, 5 kHz, and 10 kHz
• 12 kHz to 20 kHz in 1 kHz increments

Set the audio oscillator to these various frequencies, noting the mixer's output level for each frequency. The output level of the audio oscillator shouldn't be changed. If it was changed, the frequency response test is invalid. The test should be rerun.

If desired, the test should be performed on all inputs to all outputs if a problem is suspected with the mixer. These tests are equally valid for signal-processing devices. With any signal-processing device, there should be no controls or adjustments set that would intentionally change the frequency response of the device. The test should be made at +4 dBu or the stated nominal output level of the device.

Procedure for measuring maximum output levels of mixers and signal processors

Provide the same setup as with the procedure for frequency response. However, terminate the mixer left output bus with a 604-ohm, 1%, or 620-ohm resistor. A power rating of 1/2 watt is adequate. Connect the oscilloscope input to the left output bus of the mixer.

Set the input fader at the zero setting on the dial, and the submaster or master at its zero setting. Adjust the input trim so that the output level of the mixer is +4 dB. Depending on the mixer's gain parameters, you may have to change the audio oscillator's output level so that the trim control is in the middle of its range.

While watching the oscilloscope trace, increase the input fader level until you see the positive or negative peak of the sine wave just begin to flatten. This is usually called the maximum output level or the clip level. If the input fader is at the top, with no clipping, leave it at that setting, then increase the submaster control until you see the positive or negative peak of the sine wave just begin to flatten.

You may want to decrease the oscilloscope gain and adjust the vertical position so you can see the positive peak of the sine wave in greater magnification. For any well-designed mixer, both the positive and negative peaks should flatten at the same level.

Decrease the submaster control to just below the clipping level. Note the output level, that is, the maximum output level of the mixer. It should be +24 dBu, but check the manufacturer's specifications to verify the number. The maximum output level may be higher, but it shouldn't be any less than +22 dBu. The procedure for testing a signal-processing device is basically the same, but verify that there are no controls or adjustments set that might change the clip level of the device.

Procedure to measure total harmonic distortion of mixers and signal processors

A word or two about mixers: there are at least five variable elements in a mixer.

1. The input levels
2. The input trims
3. The input faders
4. The equalizers
5. The submaster

Because of these five variable elements and the amplifiers associated with them, any of those amplifiers may be driven into clipping, depending on the input level and the setting of a variable element. A mixer should be designed so that clip levels for all amplifiers are the same. The left combining amplifier, for example, is literally combining all inputs directed to it. These combining amplifiers may clip first, unless the designer has taken precautions to prevent that.

A signal-processing device normally has one input level, +4 dBu, and the variable elements usually do not control level. A compressor or limiter is an exception, usually with one variable element.

Provide the same setup as the procedure for maximum output levels. Be sure a terminating resistor is connected across the appropriate output bus. Connect the audio oscillator to microphone input #1 (by convention) of the mixer together with the audio voltmeter. Set the audio oscillator's output level to −50 dBu at 1 kHz. Then connect the audio voltmeter to the mixer's left output bus.

Set the input fader at the zero setting on the dial and the submaster or master at its zero setting. Adjust the input trim so that the output level of the mixer is +4 dBu. Depending on the mixer's gain parameters, you may have to change the audio oscillator's output level so that the trim control is in the middle of its range.

Measure the THD at this level and frequency. It should be 0.01% or less. Then set the input fader to maximum and adjust the submaster until you see clipping on the left output bus. Decrease the submaster control to just below the clipping level. Then measure the THD. It should be 0.01% or less. Watch the THD reading as you very slowly increase the submaster setting. You'll reach a level where a very slight change in the submaster setting will cause the THD reading to rapidly increase. That is the maximum output level at 1 kHz, with the loading you've placed on the output bus. The loading includes the terminating resistor and the equipment connected to the bus.

Now set the audio oscillator's frequency to 20 Hz. Then measure the THD. It will probably be higher. You may find it necessary to slightly decrease the submaster control so that the output level isn't clipping. If the audio oscillator has a calibrated output level control, or if you're monitoring the oscillator level, it may be better to reduce the oscillator output level. If the reduction is more than 1 dB, that should be noted. If the reduction is more than 2 dB, it may be necessary to use 30 Hz or even 40 Hz as the low-frequency limit.

If 30 Hz or 40 Hz becomes the low-frequency limit, check the manufacturer's specifications as to their stated THD measurements. It may be that the unit you are testing is defective or the quality of the device is less than average. If the device has an acceptable 20 Hz THD figure, continue with the balance of the THD measurements. It's recommended to use the same frequencies as those used for frequency response measurements.

If you're working with a signal-processing device, the process is the same. Usually there are no level controls, so the higher output level is achieved by increasing the level from the audio oscillator.

Procedure to measure signal-to-noise ratio of mixers and signal processors

If an audio voltmeter is available with a higher sensitivity figure than –60 dBu, use it. The electrical environment must be clean; no radio stations next door, no computers on the next bench, no stray magnetic or electrical fields. You want to find out how quiet the mixer is, not how quiet the environment is.

The test setup should be the same as that for frequency response. Set the audio oscillator output level, and the mixer's output level to +4 dBu. Disconnect the audio oscillator from the mixer, and move the connector away from the mixer to prevent signal leakage. Don't change any settings on the mixer. Solder a 150-ohm resistor across a male plug that matches the microphone input connector. Plug that into microphone input #1. Be sure that all other input faders are down or at the infinity setting.

If the audio voltmeter has an output connector, connect the oscilloscope to that connector. If the audio voltmeter doesn't have an output connector, parallel the oscilloscope across the output bus with the audio voltmeter. Range down on the audio voltmeter until you see a random movement of the meter needle. You'll probably see a 5 dB (or thereabouts) variation in the meter reading.

If the meter is indicating a specific level without deviation of the needle, be sure that the internal audio oscillator on the mixer (if there is one) is off. Then check the oscilloscope for an unwanted waveform. This indicates either an unwanted oscillation in the mixer or an external field being picked up by the mixer. Review Work Element 15016 for a discussion on troubleshooting techniques for this type of problem.

If there are no unwanted waveforms, just random noise, then note the reading on the audio voltmeter. If the needle fluctuates between –78 and –72 dBu, then a good approximation for the noise level is –75 dBu. This noise reading is wideband, meaning the measurement includes random noise up to the upper bandpass of the audio voltmeter. For example, that upper bandpass might be 100 kHz. If more accurate noise figures are desired, the use of a computer-based test system is desirable and sometimes necessary.

The same procedure is followed for signal-processing devices. However, for the majority of these devices, the nominal input and output levels are +4 dBu and the attendant noise levels are often in the region of –100 dBu, requiring sophisticated or computer-based test systems necessary to achieve useful numbers.

How to conduct measurement of crossover points and slopes of electronic crossovers

Crossover filters, whether electronic or passive, will have slopes of anywhere from 3 dB per octave to 24 dB per octave. If a given low-pass filter has a specified crossover frequency of 440 Hz, referred to as the F_C point, and the filter has a slope of 18 dB per octave, then at 880 Hz, the filter response will be down 18 dB from the F_C.

Because of small variations in the filter slope where the filter just begins to depart from a flat response, F_C is stated at the 3 dB down point. In other words, the filter just discussed will begin to depart from a flat response at some frequency slightly lower than 440 Hz. If you attempt to measure the frequency at which the filter begins to depart from a flat response, you will be splitting hairs in determining that frequency. Hence the reason for the 3 dB point. There are good mathematical reasons for the 3 dB point, but they are above the level of this discussion.

Once this important parameter has been established, the actual measurement is not difficult. You will require an audio oscillator with accurate frequency markings, and an audio voltmeter. If accurate frequency measurements are required, a frequency counter is a necessity.

The oscillator is connected to the device under test, and the audio voltmeter is connected to the output. Set the crossover to the desired frequency, set the audio oscillator's frequency to well within the passband of the crossover, and adjust the audio oscillator to provide zero dBu or another level at least 20 dB below the maximum output capability of the device.

Adjust the audio oscillator's frequency toward the crossover frequency until the audio voltmeter reads 3 dB less than the level within the passband. Note that frequency, and see if it agrees with the selected crossover frequency on the device. Determine from the manufacturer's specifications for the crossover the slope of the crossover, unless it can be adjusted from the front panel. For this example, we will assume the crossover is a high-pass unit, the slope is 12 dB per octave, and the F_c is 100 Hz.

Therefore, at 50 Hz, one octave below 100 Hz, the level measured should be –15 dB from the level well within the passband. Or, the level measured should be –12 dB from the level at the F_c.

If the crossover frequency and slope aren't known, you can determine them by the above process. Vary the audio oscillator's frequency to find the frequency range making up the passband. Then vary the frequency to find the frequency range making up the slope of the crossover or filter. Again vary the frequency to locate where the level is 3 dB down from within the passband. That is the F_c of the crossover. Then adjust the oscillator to one octave above (or below) the F_c just measured. Note the level at that frequency. Subtract 3 dB from that level and the result is the slope of the crossover. Because of practical limits in component tolerances, you may find the level to be slightly different from what you expect.

This work element is concerned with electronic crossovers. They should not be confused with 1/3-octave equalizers, channel equalizers as used in mixers, or unique equalizers in signal processing devices. Crossovers will have a fixed slope beginning with the 3 dB point, whereas other equalizers may have a gradual slope.

Advanced Assembly

The rack has been turned over to you by the techs for inspection and test. Do you reach for a power cable? No. Instead, get a copy of the original block diagram as delivered to the shop, the marked-up block diagram, a flashlight, a yellow highlighter pen, and a red pen. Mark the original copy with any major changes from the marked-up block diagram, probably in green. You should also have a copy of the contract, and the system specifications. The usual reference for marking up drawings is red for changes, green for reference notes, and yellow for items checked.

Visual inspection procedures

Study the block diagram and the rack until you're acquainted with the various devices and their function in the system. You want to examine connections, connectors, wire supports, and terminations at each device. Working down the rack from top to bottom, and from left to right on each device is the easiest method to remember where you are in case of interruption.

Pick an XLR-type connector. Is the cable preparation and soldering acceptable? Examine a number of spade lugs. Are they properly crimped and are wires secure? If there are multipin connectors, are the wires securely crimped, and do all pins appear evenly seated? Are the cable supports securely fastened, and are the cables neatly tied to the supports? Are all cable ties the same color? (Don't laugh; it looks messy if they aren't.)

Is each AC power cable bundled and neatly tie-wrapped? Are there any ground isolators to be removed? By inspection or measurement, are the AC power connections properly connected for hot, neutral, and ground?

Do cable numbers appear on all cables other than AC power cables? Do they match the block diagram for location? Does the rack, front and rear, have a neat appearance?

Test equipment needed
for checking a completed rack system

At a minimum, you should have an audio oscillator covering the range from 20 Hz to 100 kHz, an audio voltmeter with a range of −80 dBu to +30 dBu, a 100 MHz oscilloscope, a DVM (digital voltmeter), and 8-ohm and 16-ohm dummy loads, (200 watts each). Also handy would be a pink noise generator and a 1/3-octave analyzer. Ivie and Gold Line are two manufacturers that come to mind. You'll also need a pair of hearing protectors, commonly known as earmuffs.

Review the specifications. You may also need a harmonic distortion analyzer. If you have access to a computer-operated test system, use that and forget everything else except the oscilloscope and DVM. We didn't forget test cables, as the specific types depend on your test equipment and the cable normally used in your shop.

A point on grounding and test cables: for most system testing, it's better to have everything grounded both ways. Both the source and destination ends of the cable should have the ground wires on a separate clip or single banana plug. Each test equipment device should have a three-wire AC plug with the U-ground pin intact. The power strip should have the U-ground pin intact on the three-wire AC plug. No ground lifters should be used, except to test for suspicious ground conditions.

Why should the oscillator have a range to 100 kHz? It is a good idea to view the system output on the audio voltmeter and oscilloscope and to sweep the oscillator all the way to 100 kHz. The system response should smoothly fall off beginning about 15 or 20 kHz. However, it is possible that parasitic oscillations are lurking in the system, and they will show up when the oscillator's frequency is one or two octaves above or below the oscillation.

If your test equipment is calibrated or checked at regular intervals, so much the better. If your test equipment is calibrated only when you have a problem with the device you might be hard-pressed to justify the performance specifications for the system.

Operational test procedures

Now is the time to test. Gather the test equipment. Disconnect all power cables from the power strip, then energize the incoming AC and check all receptacles with a grounded outlet tester. These devices go under various names, but they check correct polarity and a proper ground for each receptacle. Once that is done, de-energize the incoming AC and reconnect all power cables.

Some techs and engineers prefer to power up all equipment while sniffing inside the rack and watching for smoke. Others prefer to power up one device at a time while sniffing and watching for smoke. Regardless of your preference, this is a valid procedure. Even the best manufacturer makes a mistake once in a while.

To clarify the description of the system you're testing, this is a sound reinforcement system for a church with a congregation of about 300 people. The system isn't large enough to justify a mixer in the nave or the balcony. The system includes an 8-input mixer, a 1/3-octave equalizer, a cassette tape recorder, a 100-watt power amplifier, a local monitor amplifier and speaker, and a video camera and monitor.

These tests are an example of a procedure you might follow. Your company may already have test procedures established. In that case, refer to these for the NICET exam only. We haven't discussed the equivalent procedure if you are using a computer-operated test system. If you have used such a system, by necessity you will be familiar with the operating procedure. Nevertheless, the data obtained will still apply.

Once you've finished the AC test, turn all gain controls down to maximum CCW position. Connect a reasonably sized loudspeaker in a cabinet to the power amplifier output. Send a microphone level (about –60 dBu) from the oscillator to the mixer. If you have a pink noise generator, that's even better. In that case, set the pink noise level using the audio voltmeter. Adjust the level so that it reads in the neighborhood of –60 dB on the meter. Use the channel 1 input. Set the mixer so the signal is being fed to the left output channel. Turn up the level on channel 1 until the VU meter shows approximately zero level.

Set the individual knobs on the 1/3-octave equalizer at zero, as well as the gain control (if it exists). Then turn up the gain control on the power amplifier until you hear the oscillator tone. Or if you're using the pink noise generator, you hear the characteristic sound of pink noise. Classically, 1 kHz is used, but for a listening test, 800 or

880 Hz is more musical to the ear. Why 880 Hz? Because that's one octave above middle A, 440 Hz, on the piano.

Move the oscillator to each input channel in turn. Operate the controls common to each input channel and verify operation. Note that the fader and other settings should be almost identical in position from channel to channel.

Whether you're using the oscillator or the pink noise generator, note that the tone or the noise sound basically alike as you're moving from channel to channel and adjusting the various controls.

Now we want to check system gain through the power amplifier. We'll make use of the appropriate equation from Ohm's Law:

$$E = \sqrt{PR}$$

We'll assume for argument that you're using a 16-ohm load. We want to drive the power amplifier to its full output of 100 watts. Therefore, the output should be 40 volts. Do we agree? With the oscillator set to 1 kHz into channel 1, connect the audio voltmeter and oscilloscope across the power amplifier output, and connect the appropriate dummy load in place of the loudspeaker.

Then adjust the power amplifier gain so that you're reading 40 volts on the audio voltmeter. The VU meter on the mixer should still show an approximately zero level. Now sweep through the audio range and check for flatness of system response. In the absence of other specifications, you should measure plus or minus 1 dB from 40 Hz to 15 kHz relative to 1 kHz at 100 watts. While you're doing that, you should watch the waveform on the oscilloscope to be sure the power amplifier wasn't clipping.

Now adjust the input fader so that you're reading about 10 volts on the power amplifier output. Set the oscillator to match each of the frequency settings on the 1/3-octave equalizer. Adjust the control for that frequency to assure that the equalizer is working correctly. This might be easier with two people—one to set the frequency, the other to adjust the equalizer for that frequency.

If a pink noise generator and 1/3-octave analyzer are available, you'll find the procedure much faster.

We won't go through the procedure, but if you have a harmonic distortion analyzer, perform a distortion test on the system. Use 100 Hz, 1 kHz, and 10 kHz as the test frequencies.

For the last test, connect the video camera to the video monitor. Verify picture quality and video resolution. Verify operation with low light levels and high contrast images.

We admit we have gone slightly beyond NICET's description, *"Inspect and test completed rack systems for proper assembly and operation...",* but to the technical side, the above measurements are operational.

Maintaining as-built documentation

For rack elevations, you should verify that the drawing shows the equipment installed in the rack, the amount of rack space each device occupies, and the serial number of the device (if applicable).

Wiring details for the mixer and other equipment provided should appear on separate drawings. The connectors on each device should be shown, preferably on a pictorial drawing. Each connector should be identified as to type, wire number, and circuit purpose. If the device is plugged into an AC receptacle, the circuit number should later appear on the drawing.

Mark the block diagram with your initials and the date you started testing. This isn't for self-protection, but in case the drawing is borrowed, you can identify it. As you test the system, mark the block diagram with the yellow highlighter to show that the system works where you've done the highlighting and to remind yourself how far you've gone in testing.

If you find a wiring error, have one of the techs correct the problem. Depending on the nature of the problem, you might want to hold the correcting until you have more problems to correct. You may find it more expedient to correct the problem yourself.

If you have a faulty device, you either replace it or trouble-shoot the problem. You might check the manufacturer's warranty to see if your work on the device invalidates the warranty in case of later problems.

When you're finished with system testing, your markups should be turned over to the draftsman so that the original drawings can be brought up to date.

Techniques for on-site connecting

The quickest and most expensive technique is using multipoint connectors. The appropriate half is wired in the shop, the other half is wired in the field. This technique is appropriate when the connection time in the field is at a minimum.

Jones-type barrier strips are usable, but they take up space and tend to look rather messy after wiring. DIN rail terminal blocks and panel-mount terminal blocks are better for appearance and provide easier connection of individual wires.

XLR-type connectors are often used on systems of this size. If the rack is a wall-mounted unit, they might be mounted on either fixed side, not to the movable portion. Do not mount any XLR-type connector on a horizontal surface with the connectors facing upward. Dust and dirt will make your life difficult.

If the rack is a freestanding unit, the XLR connectors might be placed on an interior panel facing to the rear of the cabinet. They might be placed on either side, no less than 2 feet above the floor. If the connectors are neatly lined up and have adequate space around them for legends, they will enhance the appearance of the system.

Questions

1. Inductance measurements to find cable faults should always be performed with system power on and the destination end of the cable connected. True or false?

2. Inductance measurements for cable faults should be performed using which of these choices:

    a. +4 dBu.

    b. 10 kHz.

    c. Microphone level.

    d. Whatever is available on the impedance bridge.

3. Shorts are best located with an impedance bridge. True or false?

4. A cable should always be repaired rather than replaced or abandoned. True or false?

5. A computer-based test system should be used for problem verification:

    a. When nothing else is available.

    b. As the first choice.

    c. When the consultant requests it.

    d. As a last resort.

6. "Robert's Rules" of Orderly Problem-Solving are:

    a. A variation of Roberts Rules of Order.

    b. A useful guide.

    c. Only to be used after the shotgun approach has failed.

    d. Something gimmicked-up by the author.

7. Frequency response tests:

    a. Should be performed if square-wave tests didn't work.

    b. Are useless when performing acoustical testing.

    c. Must be performed by your chief engineer.

    d. Are useless unless documented.

8. THD measurements are better than IM measurements. True or false?

9. Signal-to-noise measurements must be performed:
   - a. Before frequency response measurements.
   - b. Using a 200 mHz oscilloscope.
   - c. Using a computer-based test system.
   - d. With system power off to avoid AC interference.

10. When testing loudspeaker systems, you should use earmuffs:
    - a. When the weather is cold.
    - b. Only for high-frequency elements.
    - c. Only if the specifications require them.
    - d. Always.

11. With a computer-based test system and cables, the only other item you need is:
    - a. An oscilloscope.
    - b. AC power.
    - c. An audio oscillator.
    - d. A square-wave generator.

12. As-built documentation should be prepared:
    - a. When requested by the consultant.
    - b. When the customer is separately paying for it.
    - c. If you have time.
    - d. For each project.

Chapter 7
System Design

by Bob Bushnell

- **NICET Work Element 16003, Architectural Mapping**
- **NICET's Description:** *"Using the principles of three-dimensional geometry, convert an architectural plan into a wire frame model. Assign absorption characteristics to room surfaces."*

- **NICET Work Element 16011, Small Systems Layout**
- **NICET's Description:** *"Verify customer needs. Determine appropriate equipment and wire routing. Interface with others as required to assure proper system installation and operation. Prepare appropriate sketches and drawings. Submit to supervisor for review and approval."*

Architectural Mapping

What will be the reverberation times for a room at various frequencies? We can, of course, build the room and then measure the reverberation times. Not a practical or feasible choice. Doing the work on paper is a better choice. The best substitute is to use an architectural or acoustical mapping application on a computer. You can explore many "what-ifs" with freedom and speed.

Wire frame modeling was in use before computers. The technique has become very powerful with the advent of computers. Architectural mapping allows us to calculate acoustic qualities of a room according to formulas developed by Sabine, Fitzroy, and Norris-Eyring.

If you are good at visualizing spatial relationships, understanding architectural mapping will be almost intuitive. Five computer applications are available to you for this technique. They are: EASE, published by ADA in Germany and available in the United States; JBL CADP2, now out of print, but still used by many contractors; AcoustaCADD, now out of print, but also used by many contractors; ArraySHOW, published by EVI; and CATT, published in Sweden, and available in the United States.

Understand X-Y-Z coordinate system
and how it is used in creating wire frame models

An oscilloscope display is an easy way to see the use of X and Y axes (plural of axis). X-Y-Z coordinates are used in mathematics, architecture, construction, and electronics. As you may recall, the X dimension is horizontal, and the Y dimension is vertical. The same technique is used in architecture, with the Z dimension as the third dimension, which is height.

If you've drawn a plan view of a room, you've used X and Y dimensions. If you have drawn an elevation of the wall of a room, you've used X or Y and Z dimensions. In all cases, you provided details for the walls, floors, and ceilings, usually in a pictorial form.

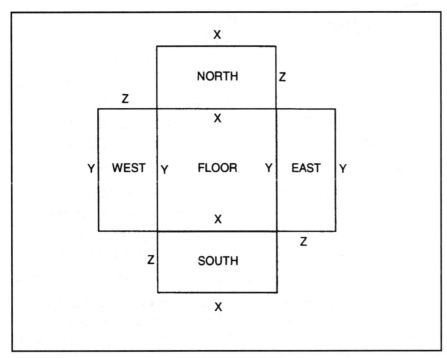

Figure 16003-1. A plan view of a room with the walls laid out flat

Shown above is a plan view of a room with the walls laid out flat. The dimensions of the room are not important, but the relationships between the four walls and the floor are important. Notice the X, Y, and Z dimensions placed by the various elements. You may think that we've taken liberties with the Z dimension, but remember this drawing has the walls laid out flat. Therefore, the Z dimension is the height of the room.

Now fold up each of the four walls, so that you have a room. Since the walls are perpendicular to the floor, consider that the ceiling has the same dimensions as the floor. You have created a six-sided or six-faced room. Regardless of how you view the room, the three axes retain their relationship. Those relationships hold for any room, and any size of room. If the room has nonparallel faces, then you'll treat each of those faces as a separate entity. Now we'll put dimensions on the room. The floor size is 15 feet by 15 feet, and the ceiling height is 10 feet.

Let's change the way we're looking at the room. Each line is the junction between a wall and the floor, or between two walls, or between a wall and the ceiling; we'll call those junctions "wires." Where three wires come together at a corner, we'll call a "vertex." For this room, if you count them, you'll find 12 wires and eight vertices (the plural of vertex).

If we look at the collection of wires and vertices as a three-dimensional unit, we have a wire frame. Again, we can turn that frame any way we want, and the three axes maintain their relationship. So far, that wire frame is strictly a wire frame with dimensions.

Let's apply the XYZ coordinates to the wire frame. Figure 16003-2 is a two-dimensional representation. Since the Z dimension is height, we'll put the zero XYZ coordinates at a lower corner. We'll further state that P1 is the zero XYZ coordinate location. Now the wire frame has some relation to reality, by virtue of dimensions and coordinates. Remember, we can view that wire frame (and the two-dimensional representation) from any direction we desire.

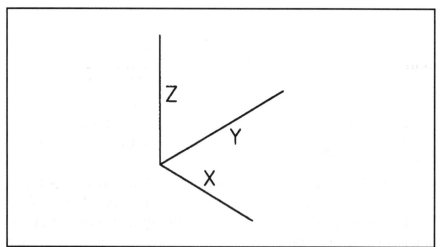

Figure 16003-2. The X-Y-Z relationship

We've labeled the vertices beginning from P1. Later in this chapter we'll show how you'll label the vertices. The labeling isn't random, but planned. Since we have the vertices or points labeled, we can refer to the floor, the four walls, and the ceiling by four points that enclose the face in question.

You probably see where we're going with this idea. Keep your understanding of the XYZ relationship as you study the rest of this chapter. Figure 16003-2 will help you remember this XYZ relationship.

Identification and entering room faces

Since we have a wire frame with dimensions and a reference point, let's start with the floor, which has P1, P2, P3, and P4 as its vertices. We don't have to start with the floor, but it's easier to assign and track the faces in a logical sequence. This is especially advantageous when building a large room with many faces.

Bear in mind that we're discussing architectural or acoustical mapping using one of the wire frame modeling applications. As you use the program, it is worthwhile to use paper and pencil to help you keep track of where you are. In writing this, we were using EASE, because it was available to us. Any of these applications will do quite well.

In working with one of the wire frame modeling applications, the application will place a point at each vertex as you click on it. The floor is a face. Referring to Figure 16003-2, and working in a clockwise direction since you're viewing the face from the inside, you click first on P1, then click on P2, then click on P3, and finally click on P4. As you move the mouse after the initial click, you'll see a yellow dotted line following the cursor, which indicates you're enclosing a face. When you complete the face, the dotted lines will disappear and be replaced by a label, F1 in this case. Since we're working on paper, you'll put the label of F1 on that face.

Let's create a face for one of the walls. Here's where your spatial visualization comes in use. Viewing from the inside of the room, you'll click on P1, then P5, then P6, and finally P2. Which wall did you enclose? If you determined that F2 is the face, you're correct.

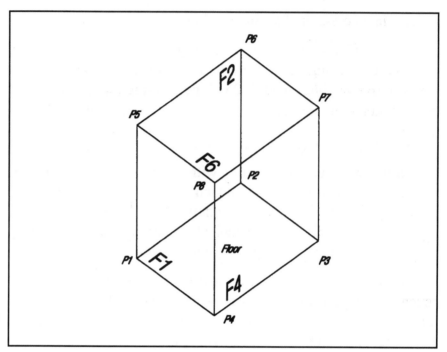

*Figure 16003-3. A
spatial visualization*

Then clicking on P2, P6, P7, and P3, you'll enclose F3. Then clicking on P7, P8, P4, and P3, you enclose F4. Then clicking on P5, P1, P4, and P8, you enclose F5. For the ceiling, click on P8, P7, P6, and P5. Due to the limitation with the CAD application used to draw the figure, we can't properly place the labels for F3 and F5. We realize this is confusing, but if you spend some time doing sketches on paper, it will help. If you have access to one of the applications, it will serve as the best guide. As you clicked on each vertex, you were working in a clockwise direction, as though you were viewing the face from within the room.

If you wanted to enclose a face by viewing it from the outside, you'd click on each vertex in a counterclockwise direction. However, it's better to visualize the room from the inside, as that's where the acoustical action is.

Stop, review, and think about what you've learned. You're looking at a room, but instead of the usual walls, floor, and ceiling, you have vertices, which enclose faces. You've identified the faces. Sound reflects in a room from faces. Sound is absorbed by faces. (That includes human faces and bodies.)

What are the acoustical properties of each face? The acoustic simulator program has a database of various floor, wall, and ceiling types. You tell the program what the face materials are. We'll state that F1, the floor, is a wood face. We'll make it easy for this first problem, and state that the four walls, F2, F3, F4, and F5, and the ceiling, F6, are Sheetrock over studs.

Now the acoustic simulator program has data from which to work. It knows the size of the room and rapidly calculates the volume of the room. Then using one of the three formulas created by Sabine, Fitzroy, or Norris and Eyring, it will provide us with the reverberation time of the room. Not just at one frequency, but at seven octave frequencies beginning at 125 Hz.

Procedures to enclose a room in a wire frame model

Now that we've gone through the wire frame modeling system, let's apply our knowledge to a real room. We suggest you start with a simple room—perhaps a meeting room at work, the office you're in, or the architectural plans of a recent project.

Referring to Figure 16003-2, the figure shows the directions and names for the XYZ coordinates. If possible, make a copy of the plan and elevations that you will use, as you will be marking up the plans. Determine where the 0,0,0 coordinates will be. We suggest the lower left corner of the room on the drawing, just because that's the way we think in the Western world. Also, most plans are drawn with north being toward the top of the plan. If that lower left corner of the room has intricate shapes, then select another corner.

Mark the XYZ symbol on the drawing near your starting coordinates, pointing the directional coordinates as you need. If you started at the lower left corner, your XYZ symbol might be oriented as Figure 16003-2. The Z direction is vertical, the X direction probably is left to right, and the Y direction probably is front to back.

If the room has a number of vertices that can't be directly read from the dimensions, it is advisable to mark the XY coordinates on the drawing, naturally placing the marking near the vertex. Go through the plan view, marking all the necessary vertices, keeping in mind the directions of the XYZ symbol. Do the same for the room elevations.

Now that you have a number of vertices describing the room in question, start up the acoustic simulation application, setting the appropriate parameters, then entering the vertices to build the wire frame. As each of the acoustic simulation applications has different methods for data entry, we won't attempt to go through the procedures for each application.

After finishing the data entry and modeling the room, the application may advise you that you have open faces, and won't continue until you've resolved them. Open faces can be one or both of two conditions, the simplest being that you entered the data for a particular face in a counterclockwise direction, therefore you and the application are viewing the face from outside the room. Since the application will consider any face as a reflector or absorber of sound waves, it sees that face as nonexistent and can't perform any calculations. In that case, you simply mark the face and invert it.

The other possible condition is where three or more of your vertices don't describe a face. Figure 16003-4 shows the condition, somewhat exaggerated for clarity. Just as with the inverted face, the acoustic simulation application doesn't see the incomplete face, and can't perform any calculations. In that case, it's probably better to check your numbers, and correct the misplaced vertex. Sometimes it's easier to delete the face, then reenter the vertices.

Any acoustic simulation application works with interior volumes only. If you attempt to model an open-air pavilion, the application considers the open volume above the seats as a nonexistent face, and will return an error message. You might set the faces above the seats, then mark them as high-absorption material types.

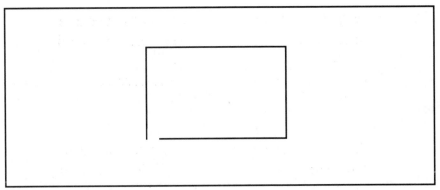

Figure 16003-4.
Where three or more
vertices don't
describe a face

Modeling curved surfaces and unusual shapes

By their very nature computers and video monitors do not calculate or show curved surfaces very adequately. We humans can draw a circle or a curved line, which is a succession of points. The number of points necessary to describe a circle is virtually infinite.

The problem is the same for the computer. We tell the computer to draw the line by a succession of points; the more points indicated, the more memory and storage space is used.

If you want to describe a circle using 100 vertices, it can be very time-consuming and subject to error. Fortunately, a misplaced vertex will be very obvious as soon as you complete the circle, and the application shows the face. How many vertices should you use?

We suspect that most modeling applications do *not* take into account the width of each face in a circle and then relate that dimension to the wavelength of the frequency of interest. Rather, the application regards each face as a reflector/absorber, using its database for the absorption coefficient for the material in question. The greater the number of faces, the closer to reality will be the results from the computer.

It seems that 10 to 20 faces is a reasonable number for a curved surface with a diameter between 10 and 50 feet.

Assign absorption values to room surfaces or objects

Now we get to the reason for building a wire frame model. We'll assume that the example room you've built is correct and that all faces of interest are facing inward. You select a given face, follow the procedure for the particular acoustic simulation application, and assign the material type to that face from the database.

You may find with at least one of the architectural mapping applications you're requested to assign the material type immediately after you've marked the face. You may assign material types or change them after you've finished constructing the faces. Once you've assigned material types to all faces, loudspeaker selection and placement are next. All of these applications have a good database of loudspeaker types to choose from. Since these are virtual systems, you may place the cluster in any location you desire then view the coverage and RT_{60} results.

The application will calculate the absorption value for each face, calculate the room area and volume, then perform the RT_{60} calculations for the room. You may select either Sabine, Fitzroy, or Norris-Eyring equations. The application will perform the calculations in a few seconds. Think about the time it would take you to perform the same calculations using paper, pencil, and a calculator!

The various applications will allow you to edit the database for material types, but this must be done with care. Your data must include the absorption coefficients for seven octave bands beginning at 125 Hz. You can also add other loudspeaker types, being sure the format is in the same form as the application you're using.

As you see, by using architectural mapping via acoustical simulation applications, you have a powerful tool at work. The idea isn't new, but the ability to make numerous choices and to receive virtually immediate answers is new. However, like all simulation applications, they are no substitute for the real world and experience.

Small Systems Layout

This section is concerned with small systems, requiring one design individual rather than a team effort. We will use a church system as an example, as it is a system design frequently encountered by many sound contractors. However, these design issues are just as relevant for sound design in other venues, such as hotels, schools, or commercial buildings.

We'll cover principles and pitfalls you should recognize and remember. Apply these principles and pitfalls whether the project has a budget of $50,000 or $5 million, and whether the project is a new or existing building.

Verify and analyze customer needs

Making an objective determination of what the customer needs may range from a simple task to a multitude of tasks. The customer may want a system that is a simple idea, yet very expensive to implement. Explaining to the customer in his or her terms why the idea is very expensive is one of your goals.

On occasion, it may appear that the customer's perceived needs are not the same as actual needs. It is necessary to understand whether the customer's perception stems from ignorance, or whether he or she is viewing the situation from a different perspective. If the perception stems from ignorance, your task is to reeducate the customer, but without making him or her feel foolish. If the customer is viewing the situation from a different perspective, you might want to look at the situation from that same perspective.

The customer sees you as the company. Your sales department made a good impression, otherwise it's unlikely that your company would have been awarded the contract. Now it's up to you to follow through. You won't have this on the NICET exam, but remember this as you are contacting your customers.

It may be desirable to attend one or two services to understand the nature of the customer's requirements. If you attend services before you meet with the representative you'll be in a better position to relate to the customer. You may see that the minister or pastor tends to move about as he is preaching. It may be his normal method of preaching, something you'll take into account. He may not know the importance of microphone technique, or it might be a good idea to recommend a lavalier or wireless microphone.

You'll hear the choir and organ firsthand, knowing that church pipe organs don't need sound reinforcement. If the church doesn't have a sound reinforcement system, perhaps the organist has varied her or his style of playing to accommodate for the lack of choir sound reinforcement. With the addition of sound reinforcement, the organist may wish to rethink her or his way of playing.

Other questions that may arise:

- Will the congregation require microphones for any reason?
- Does the church perform Christmas and festival activities in the sanctuary?
- Does the church use the foyer to accommodate congregation overflow?
- Does the church desire assisted listening?
- Do the participants (minister, choir, organist) have any difficulty hearing one another?

For this example, we shall assume:

- Your company has the contract.
- Your sales department has given you design latitude.
- The project is a good-sized church installation with lecture-hall-style seating for 700.
- The church is an existing building.
- The customer is agreeable to reasonable changes in the contract.
- Room acoustic measurements may be required; the customer is aware of the potential cost.

We shall not assume:

- The project design is correct.
- The sales department performed a complete site inspection.

Recognize factors or essential elements of a site visit

A complete site inspection is crucial, even if the sales department has already done one. As the design engineer, the responsibility is yours to assure that your company installs the system on time and correctly, and that it performs to the customer's expectations.

Coordinate your site visit with the customer. If possible, meet with one individual selected by the church as its representative. A committee in attendance can change a straightforward meeting into a rehash of many points, including some not pertinent to the sound reinforcement system. Fortunately, this doesn't happen too often, but it is a possibility to keep in mind. Depending on the church, the representative may be able to resolve questions during the site visit. If there are unanswered questions, set a clear agenda to resolve them.

You should present yourself to the customer as an intelligent, knowledgeable individual who understands the needs of the church balanced against a practical system.

You should complete the site visit or inspection with these topics clearly understood and agreed to by the customer and you:

- Room size and volume
- Main equipment location
- Mixing console location
- Cluster location
- Distributed loudspeaker locations
- Microphone locations
- Microphones to be furnished by your company
- Ancillary cables to be furnished by your company
- Cable raceways and locations
- Clean power availability
- Cabinet colors or finishes
- Aesthetic considerations
- Existing equipment to be accommodated or used
- Unique circumstances requested by the customer

- Sound reinforcement in other areas
- Telephone receptacle and cable for broadcast connections
- EMI (Electromagnetic interference) conditions from nearby broadcast facilities or other sources
- Completion date
- Working schedule and possible conflicts with customer's activities

These topics may not apply in every project, but they form a checklist for your reference.

Equipment location may need some study. The customer may have a desired location in mind, but the problem of running cable wireways and conduits from that location may be difficult and expensive. The location may be good, but verify that adequate AC power is available at that location. If the representative knows the physical layout, use his/her input, as it will save you time. Ask if an architectural drawing set is available for inspection and review.

Most doorways are 2 feet, 6 inches wide at a minimum. Be sure that all equipment and cluster components may be brought in without damage to the building. Verify that there is room to set up a scaffold, or it may be more practical to use a scissors lift.

Be on time for your site inspection. Don't antagonize the representative by being even 10 minutes late. It is better to show up 10 minutes ahead of time. Being late may negate all of your excellent efforts during the meeting. When the representative asks you a question, answer that question. Don't anticipate what you think he or she wants to find out about, as your response may not directly answer the question. If the question appears stupid or naive, answer it professionally.

For the initial job-site visit, arrive with everything you need, or may need. Here is a suggested list:

- Project folder
- Letter-sized pad and holder, but not a fancy tooled leather item that may be easily damaged

- Pens, pencils, and erasers
- Tape measure or measures; 100-foot minimum
- A protractor or 45-degree triangle for measuring ceiling heights
- A good (not Radio Shack) sound-level meter
- A pink noise generator
- An RTA
- Test leads for the above, with various adapters
- A pair of binoculars
- Your business cards
- Your telephone credit card
- A cell phone (if your company provides them)
- Your toolbox

Let's review some of the more unusual items. If the church doesn't have a good set of architectural prints available, you can measure the ceiling height to a good approximation with a 45-degree triangle.

The procedure is this:
1. Stand away from a wall leading to the ceiling height in question.
2. Hold the triangle so that one of the 90-degree included angle sides is parallel to the floor, and the other side is parallel to the wall.
3. Sight up the 45-degree angle until you're looking at the wall or the ceiling.
4. Then move toward or away from the wall until you're looking at the wall/ceiling joint.
5. Measure the distance from the wall to your standing location, and add your eye height to that number.

If you remember your trigonometry lessons, or Work Element 13003 that you studied in Level II, you'll probably have the technique for solving this problem. If not, this is the equation to use:

$$\tan \varnothing = \text{opposite side} / \text{adjacent side}$$

For a 45-degree angle, the tangent is 1.00. If we restate the equation as:

$$\text{opposite side} = \tan \varnothing \times \text{adjacent side}$$

Then we substitute and solve. You'll find that the distance from the wall to where you were standing plus your eye height is equal to the wall height.

Why the test equipment? It may be necessary to measure the frequency response of the existing system to have an objective understanding of the system.

Why a pair of binoculars? You may want to see some detail overhead that would normally require a ladder or scaffold.

Why a telephone credit card? If you're making a toll call, it's a sign of professionalism that you don't want to inconvenience or annoy the customer. The same reasoning applies to the cell phone.

A site inspection may not require a toolbox, but you may need access to a cabinet or an area that requires tools. Asking for tools won't impress the customer.

Select appropriate equipment

Even though the sales department has selected the equipment as part of the contract, the responsibility is yours to assure that your company installs the appropriate equipment. You've seen the site, and heard the church services; you're in a better position to be sure the appropriate equipment is selected.

We'll make a further assumption that the project calls for a central cluster. In this case, it provides the best coverage for the sanctuary, and an acoustically transparent housing will be constructed on site. You might request the services of a structural engineer to verify the cluster support elements.

In all sound reinforcement systems, system design begins with the loudspeaker elements. In this case, we'll assume that 300 Hz horns are to be used, with no low-frequency loudspeakers. The church organ needs no reinforcement, the choir loft is in an excellent acoustic location, and the church doesn't expect to use the sanctuary for any occasions requiring a full-range system. With ease and courage, you use one of the better acoustic modeling programs and determine the cluster elements and coverage. From this, you know the desired power amplifier wattage. Your supervisor has suggested a power amplifier series to use, so you select the appropriate amplifier.

Our site inspection has determined that the church does not need nor want a mixing location in the sanctuary. In a room behind the pulpit, we will install a central rack location containing all the electronic equipment.

Coordinate with other trades and Owner

We've used the terms "customer" and "representative" throughout this chapter. The usual term for customer that you'll encounter when working with architects, construction companies, and subcontractors is "Owner." Always capitalized, the term refers to the owner and the individuals making decisions for the company paying for the work. Other than the AHJ (Authority Having Jurisdiction) relating to building codes, the Owner has the final decision. In this example project, no other trades are involved.

In many projects, you may be a subcontractor to the GC (General Contractor), or you may be a contractor working directly for the Owner. In either case, coordination is essential. Your work in an area should not fall behind other subcontractors, nor should you install equipment before the room is ready.

When you and your crew are due at the job site, be sure to let the representative know you're coming. If this is a church project, and the representative isn't apt to be there, let the church office know. If you're scheduled to arrive at 10 a.m., be on time. When you leave, let the church office know you're leaving. Coordination extends directly to the customer.

As you work on the project, keep your customer informed. Not on a daily basis, but when something significant happens. The customer may desire changes to the project. Immediately respond to these requests rather than when convenient for you. The change requests may simplify the project, making the task easier for you.

Create sketches and documentation

After you've completed the installation and the Owner has accepted the system, you complete the paperwork. Since your company employs experienced CAD draftsmen, you mark up your working drawings and equipment lists for their completion. The Owner's equipment manual should include:

- Single line drawings of the system
- Equipment lists with serial numbers
- Rack elevation drawings
- Detailed cluster drawings
- Detailed schematic and physical drawings of any custom assembly or item
- Cable running sheets
- Cable wireway layouts (if appropriate)
- System specifications (if appropriate)
- Your company telephone numbers and contacts
- Room acoustical measurements (if appropriate)
- Room response curves (if appropriate)
- System description (if appropriate)

Generally, two copies of the operating manual are provided to the Owner. One copy is for his or her use, while the other copy is kept on site for use by your technicians on a service call. In some cases, the contract may call for more copies of the operating manual. You may also find that the contract is not considered complete until the manuals have been delivered to the GC or another party.

If you made acoustical measurements of the room they should be included, as well as the final room response curves.

Why submit sketches and documentation to your supervisor? The project was yours, you kept your supervisor informed as to job progress, so you complete the job by submitting the information for his review and comment.

Questions:

1. Architectural mapping techniques were unknown before computers. True or false?

2. Paper-based architectural drawings do not utilize X-Y coordinates. True or false?

3. XYZ coordinates should begin at which corner of the paper or screen?

    a. Upper left corner.

    b. Lower right corner.

    c. Centered left to right.

    d. Any location you desire.

4. Room faces are:

    a. Any face of the room.

    b. The walls only.

    c. The ceiling only.

    d. As defined by the consultant.

5. The normal view of a room using architectural mapping is from the outside. True or false?

6. Architectural mapping isn't valid for:

    a. Free-field conditions.

    b. Recording studios.

    c. Architects.

    d. Rooms with a dirt floor.

7. Architectural mapping provides poor results when:

    a. The technician doesn't understand the system.

    b. The room is smaller than 10 feet by 10 feet.

    c. The reverberation time is unknown.

    d. The room hasn't been designed by an architect.

8. In system layout, the customer should be contacted:
   a. Only if necessary.
   b. Just before installation.
   c. When first starting the project.
   d. Only with approval of the architect.

9. Since you're a technician, and not the owner of the company you work for, the impression you make on the customer is:
   a. Very important.
   b. Not at all important.
   c. Important if you think the customer deserves it.
   d. Not really part of your job.

10. Knowing firsthand the purpose for the system is:
    a. Incidental to the project.
    b. A vital part of the project.
    c. Necessary if the boss says so.
    d. Necessary if the system is higher quality than a paging system.

11. A site visit should:
    a. Be a surprise to the customer.
    b. An afterthought.
    c. Disregard any input from the customer, as he or she is not designing the system.
    d. Carefully planned in advance.

12. After a site inspection, the customer:
    a. Doesn't need to know the technical details.
    b. Isn't as knowledgeable as you are.
    c. Should be made aware of various details of the project.
    d. Shouldn't be contacted unless absolutely necessary.

Chapter 8

System Equalization, Alignment, & Adjustment

by Bob Bushnell

- **NICET Work Element 16016, Basic Equalization**
- **NICET's Description:** "*Define broadband and narrowband terminology and recognize typical applications of each. Identity the functions served by a spectrum analyzer, and differentiate between graphic and parametric equalizers. Follow proper procedures for the use of multiple equalizers. Recognize the significance of, and perform equalization adjustments at crossover points.*"

- **NICET Work Element 16017, System Signal Alignment**
- **NICET's Description:** "*Conduct and/or supervise the system signal alignment process including measurement and adjustment of signal delays and phase alignment of loudspeakers. Consult with supervisor as needed. Document all control settings.*"

- **NICET Work Element 16013, Signal Processing Adjustment**
- **NICET's Description:** "*Calibrate and adjust signal processing equipment such as compressor/limiters, signal delays, multieffects processors, etc.*"

Basic Equalization

The tone controls on your car stereo or your music system are equalizers. If you have a graphic equalizer in your stereo system, that's a simpler form of a graphic equalizer compared to the 1/3-octave units you've encountered in sound reinforcement. Graphic equalizers are installed in sound reinforcement systems for two purposes:

1. To increase gain before feedback.
2. To provide a desired frequency response curve to the system.

Octave and 1/3-octave band (ISO band center frequencies)

An 880 Hz tone is one octave above a 440 Hz tone. By way of reference, 440 Hz is middle A on the piano. A 5 kHz tone is one octave below a 10 kHz tone. Octaves are primarily used in music. 1/3-octave increments are simply the division of an octave into three equal parts.

For acoustical measurements, the audio frequency range, 16 Hz to 16 kHz, has been divided into octave and 1/3-octave bands. This was done through international agreement by ISO (International Organization for Standardization). The band center frequencies are selected so that even though 1/3-octave increments are available, there is even overlap between band center frequencies.

Depending on the instrument, various bandwidths are available. These bandwidths are accepted by several international organizations; ANSI (American National Standards Institute), DIN (Deutsche Industrie Normal), and IEC (International Electronics Committee). These bandwidths are divided into classes. The divisions relate to the filter slope. The table at the top of the following page displays the band center frequencies for most 1/3-octave analyzers.

The role of the spectrum analyzer in equalization

A more specific description of the device is a "real-time audio spectrum analyzer." Basically, the device displays frequency

Band Center Frequencies for Most 1/3-Octave Analyzers

25	250	2500
31.5	315	3150
40	400	4000
50	500	5000
63	630	6300
80	800	8000
100	1000	10,000
125	1250	12,500
160	1600	16,000
200	2000	

versus amplitude. An audio spectrum analyzer is essential for effective room tuning or system equalization. Spectrum analyzers are available that will measure well into the gHz range, but these are RF, not audio devices.

The functions described apply to some or all of the various instruments available on the market. The device displays either octave or 1/3-octave band frequencies on the "x" axis, versus amplitude on the "y" axis. LEDs (light emitting diodes) or an LCD (liquid crystal display) panel are the most common display techniques. Older instruments utilized a CRT (cathode ray tube) for display. The amplitude scale may be anywhere from 1/4 dB to 5 dB per indicator or division.

Generally one to three time domain weightings are applied to the display, providing continual monitoring, peak readings, or integration for pink noise measurements. We are most concerned with continual monitoring of the acoustic signal.

Frequency weightings are also applied to the display corresponding to ANSI "A" or "C" curves. Flat response may also be applied. The "C" weighting is used at SPL (sound pressure level) above 85 dB. Some instruments also apply "B" weighting, which is used between 55 and 85 dB SPL. The "A" weighting approximates the human ear at SPL figures below 55 dB. "B" weighting is not often available, as there is not a drastic difference between "B" and "C" curves.

An audio spectrum analyzer is used as a calibrated measurement device in conjunction with a calibrated microphone, which is usually provided with the analyzer.

Characteristics of graphic and parametric equalizers

A graphic equalizer takes its name from its physical appearance. Just as a graph is used to show a frequency response plot, a graphic equalizer shows a plot of the desired frequency response of an audio system, or the changes from a flat response. The plot is shown by the placement of the vertical slider-type level controls in relation to their position on the panel, and the panel markings.

There may be up to 30 level controls on the equalizer panel, each control adjusting the level of a 1/3-octave frequency band. These bands correspond to the frequency bands earlier discussed in the section *Octave and 1/3-octave band (ISO band center frequencies)*. The equalizer panel is marked and calibrated in dB steps. Some equalizers are manufactured with detented sliders, while others have sliders without detents.

The slope or "Q" of the equalization curve is a fixed bell curve. The amount of boost or attenuation is changed by the slider control. Some equalizers are designed to boost/attenuate, while some are designed to attenuate only. Extensive research, both empirical and theoretical, has been accomplished on filters and equalizers relating to room equalization. Many sources indicate that "attenuation only" is preferred for room equalization, due to the probability of exciting room nodes with resultant feedback or near-feedback conditions.

For special situations, notch filters are used. These are filters with a bandwidth considerably narrower than a 1/3-octave equalizer. However, these must be used with great care, as the resultant sound to the ear may be less than satisfactory, in spite of the increase of gain before feedback.

Parametric equalizers are another breed entirely. The name "parametric" was adopted because an additional control varies the parameter of the equalization curve. In this case the slope of the equalization is varied by adjusting the "Q" of the circuit. Therefore, the slope is no longer a fixed bell curve. There are variations on this technique. One variation narrows the bell curve, increasing the "Q," as the amount of boost or attenuation is increased. However, the "Q" cannot be independently adjusted.

There aren't many parametric equalizers yet designed for room tuning. There are a number of parametric equalizers for studio use. However, they have fewer frequency selections and are not designed for room equalization.

Test and measurement setup for room equalization using pink noise source

A noise generator provides noise spikes of random amplitude and frequency distribution. The majority of noise generators are based on digital circuitry, which generates pseudo-random noise. Pseudo-random noise will have various repetition rates, depending on the design. True random noise will never exhibit repetition rates, but very few true random noise generators are manufactured.

White noise contains the same amount of energy or power per unit bandwidth. When viewed on an audio spectrum analyzer, the noise content will increase at a rate of 3 dB per octave as the frequency increases. Tuning interstation on an FM tuner with muting off will provide approximate white noise. It is a poor idea to use white noise when doing room tuning, because the increasingly higher sound level as the frequency increases may overload the high-frequency loudspeakers before an adequate level is obtained in the room.

Pink noise contains the same amount of energy or power per unit octave. Viewing pink noise on a 1/3-octave analyzer will show basically a flat frequency response. Pink noise should be used for room tuning or system equalization.

Equalizing a sound reinforcement system is performed after the system is installed and operational. The electronics of the system have been tested and approved. All loudspeaker elements are in place and sweep tones have been fed through the cluster to verify that no rattles or buzzes are present. The room itself is architecturally and aesthetically finished. All carpets and wall treatments are finished; the room is ready for occupancy.

If these conditions haven't been met, the equalization process must be delayed until they are completed. The equalization process, by its very nature, takes into account the system electronics, the cluster, the room, all furnishings, and all floor, wall, and ceiling treatments. For example, if equalization is performed before the carpet and padding are installed, then the overall response of the sound reinforcement system will change after the carpet is installed. It will be found necessary to retune the room, and possibly re-aim the cluster elements.

Equipment required? A pink noise generator, a real-time audio spectrum analyzer, connecting cable between the measuring microphone and the audio spectrum analyzer, an oscilloscope, an "A" size (8½ x 11 paper) plotter (if available), and ear protectors for the number of people in the room. If a plotter is available, and depending on the audio spectrum analyzer used, the various measurements may be plotted for later reference. The audio spectrum analyzer is set near the 1/3-octave equalizers, and the measuring microphone is set up in the room at various locations.

Connect the pink noise generator to a high-level input at the mixer. Be sure that any equalization is switched out, and that the 1/3-octave equalizer has all band level controls set at the zero position. If the equalizer has a gain control, be sure that it is set at the marked position determined during the system test. Connect the oscilloscope across the power amplifier output.

Set the master gain for the mixer to the marked position determined during the system test. Set the output level of the pink noise generator at a suitable level, possibly referring to the manufacturer's data. Gradually increase the input fader until the VU meter or bar graph on the mixer indicates about -10 to -15 dB. On the oscilloscope, set the time base so that the peaks of the pink noise may be easily seen as an individual trace. Set the sensitivity so that the peaks aren't off-screen.

The peaks should be sharp, indicating that clipping isn't taking place anywhere through the chain. The sound level in the room should be within specifications, usually 85 to 90 dB SPL, "C" weighting. Now you know the reason for the ear protectors. Where should the measuring microphone be placed? If the room design and the sound system design are perfect, a listening position should be anywhere in the room. Therefore, the measuring microphone should be anywhere in the room.

The first step, then, is walking the room with the analyzer using the SLM (sound-level meter) portion of the instrument. Check the manufacturer's instruction manual for the best direction to aim the microphone. While walking the room, and watching the 1/3-octave display, track the sound level.

We will assume that the sound level throughout the room is within acceptable limits for all listening positions. That's a nice assumption, and sometimes it's even realistic. Since the coverage is even, place the measuring microphone in the center (L to R) of the room, and approximately 1/3 of the distance from the cluster to the rear wall. Set the pink noise to the specified SPL, probably about 85 dB.

Now, through a process of adjusting the 1/3-octave equalizer, then talking the room, you should arrive at a respectable-sounding system. By talking the room, you are speaking either specific sentences or reading through the normal microphone at that microphone's normal location. This might be done using two or more persons, all preferably speaking the same material. If there is more than one microphone location, the same procedure should be performed at all locations.

After the first or second use of the room, you might request comments from the Owner and other individuals regarding the sound reinforcement system quality.

Unique EQ considerations at crossover points

Due to the nature of crossover filters, whether active or passive, definite phase shifts occur just below, at, and above the crossover frequency. By agreement, the level at the crossover frequency is designed and measured at –3 dB from within the passband of the filter. If the low-pass and high-pass filter curves are superimposed over one another, a notch of approximately 3 dB will be seen at the crossover frequency.

For the sake of argument, we shall assume we are working with a three-way system: low-frequency, midrange, and high-frequency elements. We will further assume that a pink noise generator, and a real-time audio spectrum analyzer are being used. Depending on the loudspeaker elements, various anomalies may be measured and heard around the crossover frequencies.

The sound level may rise or fall, or acoustic anomalies may be heard when listening to pink noise, sweep tones from an oscillator, or sentences talked through the system. It may be necessary to reverse polarity to one or more elements and adjust the 1/3-octave equalizer as necessary to correct the condition. The phase shift discussed earlier contributes to these anomalies.

No two systems will be the same. One system may require extensive measuring and listening, another system may be correct at the start. The condition may not be as severe when working with active crossovers working into individual power amplifiers as compared to passive crossovers. One possible answer may be that with active crossovers, nothing is between the power amplifier and the loudspeaker except cable. With passive crossovers, the reactive nature of loudspeakers may be reacting with the elements of the passive crossover.

We must stress the need for listening to the system. If you don't feel your ear/brain combination is sufficiently trained to analyze what you're hearing, bring someone else into the picture. Youth alone, with its attendant hearing sensitivity, isn't adequate. An individual trained, usually by vocation, to accurately perceive what is being heard is required.

Talking the system is also mandatory. If you're not familiar with the unamplified voice of the talker, have that person talk to you face to face until you are familiar with the sound and the various nuances of his or her voice. All of the intonations are important; the particular sound of an "s," whether at the beginning, middle, or end of a word, or a "t" sound as in "truck," for example.

System Signal Alignment

Why are we concerned with signal delays, delay devices, and phase alignment of loudspeakers? It all comes back to the use of sound systems by people, our listening mechanisms, and the fact that sound travels rather slowly. When you are at a large venue watching and hearing a rock concert, in spite of the fact that lights may be all over the auditorium, there is no need for light delay devices, nor light phase alignment devices, as our eyes and brains perceive light as arriving at the same instant.

On the other hand, our ears and brains can recognize the difference in arrival times of sound waves when the difference is greater than approximately 30 ms. This is called the Hääs effect, which is discussed later in this chapter.

Calculate conversion of distance to delay

Unlike the velocity of light, which is rather fast, the velocity of sound is a real and finite factor in sound reinforcement. The approximate velocity of sound at sea level at a temperature of 72° F, and 20% RH (Relative Humidity) is 1130 feet per second, or 745 mph. If you are in a large meeting room speaking into a microphone and the loudspeaker cluster is about 1000 feet from you at the other end of the room, you will hear your amplified voice delayed by almost two seconds. Consider the aural effect on someone standing 6 feet to your side, listening to your natural and amplified voice at the same time.

The velocity of sound in air is primarily affected by temperature and very slightly affected by altitude. The equation for calculating the temperature effect is:

$$c = 49\sqrt{459.4 + °F}$$

Although this equation isn't exact, it will be adequate for our purposes. Doing a brief calculation, assuming that the temperature is 72° F, you should have calculated 1129.55, or rounding off, the answer is 1130 feet per second. If we assume the temperature to be 100° F, the answer is 1159 feet per second, about 3% faster. If the temperature is about -50° F, you should have calculated about 1004 feet per second, slower by about 11%.

Sound travels slightly faster as the humidity increases, probably because the increased number of water molecules in the air provide for faster transmission of the sound wave. The humidity factor can be disregarded for general calculations.

If you assume the temperature to be 72° F, which is also a good temperature for human comfort, and use a velocity of 1130 feet per second, this is a good basis for many calculations.

The equation to determine the delay according to the distance will be:

$$D = d \div 1130$$

where **D** is the delay to be calculated, and **d** is the distance in feet. Later in this element, we'll discuss the Häas effect, which relates to time and distances.

Methods to measure signal delay

Several methods exist for measuring signal delay, ranging from simple to complex techniques. The simplest technique is to physically measure the distance in question, then calculate the signal delay. Obviously, for large halls and vertical distances, this technique isn't too practical.

The next technique involves two microphones, a mixer, and a calibrated oscilloscope. Place one microphone at the normal talking location, the other microphone at the far end of the hall. Feed both microphones into two of the mixer's inputs. Connect the mixer's output to the "Y" or vertical input of the oscilloscope. Set the oscilloscope's time base at 0.5 or 1 second per division, depending on the hall.

Generate an impulse sound approximately 1 foot from the microphone at the talking location. The impulse sound should be less than about 50 milliseconds in duration, and loud enough to be picked up by the second microphone. Adjust the oscilloscope's time base trigger so that the sweep is activated by the first signal from the mixer. Depending on the oscilloscope, you may have to estimate the first pulse's location on the oscilloscope graticule. A graticule, by the way, is the engraved or printed screen in front of the CRT. This graticule allows you to calculate voltages, and estimate frequency dependent conditions and short time periods.

Working against the time base and the calculated distance on the screen between the two impulse waveforms, you can then calculate the delay between the two microphones.

The most complex technique involves the use of a TEF (Time/Energy/Frequency) analyzer, versions of which are manufactured by at least two companies. Incidentally, the term TEF is a registered trademark of Gold Line. We won't go into the operational details, except to note that a TEF analyzer will perform a number of acoustical measurements.

Specifications of delay devices

Delay devices provide a wide range of delays, ranging from less than a millisecond to 5 seconds, depending on the manufacturer. The delay is usually indicated in milliseconds, although some manufacturers provide indications in other modes more directed to motion picture postproduction or recording studio applications. In the sound reinforcement industry, delay devices are used to provide aural synchronization of direct versus amplified sound, or synchronization of sound from two loudspeakers spaced some distance apart.

Although various measuring devices are used, often the final setting of delay devices relies on the educated human ear during walks of the hall. One or more persons will talk over the system using a variety of material, ranging from complete sentences to nonsense words.

Nonsense words are useful to determine if the listener truly heard the word or was interpolating based on complete sentences. If I'm telling you about some event that I read in the news, and all the words and general topic are known to you, and I mispronounce or garble a word, you'll probably recognize the word because you're interpolating the sentence to recognize that garbled word. This is the reason for nonsense words. If I use the word "gribblefy," you may not know the word, but with a well-designed sound system, you'll hear the word and be able to spell it.

Hääs Effect

The Hääs Effect was discovered by Helmut Hääs and published by him as his doctoral dissertation presented to the University of Gottingen, Germany, in the late 1940s. It is also called the precedence effect. The effect is possible because we have two hearing mechanisms: our left and right ears.

Let's try a brief experiment. Stop up one ear, close your eyes, then walking around, localize a particular point sound source. If you're walking around with your eyes closed, don't run into things.

Because of your head geometry, you're able to localize a sound source because the sound may or may not arrive at your ears at the same time. With one ear stopped up, you'll find it difficult to localize a point source. If the sound arrives at your ears at the same time, the sound source will either be directly in front of you, or directly behind you. Oddly enough, in most cases, you'll be able to tell the difference. We don't know why.

You may say, "I already knew that," but the important part of Häas's work is this: the Häas Effect states that we localize a sound source based on the arrival of the first sound if the later sound arrives within 25 to 35 milliseconds. If the later sound is later than 25 to 30 milliseconds, then we hear two distinct sounds. This effect is true even when the second sound is louder than the first, by as much as 10 dB.

Because of our outer ears, it is possible to provide some localization with one ear. The different parts of the outer ear reflect sound at slightly different times, providing the listener with some degree of sound localization.

Alignment of adjacent loudspeaker devices using high-resolution signal delays

Providing alignment of adjacent loudspeaker devices using high-resolution signal delays must be done with extreme care and the use of TEF analyzers or similar devices. Because the sound sources originate in close proximity to one another, the probability of comb filter effects is high.

A comb filter effect may be heard and understood by an individual trained to hear these effects. However, the use of a TEF analyzer or similar device is necessary to measure the depth of attenuation and spacing of each comb. Figure 8-1 shows the comb filter effect.

This is an idealized graph of the comb filter effect. The effect is caused by cancellation of specific frequencies generated by two or more loudspeakers in close proximity.

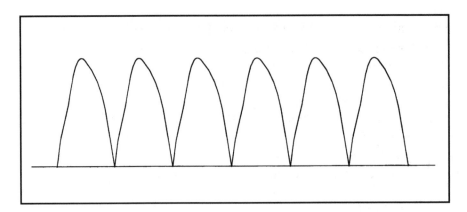

Figure 8-1. Comb filter effect

If it is necessary to have adjacent loudspeaker devices, an individual delay must be used for each loudspeaker or group of loudspeakers not in time alignment. Measurements must be made to determine comb effects, and to determine the specific delay required for each element. Individual variations in the millisecond range can be expected. Careful listening by qualified listeners should be part of the process.

Signal Processing Adjustment

Most signal processing devices are unity gain—+4 dBu input and +4 dBu output. In a well-designed system, they should not be called on to provide gain functions, as that is the mixer's purpose. The purpose for any signal processing device included in the system should be reviewed, and the setup for that device should be performed according to the manufacturer's instructions. Some system complaints can be traced to the inappropriate use of signal processing devices.

Setup procedure for compressor/limiters

We are restricting this discussion to fixed sound reinforcement systems, not large-scale road-show systems. Use of an AGC (Automatic Gain Control) device in sound reinforcement must be done with extreme care. An example: The device is limiting 5 to 8 dB during speech. After a 3-second speech lull, the AGC device returns to its normal setting. That normal setting increases the system gain by about 6 dB.

Under these conditions, it is likely for the system to go into feedback, which will annoy all listeners, and confuse the talker and the sound system operator. The system might exhibit traces of feedback, causing the operator to reduce the system level, thus undoing the advantage of using a limiter.

A compressor or limiter serves two functions: system protection and aural effects creation. Use of the latter function, aural effects creation, is primarily in recording and postproduction work.

There is no clear-cut difference between a compressor and a limiter. Usually the difference lies in the compression ratio of the device—the input level vs. the output level. If the ratio is 10:1 or lower, it is generally called a compressor; if the ratio is 10:1 or higher, it is generally called a limiter.

The AGC device should have a high compression ratio of 12:1 or higher. The limiting should be no more than 3 dB with the loudest speech expected through the system. Alternatively, pink noise might be used to set 3 dB of limiting, with a 95 dB SPL (Sound Pressure Level).

Setup procedure for speaker alignment signal delay unit

In a large hall, the time delay usually is quite significant between the main cluster and the rear of the hall. Under-balcony loudspeakers provide coverage to areas in acoustical shadows created by the balcony overhang. In these cases, the later arrival of the sound from the main cluster conflicts with the near-instant arrival of the signal from the under-balcony loudspeakers.

An electronic signal delay is installed for these situations. Setup of the electronic delay may be accomplished aurally or with the use of a TEF analyzer. In either event, qualified listeners should approve the final adjustments. The delay time may be measured or calculated in advance. Often it is easier simply to increase the signal delay to the under-balcony loudspeakers until the time arrival of the two signals coincides. The area should be walked to verify the correctness of the setting.

Setup for electronic crossovers

Electronic crossovers usually have provisions to adjust the crossover frequency. The manufacturer's specifications for each loudspeaker should be consulted to determine the recommended crossover frequency and the high- or low-frequency limit of the device. Any special precautions stated by the manufacturer also should be noted.

We shall assume that the loudspeaker cluster has three elements; low frequency, midfrequency, and high frequency. We shall further assume that the electronic crossover is an active device, meaning that three power amplifiers have been connected; that is, one power amplifier to each loudspeaker.

As a start, one tech should talk the system as the other tech is adjusting the crossovers. Set the crossover to the recommended frequencies, turn down all level controls on the power amplifier, then turn up the midrange power amplifier level control while the system is being talked. When a reasonable sound pressure level is attained in the hall, the low-frequency power amplifier should be turned up until the low-frequency voice content sounds in balance with the midrange.

Then the high-frequency power amplifier level control is turned up until the high-frequency voice content sounds in balance with the midrange. At this point, the system should be tested using a pink noise generator and a 1/3-octave analyzer. See Work Element 16016 for further discussion of this topic. Alternatively, a pink noise generator and a 1/3-octave analyzer might be used to set the crossover.

Particular attention should be paid to the region around the crossover frequencies to determine whether the signals from the separate loudspeakers are adding or subtracting. It may be necessary to reverse the polarity of either loudspeaker. This should be accomplished with the aid of qualified listeners.

Correct gain structure setup

In spite of the fact that the Potential Acoustic Gain may be easily above the Needed Acoustical Gain, the various gain elements of the system should accommodate minor incorrect settings. At the same time, the gain structure should provide electronic clipping for any of the devices before the loudspeakers have been overdriven.

To simplify the situation, a 200-watt power amplifier should not be driving a 50-watt loudspeaker. Either the devices should be approximately matched as to power or the loudspeaker should have a higher power rating than the power amplifier. A damaged power amplifier can be quickly exchanged for a good unit, whereas the majority of loudspeakers are in a location where replacement is neither easy or quick.

Review the basic procedures in *Advanced Assembly, Element 15014*. Setting up the gain structure can be accomplished with a talker at the microphone, but providing evenness of sound level is difficult. Using a pink noise generator is preferred, with a "C" weighting curve. The pink noise generator is connected to a microphone input on the mixer, and the level is adjusted to read about –5 dB to zero on the meter or bar graph. The power amplifier should then be adjusted to provide approximately 95 dB SPL or the specified level in the hall. Use an oscilloscope to verify that clipping is not occurring in the system.

The system design should be such that system gain is accomplished in the mixer, not elsewhere in the system. The output level from the mixer should be +4 dBu and maintained as such throughout the system to the power amplifier input. With this technique, maximum signal-to-noise ratios may be maintained, in addition to freedom from unwanted clipping.

The system must be talked to verify levels and freedom from clipping throughout the system. Complete sentences and nonsense words should be used.

In this section, we have stressed the need for talking and listening to the system. Regardless of the quality and sophistication of the test equipment, qualified talkers and listeners must be used. In spite of computer-based test systems and TEF analyzers, which are primarily quantitative, the human voice and ear/brain combination provide a premium level of qualitative analysis.

Questions

1. Real time analyzers can't be used with sine waves. True or false?
2. Which one of these weighting curves isn't valid?
   - a. A
   - b. C
   - c. E
   - d. B
3. Parametric equalizers are preferred over fixed-Q equalizers for room equalization. True or false? Explain your answer.
4. White noise is preferred over pink noise for room equalization, as white noise is purer. True or false?
5. Room equalization should be performed:
   - a. When the room is ready for occupancy.
   - b. Before the carpet is installed.
   - c. When the room is filled with people.
   - d. When the architect is ready.
6. Sound delay is independent of:
   - a. Time.
   - b. Frequency.
   - c. Temperature.
   - d. Humidity.
7. A TEF analyzer must be used to measure sound delay. True or false?

8. The Häas Effect isn't apparent:
   - a. To a blind individual.
   - b. To an untrained ear.
   - c. In a room less than 8 feet square.
   - d. Without a sound reinforcement system.

9. Comb filtering is an essential part of any sound reinforcement system. True or false?

10. An AGC device is:
    - a. A compressor.
    - b. A limiter.
    - c. Part of any sound reinforcement system.
    - d. Used in broadcast chains.

11. Passive crossovers have more flexibility than electronic crossovers. True or false?

12. In a sound reinforcement system where the gain may be adjusted at several points, it is better to:
    - a. Set all controls to maximum, then adjust system gain by the fader or volume control on the mixer.
    - b. Leave the adjustments to the customer.
    - c. Refer to the operating manual for the mixer.
    - d. Set controls throughout the system so that increasing the control for that section will cause clipping.

Chapter 9

Project Management

by Bob Bushnell

- **NICET Work Element 16001, Interpersonal Communications**
- **NICET's Description:** *"Use negotiation and conflict avoidance/resolution skills, cultural sensitivity, and understanding of the organization of trades to communicate effectively with members of other trades working on your project."*

- **NICET Work Element 16023, Project Analysis**
- **NICET's Description:** *"Review plans, specifications, and equipment lists. Recognize deficiencies and mistakes, and determine appropriate corrective actions. Determine applicability of equipment to specific jobs. Prepare recommendations for presentation to the appropriate person in charge."*

- **NICET Work Element 16024, Customer Training**
- **NICET's Description:** *"Conduct or provide hands-on training in the operation of installed systems. Familiarize the owner with the functions, maintenance requirements, and warranty provisions of each element of the system."*

- **NICET Work Element 15006, As-Built Documentation**
- **NICET's Description:** *"Maintain accurate drawings and notes which record changes to the original plans, equipment, wiring, and physical layout of your project. Report changes as appropriate."*

Interpersonal Communications

Basic negotiation skills

If you're the sort of individual who deals with everything in black and white, then you're going to be working hard on your interpersonal communications skills. You'll find in working with other trades that you ask; you don't demand. If you get a reputation for being hard to get along with, other trades will tend to ignore you. That can make your work more difficult, as a foreman from another trade won't mention that he's closing up a particular room. You'll find it out the hard way.

Even though you may feel your profession is better than anybody else on the project, don't take yourself too seriously, as the other trades are just as professional as yours. On the other hand, don't be a pushover, as the other trades may take advantage of your good nature. You'll find yourself doing favors, just for the sake of doing favors.

Conflict avoidance/resolution skills

In building construction, there are a number of trades involved. Most of these trades are coordinated and directed by the General Contractor, referred to as the "GC." The Owner, who is paying for the project, usually hires the Architect and the GC. Typically, the GC hires the subcontractors by the bid system. The Architect, in addition to designing the building, and drawing the plans, will consult with the Owner, the GC, and the various trades as necessary.

In smaller projects, specialized trades such as sound and video may be hired directly by the Owner. This usually happens because the GC doesn't want to be involved with the technical details. However, the GC is indirectly involved because the Electrical Contractor, referred to as the "EC," is one of his subcontractors. The EC installs all power wiring for the project, in addition to empty conduits and boxes that you, the Sound Contractor, will later fill with the required cables.

In larger projects, because of the required coordination between trades, the Sound Contractor will be a subcontractor to the GC. The plans and various contracts are the keystones of the project. In case of any construction conflict, the plans are referred to, and the conflict between the Owner and Architect is usually resolved.

You are working for the Owner in the long run. He's paying the bills, and your contract. But don't attempt to side with the Owner just because he's got the money. Don't put yourself in the middle of any argument, even if it directly concerns your work. And don't ever attempt to pit one party against the other because you think you'll win your point when the dust settles. They may realize you started the argument, and both of them will be angry with you. By that time it's too late, and you're in trouble.

Don't put yourself in the middle of an argument even if you think that you can solve the problem by your intervention. On the other hand, if the argument directly concerns your work, listen to the two arguments, then see if you can come up with a solution that can appease both parties.

Then, if you can, politely interrupt, and offhandedly suggest your solution. Don't force the idea on either party, but let them think about the idea. You want to provide the solution, not put yourself in the middle of the problem.

If another trade is trying to start an argument with you, be careful. If they're doing it for fun, then respond accordingly. If they're doing it for almost any other reason, be careful. Don't let yourself be drawn into the argument. Sort out to yourself what their complaint is, and respond to the complaint, not to them.

How is that possible? If you respond to the complaint, and address that issue rather than continuing the argument, person-to-person, you're ahead. For example, you might have installed ceiling loudspeakers and baffles in an area. The painter thinks you damaged the ceiling 15 feet above the floor because, as far as he knows, you were the last trade in the area. If you respond to him by saying that you didn't do it, you've responded to the individual, not the complaint.

If you go to the area with the painter, review the situation, then promise him you'll get back within the day; you've responded to the complaint. Then you can go back to your crew, and to the GC, and determine a useful course of action. It may be that one of your crew inadvertently damaged the ceiling, and by contact with the GC, you resolve the problem. You may have to incur a back charge from the GC, or if you're on good terms with him, he may trade off with the painter to repair the ceiling.

If the damage was actually caused by another trade, you've still solved the problem. Then after the GC has contacted the painter, you can go back to the painter, and advise him as to what *you* did or are going to do. Don't tell him what the GC is going to do, that's putting you in the middle.

Compromise

In any successful negotiation, compromise is the rule. Decide before you go into a negotiating session what you really want, and what you're willing to give up. Even if the session is simply a discussion of where a particular wall box will be placed, don't lose sight of your goal. If you begin discussion on the placement with the outspoken attitude that an arbitrary location selected by you is where the box must go, and that any discussion is useless, you're in trouble.

The other foreman you're discussing the problem with will realize very quickly that you're being stubborn without reason, and possibly give up in disgust. But the next time you're in a similar situation, word will have gotten around that you're hard to get along with, and the other trades may see you coming and be ready.

When you decide what you really need out of the negotiation, pick a couple of small points that you're willing to give up on. But don't make it easy. You can even use reverse psychology. You bring up one of the small points, but as a larger issue. Then hesitantly allow the other negotiator to win you over to his point of view. He (or she) now thinks he's ahead of the game. Depending on your read of the situation, you might do this for another point.

Then you offhandedly bring up the issue that you really want to resolve to your advantage. In most cases, the other negotiator having won his points, will give up to you. In effect, you're playing a hand of poker, and bluffing is part of the game.

The most important point to remember is not to lose your cool and not to lose your temper. If you do that, you not only lose any control you had over the situation, but you have made the situation a personal matter. The other negotiator feels personally attacked and will defend himself against any issue that you may bring up.

Role of construction contract as guideline for negotiation

The contract is gospel, or at least an excellent starting point. Some contracts are so ambiguously worded that even a lawyer has problems understanding them. Some contracts are so strict that there's no latitude for defining a particular section.

As we stated before, when you're in a negotiating session, even regarding contracts, don't lose your temper, and don't make the discussion a personal matter between you and the other person.

If you've studied the contract during one of those evening sessions, and are familiar with it, you're ahead of the game. If, during negotiation, you can respond to a question by giving the page number and section of the item in question, you're ahead of the game. The other party will realize that you're thoroughly acquainted with the contract, and can't be taken advantage of very easily.

Remember that the documents and drawings your company submitted as part of the bid were later included as part of the contract. If you keep on hand an unmarked set of those documents and drawings, and are familiar with them, that will be of benefit to you during negotiating sessions. If you respond to a question with a reply on the order of: "I thought that information was here someplace, let me find it," you're at a loss because you've shown your unfamiliarity with the contract.

If a question comes up concerning the details of your installation, and you're familiar with the contract, again you're ahead of the game. You might respond to a question about a device by stating the information is on a given page. The other party spends time looking for that page and information; you know exactly where to look. As we said, negotiation is a lot like playing poker.

If you're discussing a part of the contract concerning the details of your installation and equipment, it may be that the other party doesn't understand those details. Rather than admit their ignorance, they've chosen to attack you rather than understand them. If you use the contract to your advantage by explaining in terms recognizable to them, you can probably resolve the conflict. Note that you haven't attacked the other party, you've defined your position.

On a job site, you are the representative of your company. As far as the other party is concerned, you are the company. If you feel that the nature of a discussion is over your head, either legally or by some element of the design, don't hesitate to say so. If you attempt to bull your way through, you may put yourself and your company in a bad situation simply because you made statements on behalf of your company. On the other hand, if you admit your ignorance and suggest you will have the appropriate individual from your company contact the other party, you will defuse a potentially bad situation.

Project Analysis

*Review specifications, including general
and special conditions*

You've been assigned to review a new project on which your company was the successful bidder. The plans and specs came from an outside consulting firm. Your task is to review these plans and specs. We'll use part of the sentences from the NICET work element description: *"Recognize deficiencies and mistakes, and determine appropriate corrective actions. Determine applicability of equipment to specific jobs. Prepare recommendations for presentation to the appropriate person in charge."*

This is a straightforward task description, but not a simple task. Your task is to determine if the project can be successfully completed by your company. Is the project appropriately sized? Do you have the financial and human resources to successfully finish the project?

Where might you begin? Start by going over the entire package to get an understanding of the intent of the completed system. In one sense, you're second-guessing the designer. You're not looking for details, or "gotcha's," but whether the project is Madison Square Garden, or a 100-seat off-Broadway theatre.

After you've reviewed the package, you have a good understanding of the system design. You know their intent, but you don't know if they made mistakes. The policy of some contractors is to bid "per spec," then later offer to make the system operate at extra cost. While this is legal, it is unethical. Some specifications state that the system must work, regardless of the plans and specs, and that it is the contractor's responsibility to advise in advance of known problems.

Once you've done a once over, then turn to the specifications and go through them. Even though many consultants use similar "boiler plate" items in their specs, you may encounter a change that radically alters your company's view of the project. Pitfalls such as submitting equipment for technical review, verification of local codes, aesthetic considerations, or money deposits with the bid; any of these could be an unpleasant surprise if not discovered in advance. Even if no surprises are encountered, a thorough study of the specs will provide needed information, such as "or equal" specifications, bid due dates, and similar qualifying information.

When you're through reading the specs, (You did make notes while reading, didn't you?), review your notes to see what you overlooked.

Analyze scope of project

Then you turn to the plans, starting with the most general sheets, to understand the project. If the architect was thorough, your set begins with "A" drawings, which are the architectural drawings. If the architect was saving money, your set probably begins with "E" drawings, which are the electrical drawings. Sometimes the sound drawings are a subset of "E."

Once you've gone through the drawings and made notes, stop and think about what you've read and learned. Summarize on paper the scope of the project so that you can present your results at a meeting.

Recognize special requirements

Are there some parts of the project that are beyond your company's capabilities? Would it be worthwhile letting a subcontract, assuming that is not prohibited by the bid specifications? Is the project too small for your company? Will unique test equipment be required that your company should rent, rather than buy? Will your company be required to provide a cash deposit with the bid? Is this a set-aside project to promote hiring of minorities?

If the project is out of your state, will temporary per diem costs for the work crew make your bid too high? It may be that your company has an edge that will reduce the effect of those additional costs. Must your company provide equipment in advance for technical review? Do you foresee that special plates and panels will have to be fabricated? Are there union restrictions, assuming your company runs an open shop?

Determine applicability of system specified to plans

Have you found discrepancies between the plans and specs that should be brought to the attention of the architect? If the architect or consultant has made an error that will affect all bids, the architect may issue an addendum advising of the error. If you hope to use the error to your favor, you won't have much success; frequently there are clauses requiring that known errors be brought to the attention of the architect.

Develop appropriate recommendations for known errors

If you respond to the architect with a recommendation for correction of an error you've found, unofficially you've put your company ahead of other bidders. In spite of plans and specs, architects and consultants are human, and if you make their life a bit easier, they'll remember those suggestions.

With the project scope summary, and your error correction recommendations, add your project comments and any special requirements noted. If you have all these comments together in a neat form, you'll be ready to present those results at your next company meeting. You may not be able to present a bid for the project, but you should be able to "ballpark" a good figure for your company's bid.

Determine functions of system and compile related literature

The project is in the final stages of completion at the customer's site, a church. You've been requested to build a systems manual, and educate the various individuals in the effective operation of the system. Unfortunately, because of commitment to other projects, you haven't been involved in the system up to now.

Where do you begin? You get the project file and study that. Then to the block diagram, probably the shop working drawing, as that will have the latest markups. After you've studied the block diagram, then you accumulate the various manuals and literature for the system.

Fortunately, you don't have to prepare a step-by-step instruction manual at this time, just the factual information on the system. There will be some electronic drafting, however. Since you have all the project documentation, you assemble the information into a useful order.

There are several techniques for organizing the information. First, you might group the various manuals by function: microphones, signal processing devices, power amplifiers, and ancillary devices. Second, you might group the manuals sequentially as you go through the block diagram. Using the second technique indicates your customer is technically acquainted with the system—possibly an invalid assumption. The information could be collated alphabetically by manufacturers' names.

The first technique is the most often used, as it steers the customer toward the device of interest. For example, if he or she wants to know about a delay device, he/she will assume the section labeled "Signal Processing Devices" is applicable.

Documentation you've prepared in-house should be at the end. Why? If the customer is reading the manual, he or she may fold out the system diagrams and be able to go back to individual sections to review the applicable data. If the in-house documentation is at front, the customer will have a cumbersome task folding the diagrams back and forth.

Since each manufacturer prints its manual in a slightly different form, and you're going to make xerographic copies for the manual, you review the manuals for form and see what modifications you must make before copying. Color copies would be nice, but can be expensive. Nevertheless, you review the contract to see the number of copies required, and check if there are any special requirements such as color copies. For in-house use, two additional copies should be made.

Manuals delivered to the customer may disappear, particularly at churches, as the volunteer staff may change from year to year. Depending on your point of view, you might make more copies and file them away. If the customer needs another set of manuals, it could be a source of revenue.

Determine how specific functions fulfill customer needs

Start by reviewing the original notes on the project, looking for the basic reason for the system. It may be as obvious as the need for a church sound reinforcement system, or a corporation boardroom system, or there may be another more subtle reason. Then review the system functions and see where they relate to the customer's needs. It may be useful to talk with the sales manager or the specific salesperson who dealt with the customer.

In your hands-on training in the system operation, you'll want to show how your system fulfills the customer's needs and desires. The customer will want to feel he made a good choice in selecting your company, and if you can successfully introduce him to the new system, you've supported that choice.

Locate/prepare documentation on how system is interconnected

These documents are usually in-house, possibly as simple as hand-drawn sheets you found in the project folder. These will require electronic drafting (computer-aided design software, also known as CAD) before copies can be included in the manual.

There are a number of CAD programs on the market, ranging from those costing several thousand dollars to less expensive programs for occasional use. Doubtless your company has selected one of them. If not, now is the time. Almost all of them require a contemporary computer, running the most popular operating system. If you have learned how to operate the CAD program your company uses, you might wish to do your own electronic drafting. If not, contact your draftsman and go over the documentation you want prepared. If the shop has signed off on the block diagram, the draftsman may have completed updating and is ready for your work.

These interconnect documents should be prepared in a consistent style for ease of understanding. You may be familiar with the system, having studied all documents, but one of your service techs won't have that luxury. He may be called on to repair the system and if he must decipher a particular drawing, that can cost your company extra money.

In addition, if the customer is doing his own maintenance and repair after the end of the warranty period, he should be able to understand the documentation one or two years later.

Identify/document maintenance requirements

In the case of electronic devices, which for mechanical controls have nothing more mechanically complex than pots and switches, routine maintenance might be simply system electronic tests. For mechanical devices, routine lubrication may be in order. You might have a ceiling-mounted lift for a video projector that requires routine mechanical maintenance.

Since you've gone through all the manufacturers' documentation, it shouldn't be much work to sort out those devices requiring routine maintenance. Preparing a spreadsheet showing the maintenance intervals required shouldn't be much work. Then the spreadsheet may be printed out, and included in the manual.

It may be that a manufacturer requires a special maintenance procedure. It's up to you to flag that procedure and include it in the manual. At the same time, you should implement a system so that your service techs can follow through on that maintenance procedure at the appropriate time. Normally this is necessary only with mechanical or projection devices. With power amplifiers, the cooling fan might require regular vacuuming or an air filter replaced.

Warranties (both manufacturers' and your company's)

In most states, the warranty is limited in terms of time or components covered. The major difference between a limited warranty and an unlimited warranty is the aspect of consequential damages.

With an unlimited warranty, if a device fails and a company loses revenue as a result of that failure, the manufacturer of the device is responsible for consequential damages. Even though many manufacturers have faith in the quality of their products, they don't want to be in the position of paying out large sums of money if their product fails.

Your employer should have (or should prepare) a warranty statement to cover your company's work. Not having a warranty leaves your employer open to a lawsuit. Laws vary from state to state, so be sure that your employer is aware of the state laws applicable to your operation.

You should read through the various manuals, making notes on the warranties provided. Does your employer warrant everything in the system for some period of time, or does your employer warrant only the work of your company, leaving the individual manufacturers' warranty to cover specific devices?

After you've reviewed the various warranties, it is a good idea to provide a separate section in the manual for these warranties. This way, it is much easier to verify an individual warranty than to dig through all the manufacturers' data to find a warranty statement. In addition, it should be your responsibility for finding the various registration cards and returning them to each manufacturer. Quite often, registering the device isn't mandatory to activate the warranty. But it is better to be sure than to guess.

As-Built Documentation

(See *Installation Supervision, Work Element 16025* for related information)

You've probably seen the cartoon where the individual is finishing a personal task while holding up a roll of toilet paper and exclaiming, "The job's not done until the paperwork's finished!"

The best project you've ever done is a partial failure without adequate paperwork to guide other techs, engineers, and the customer through the system. As you install the system, it is essential to note any changes to the original plans, equipment, and physical layout of the system. You should have a single-line drawing of the system that you archive in a safe place just in case all other documentation is lost or destroyed.

The architectural and engineering drawings should also be marked up as you complete the project. Even if they're never returned to the project consultant for inclusion in final drawings, they're still an excellent source of information for your company.

Making as-built wire routing drawings

From the various markups, you build the wire routing diagrams or drawings. These will show the conduits, cable locations, and routing. If you have access to a good copy of the architectural (prefixed "A") or electrical (prefixed "E") drawings, it's best to draw on them, rather than starting from scratch.

If your company already marked up "E" drawings for the EC (Electrical Contractor) to show him conduit locations and size, you're ahead of the game. Revise the title block, then add the wire number or numbers for each conduit. These wire routing drawings must relate directly to the wire label drawings or running sheets.

They should also show the rack locations, which directly relate to the equipment drawings or rack elevations. If mixers or stand-alone equipment were provided, they should also appear on these drawings.

For rack locations and stand-alone equipment, simple rectangles are sufficient, but large enough so that the rack number or other identifying number may be easily read. It is extremely frustrating to work on a system using drawings that are either incomplete or incorrect.

Making as-built equipment drawings

For rack elevations, they should show the equipment installed in a rack, the amount of rack space each device occupies, the serial number of the device (if applicable), and the AC circuit breaker location and number or numbers for that rack.

Any mixers or stand-alone equipment provided should appear on separate drawings. The connectors on the device should be shown, preferably on a pictorial drawing. Each connector should be identified as to type, wire number, and circuit purpose. If the device is plugged into an AC receptacle, the circuit number should appear on the drawing.

Making as-built loudspeaker or cluster layout drawings

On a simple job, loudspeaker layout drawings are unnecessary. But on a stadium or performing hall, these drawings are necessary. You might have two views of each cluster, one showing the specific components, and the other view showing the aiming for each element of the cluster. The drawings should also show the appropriate cables with wire number, cable type, and source location.

It may appear that the cluster layout drawings are redundant, since the project is finished, and you don't expect the cluster layout to change. A change may be made in the hall, and with these drawings, you or another contractor can easily establish the new aiming coordinates. Otherwise, it would be necessary to replot the hall using pink noise and a 1/3-octave analyzer, which is usually time-consuming.

If the project is a distributed loudspeaker system, the drawings should also show the appropriate cables with wire number, cable type, and source location. The loudspeaker type and transformer wattage tap should appear on the drawings.

Making as-built wire label drawings

These are also referred to as running sheets. They should show:

- Wire number
- Source location
- Source connection type
- Destination location

- Destination connection type
- Cable type
- Circuit purpose
- Circuit note

If you have access to a computer at work (who doesn't?), a spreadsheet program is an excellent means for building running sheets. A template can be built up, then used as the basis for each sheet. You can add rows as necessary and change column widths as desired. Spreadsheet programs are good at work like this. Either portrait (8½ inches wide by 11 inches high) or landscape (11 inches wide by 8½ inches) high may be used.

Extra copies of blank running sheets might be provided in case you or the owner add to the system.

Creating accurate job notes

The best method is to use a spiral-bound notebook, not a loose-leaf notebook, as pages are torn out too easily. Leave a section at the front for items to track and as a tickler file, then use the pages chronologically, noting down each day's activity in detail, and the work performed.

Should you use pen or pencil? Usually a pen is better, as a pencil tends to smudge after time. If your company has provided you the luxury of a laptop computer, so much the better. Remember that computers fail, and sometimes on the wrong occasion. If you back up your information to floppy disks each night, you won't have lost any vital information. One great advantage to a notebook is the ability you have to scan through pages without opening file after file.

Your notebook is also a good place to make as-built sketches that you'll later transfer via electronic drafting for the finished manual. Nothing elaborate, just enough to remember the factual data. Just as with the drawings you guard, the notebook is also protected.

If possible, you should be the only person making notes. This way, you know what's in the notebook. As you contact your employer each night, you can advise on the job's progress by reference to the notebook and drawings, rather than simply memory. If the notes aren't accurate, you may be in trouble later on when you're attempting to remember the details in a particular room.

Questions

1. In building construction, the most important element is:
   - a. The Architect.
   - b. Teamwork.
   - c. The sound contractor.
   - d. The plans and specifications.

2. The final word on a project comes from:
   - a. The Architect.
   - b. The Owner.
   - c. The plans and specifications.
   - d. The AHJ.

3. Compromise is:
   - a. A last resort.
   - b. The rule.
   - c. Only for the short-sighted.
   - d. To be avoided.

4. Reviewing a project that you were involved in before starting design is:
   - a. A waste of time.
   - b. An unnecessary effort.
   - c. Part of the overall task.
   - d. Left to the technicians who will do the wiring.

5. You found a major error in the plans to your favor. You…
    a. Keep it a secret from the Architect and the Owner.
    b. Immediately let all parties concerned know about the error.
    c. See how much it will add to your contract.
    d. Do nothing.

6. As-built documentation:
    a. Should be prepared after the customer has requested it.
    b. Should be prepared as soon as the job is finished.
    c. Should be brief as possible, as the customer won't understand it.
    d. Usually necessary.

7. As-built drawings must be prepared on a computer, rather than hand-drawn. True or false?

8. Wire label drawings are more complete than running sheets. True or false?

9. Educating the customer about use of the system:
    a. Should be as brief as possible, since the customer doesn't understand the system.
    b. Should be restricted to use only, and not maintenance.
    c. Should be left to the salesman.
    d. Should cover all aspects of the system.

10. System training should:
    a. Be conducted with all necessary people available.
    b. Take no more than one hour.
    c. Be as complete as necessary.
    d. Disregard maintenance requirements.

11. Warranty repairs are handled:

    a. Between the customer and the manufacturer.

    b. By your company.

    c. Only if requested by the customer.

    d. For two years after startup.

12. When the customer asks an apparently stupid question during training, you should:

    a. Disregard the question.

    b. Figure out what he's trying to learn about, and answer that unspoken question.

    c. Point out that the question is stupid, and tell the customer what he should know.

    d. Answer the question.

Appendix A

NICET Level III Work Elements NOT Covered in This Book

As a Level I or II NICET-certified Audio Systems Technician, you should already be aware that each NICET level consists of work elements classified into three categories: core general work elements, noncore general work elements, and special work elements. As of this writing, to qualify for a Level III certification you must successfully pass tests for all Level III core general work elements (there are four), plus 11 Level III noncore general work elements, and 11 Level III special work elements. (This is in addition to passing numerous work elements previously in levels I and II.)

This book provides review of all Level III core work elements and covers all but three of the noncore general work elements, of which there are 13. The three not covered are *15002, Intermediate Physical Science*; *15013, Complex Switching Systems*; and *15017, Hearing Assistance Systems*.

Of the 25 Level III special work elements, this book covers 17 of them. The others were left out either in the interest of space or because they represent skill sets that are not practiced consistently throughout the industry. Typically, a technician wishing to achieve Level III status will concentrate on those special work elements that are relevant to actual experiences and knowledge gained on the job.

For your convenience we have provided the following list of work elements not covered in this book. Under each work element is a list of topics you should review if you plan on testing out of that work element. Where possible, we have also provided resources for getting additional information about the topic.

Level III Noncore General Work Elements

Intermediate Physical Science
- **NICET Work Element 15002**
- **NICET's Description:** *"Solve problems in mechanics, electricity, heat, and inorganic chemistry. (Solutions may involve algebra and trigonometry.)*

Topics to review:
- Linear dynamics
- Rotational dynamics
- Statics
- Mechanics of materials
- Fluids
- Energy and power
- Thermodynamics (heat or thermal expansion)
- Electricity (Ohm's Law or equivalent resistance)
- Electrical Power
- Inorganic Chemistry (chemical formulas/equations, acids/bases, application of molecular weights

This is a work element that you may do very well in—or become totally lost. Fortunately, this is not a "CORE" element for Level III, so you might think twice about taking the exam for this work element.

If you feel comfortable with Work Element 15003, Circuit Analysis, you'll have no difficulty with the electrical portion of this work element.

In terms of reference materials, finding a used copy of a beginning college-level textbook on physics is a start. Checking your local library might produce a copy. Isaac Asimov, the famed science writer and science-fiction writer has three excellent books with these titles: *Understanding Physics: Motion, Sound, and Heat, Under-*

stand *Physics: Light, Magnetism, and Electricity*, and *Understanding Physics: The Electron, Proton, and Neutron*. They are out of print in paperback, but still available in second-hand bookstores. Another book is *The Cartoon Guide to Physics* by Larry Gonick and Art Huffman. The title is deceiving, for it is an excellent basic guide to physics.

Complex Switching Systems

- **NICET Work Element 15013**
- **NICET's Description:** *"Install and troubleshoot complex diode matrix switches, microprocessor switching devices, sequential switchers, PLC devices, etc. Perform repairs as needed."*

Topics to review:

- How input/output matrices work
- Programming charts
- Characteristics of a good audio switch
- Ladder logic
- Sequential switchers

Hearing Assistance Systems

- **NICET Work Element 15017**
- **NICET's Description:** *"Install hearing assistance system in accordance with plans and specifications and the "American with Disabilities" Act. Interconnect to sound system as needed. Verify proper operation and coverage. Perform maintenance as needed.*

Topics to review:

- ADA requirements
- Characteristics of infrared and RF systems
- RF antenna types
- Infrared emitter types
- Testing and troubleshooting

Level III Special Work Elements

Computer-Assisted Design Programs

- **NICET Work Element 16002**
- **NICET's Description:** *"Use computer programs to provide for specified coverage and speech intelligibility. Understand the difference between programs."*

Topics to review:

- Features of typical software
- Functions of modeling programs
- Modeling requirements for calculating speech intelligibility
- Acoustical and building factors for calculating coverage patterns
- Interference effects caused by interaction of speaker components

Apparently, this element is the basis for Architectural Mapping, Work Element 16003. That work element, which is part of Chapter 7, System Design, describes the process of creating a wire frame model, and determining the acoustical properties of a room. CAD (Computer Assisted Design) is a term describing any application assisting the user in design of schematics, PCBs (Printed Circuit Boards), machined parts, and architectural drawings. Work Element 16002 is confined to acoustical simulation applications, so the element heading is somewhat of a misnomer. It does not cover CAD applications in general.

We don't suggest you take this element before you've had hands-on experience with one or more of the acoustical simulation applications. They are AcoustaCADD, published by Altec-Lansing; CADP2, published by JBL; and EASE and EASEJR, both published by ADA in Germany and sold in the United States by Renkus-Heinz. We reference these names, not by way of recommendation, but by showing the applications available.

Advanced Data Cable

- **NICET Work Element 16010**
- **NICET's Description:** *"Supervise cable installation. Certify that the installation meets specified wire and link standards using appropriate test equipment."* (EIA/TIA TSB-36, TSB-40A, TSB-53, 568A: NEMA WC-19xx)

Topics to review:
- Techniques for installing data cabling in conduit
- Techniques for installing data cable without conduit
- Level III certification techniques
- Level IV certification techniques
- Data cable documentation

Supervised Audio Systems

- **NICET Work Element 16012**
- **NICET's Description:** *"Install and calibrate detection equipment for supervision of audio system integrity. Provide transfer switching. Perform repairs as needed."*

Topics to review:
- Understand concept of supervised audio
- Fault detection technologies
- Installation of detection equipment
- Calibration and system setup
- Process of "Transfer on alarm"

Paging and Telephone Systems Interface
- **NICET Work Element 16018**
- **NICET's Description:** *"Install telephone paging interface units using various types of telephone paging circuits, common and multiple zones, page delay devices, message repeaters, etc. Use appropriate wire, wiring techniques and manufacturers' installation manuals."*

Topics to review:
- Installation of telephone paging interface units with various types of telephone page circuits
- Common and multiple zone telephone systems
- Various page delay devices
- Message repeater devices
- Wiring and wiring techniques

Microprocessor-Based Nurse Call Systems
- **NICET Work Element 16019**
- **NICET's Description:** *"Install microprocessor based nurse call systems and applicable system components. Terminate wiring at the head end and/or at junction/device boxes. Perform system programming. Interface with associated systems. Conform to applicable codes. Perform repairs as needed."* (NEC, NFPA 99, UL 1069)

Topics to review:
- Differences between microprocessor-based and analog nurse call systems
- Regulatory codes/standards
- System components
- Nurse call system signaling priorities
- Correct connections to associated systems

Sound Masking Systems

- **NICET Work Element 16020**
- **NICET's Description:** *"Install sound masking systems in accordance with plans and specifications. Understand the basic characteristics of sound masking systems and office acoustics. Conform to applicable codes. Perform repairs as needed."* (NFPA 90A, UL 2043, NEC)

Topics to review:

- Basic office acoustics
- Theory and characteristics of sound masking
- Installation methods for masking speakers
- Basic EQ and testing
- System troubleshooting

Media Retrieval Systems, Work Element 16021

- **NICET Work Element 16021**
- **NICET's Description:** *"Install media retrieval systems in accordance with plans and specifications. Understand the basic types, characteristics, and components of media retrieval systems. Conform to applicable codes. Perform repairs as needed."* (NEC)

Topics to review:

- Differences between broadband and base band distribution systems
- Methods of remote media control (IR, DTMF)
- Advantages/disadvantages of various types of cable (optical fiber, UTP, coaxial)

Master Antenna Head-End Installation
- **NICET Work Element 16010**
- **NICET's Description:** *"Install master antenna head-end components in accordance with plans and specifications. Complete system connections to antenna(s) and distribution wiring. Adjust signal strength to proper levels and supervise system performance test.* (NEC)

Topics to review:
- Proper antenna install to include orientation, grounding, and support
- Frequency allocation
- Proper gain structure: to include use of dB as used in R systems
- Coaxial cable characteristics, application, and equalization
- Termination and testing techniques and tools

In theaters, before infrared systems were developed, a section was set aside where headphones might be plugged in. With infrared systems, the patron can sit almost anywhere and receive coverage from the transmitter. It is usually located over or next to the screen to provide the best coverage. Listed are two Internet sites which will provide more information on this subject:

1. http://www.sennheiserusa.com/
2. http://www.nwbuildnet.com/nwbn/ada.html

Appendix B

Answers to Chapter Questions and Problems

Chapter 1

1. Approximately 1169 fps.
2. Approximately 1003 fps.
3. With that temperature and that large a volume, we suspect you're in outer space, therefore the answer is zero.
4. a
5. d
6. b. Either a or b could be considered correct. Specifically, sound energy is absorbed by the movement of the molecules that make up air.
7. Either c or d.
8. c, but did you solve by looking it up, or by common sense?
9. a, just to be specific.
10. Either b or c.
11. c, who else?
12. b, who else?
13. b

Chapter 2

1. C
2. D
3. C
4. D
5. D
6. C
7. C
8. E

Chapter 3

1. Your answer should be 1.8 milliamperes.

2. Your answer should be 4.5 milliamperes.

3. Only if an AC signal is being impressed on the circuit. In that case, referring to impedance is valid, even though resistances and impedances might have the same values.

4. No. This is a trick question. Both 50 Hz and 60 Hz are used throughout the world.

5. This is another trick question. If you spent any time in attempting to calculate the answer, you didn't thoroughly read the question. But to be pedantic about the subject, a capacitor will have a small amount of inductive reactance, sometimes specified by the manufacturer.

6. Your answer should be 2392 ohms as the impedance.

7. Your answer should be approximately 1569 ohms.

8. More of those trick questions. The answer is either A or B.

9. False, as heat sinks can be used for vacuum tubes, power resistors, or rectifiers, or any case where excess heat is to be dissipated.

10. False, JEDEC is a part of the EIA, which is an independent organization.

11. False, as there are hundreds of circuits designed over the years.

12. A turnstile is an "AND" gate.

13. Five inputs could be utilized; the presence of the attendant, the presence of the patron, the presence of a valid ticket, the time frame is appropriate, and the ticket matching the aisle for the turnstile.

14. None, other than a difference in terminology. In actual practice, "ground" refers to a local system and "earth" refers to the earth on which we stand. In the United Kingdom, the term "earthing" is used instead of our term "grounding."

15. Yet another trick question. The NEC has no jurisdiction of itself. When the NEC is adopted by the AHJ (Authority Having Jurisdiction) who accepts the wording of the NEC, then the NEC becomes law for that AHJ only.

16. False, as many 'balanced' circuits have been devised for transformerless designs.

Chapter 4

1. False, unless you're in a low-bid situation where quality is secondary.
2. b
3. False.
4. d, of course.
5. False.
6. False, except for some older condenser types.
7. False.
8. c
9. False.
10. False.
11. False.
12. False. We admit to a buzzword question.
13. d

Chapter 5

1. c, no kidding.
2. b, again, you have but one life.
3. Either a or d. But this is no time to try your faith.
4. a, if you don't use the same units, you've may too many assumptions.
5. b, you have but one life, and your insurance company doesn't do favors.
6. d, when's the last time you found rated hardware made of brass?
7. Either c or d, but usually c.
8. Either c or d. We just want you to think.
9. a or c or d.

10. Either c or d, and you're not concerned about liability.

11. c, yes.

12. b, false. Once your hearing loss is profound, that's it. There is no return.

13. c, mandatory. Otherwise you're kidding yourself.

14. b, useless for acoustic tests because of standing waves.

15. Either b or c are acceptable answers.

16. False, as acoustical noise can be just as detrimental as electronic noise.

17. b, unless you're profoundly deaf.

18. b, system equalization shouldn't be designed into the system unless the designer feels there may be a need.

19. c

20. Either a or c is appropriate.

Chapter 6

1. False. For what are you testing?

2. d.

3. False. A DVM or VOM is faster.

4. False, as repair is the last resort.

5. b, of course!

6. b, but then we're biased.

7. b or none of the above.

8. False.

9. Either b or c.

10. d, of course.

11. b.

12. d, of course.

Chapter 7

1. False.
2. False.
3. d, but lower left corner is a convention.
4. d.
5. False.
6. a.
7. a.
8. c, always.
9. a, always.
10. b.
11. d.
12. c, unless you shortsightedly selected b.

Chapter 8

1. False. They can be used with any audio signal.
2. c, only three weighting curves are used.
3. False. Because of the variable-Q aspect, curious effects can be encountered when tuning a room.
4. False.
5. a.
6. Either a or b.
7. False, but it will make the job easier.
8. None of the above.
9. False.
10. Either a or b or d.
11. False.
12. d.

Chapter 9

1. b, what else?
2. a, b, c, or d
3. b.
4. c, of course.
5. b, unless you're asking for trouble.
6. b.
7. False.
8. False. They are both names for the same item.
9. d.
10. c.
11. b.
12. d.

Appendix C

The NICET Audio Certification Program

The only nationally recognized certification available to installers, technicians, and designers of audio systems is offered by NICET (the National Institute for Certification in Engineering Technologies). NICET certification is a demonstration that the audio technician has competency in standard technical skills and knowledge considered essential to the audio industry. Getting certified by NICET involves meeting a number of requirements, not the least of which is a battery of written examinations. The following section describes what the NICET certification process consists of and gives suggestions for getting prepared for NICET testing. Those interested in certification should definitely contact NICET directly to request specific program details and applications. NICET may be contacted at the following address:

NICET
1420 King Street
Alexandria, Virginia 22314-2715
Call Toll-free: (888) 476-4238
www.nicet.org

Levels, Work Elements, and Requirements

NICET currently offers three levels of certification in the field of audio. Level I is intended for the entry-level or relatively inexperienced audio installation technician. To be certified at Level I it is not necessary to have any documented work experience or post-high school education. However, some familiarity with basic elec-

261

tronics and audio components is expected. Level II certification requires at least two years of experience in installation, maintenance, or design-related work, with at least one year of experience in audio. Also required is either a two-year (associate's) degree or the equivalent in on-the-job experience. Level III is much like Level II, except the requirement is that candidates have at least three years of communications systems experience, with at least two years specifically in audio. While a level IV certification has been planned, it is currently not available.

If you can prove that you meet the work experience requirements in your application to NICET, the next step is to take written exams which NICET schedules at colleges, schools, and universities throughout the United States four times a year. Each certification level has its own unique set of subject matter areas, which are referred to as "work elements." The work elements consist of sets of multiple-choice questions on a specific topic. The work elements are categorized in one of three ways: there are "general core" work elements, "general noncore" work elements, and "special" work elements. Why are there different kinds? The NICET exams are intended to be flexible. Not everyone knows or uses the same information to do audio installation and design work. NICET expects each technician to know some basic, universal things, but recognizes that some knowledge and skills differ from person to person depending on work location or what his or her job responsibilities are. The basic, universal knowledge is what is considered "core." The noncore work elements apply to most technicians, but when applying to test, only a fixed number of the total available must be passed. As the examinee, it is up to you to choose which of these noncore elements you want to attempt. This is also true of the "special" work elements, which cover special kinds of systems and skills which are not universally practiced by audio technicians, but with which you may have experience. The NICET *Program Detail Manual* (available from NICET) describes in detail what the work elements consist of and how many of each must be passed to achieve each level of certification.

Applying and Preparing for Testing

Before you begin in earnest to study for the NICET exams it is a good idea to get familiar with the application process, rules, procedures, and requirements as outlined by NICET. Make sure you read ALL of the NICET *Program Detail Manual* as well as the following sections of NICET's *General Information Booklet – Tenth Edition*: Section I – General Information; Section III – Technician General Information; Section IV – Work Element Exams; Section VII – Operational Policies. As mentioned earlier, you must apply to NICET to register for tests. The application consists of a form much like a job application on which you supply information about your work and educational history, address, etc. In addition, your supervisor or someone who is familiar with your work must verify your experience in the areas on which you plan to be tested. The other part of the application is a personal recommendation form on which someone you know attests to your positive professional and personal attributes.

A Personal Study/Review Program

It is up to you whether or not to study for the NICET exams. Some technicians are very experienced and have had a lot of training throughout the years, and they can take and pass the NICET exams without any preparation (especially Level I). This is not recommended, however. Even though the NICET tests are intended to measure whether or not you possess minimum standards of skill and knowledge in technical audio, it is important to realize that the standards are very high. This is what makes being NICET-certified truly meaningful—not just anybody can pick up a test and pass it. In most cases, it is a very good idea to prepare for the exams.

In addition to this book and the others in the NSCA Audio Technology series, there are several resources that you might want to use in your own study program. First, on pages 24 and 25 of the NICET *Program Detail Manual* you will find a list of books that contain a lot of information about audio and related systems. Most of these are available at your local bookstore, or from NSCA's on-line bookstore (www.nsca.org). Many of these titles are considered the industry "bibles" that just about every professional audio person has read or referred to at one time or another. It is a must to have a current copy of the National Electrical Code® (NEC), and you are also strongly encouraged to get your hands on a good math textbook and electronic theory book. You can take many of these items to your NICET exams (see the NICET policies concerning testing) but don't plan on blowing off your studies thinking you'll just take a whole library of books to the test. Even if you had every book in the world to refer to at test time, there's simply no way you would ever have enough time to look everything up and answer all the questions. If you plan to take *any* reference books to the test, your best bets are *this* book (and the other books in the series) and the National Electrical Code® (NEC). Part of your preparation time would be well spent highlighting tables and facts in these books, especially things that are difficult to memorize or things in which you are not so well versed.

Besides reference books, you will also want to take a good scientific calculator to the test. Part of your personal study program should involve practicing with the calculator you plan to use. Get familiar with its functions and how its notation translates into other forms of notation you may find in math textbooks or audio books. Whatever you do, make sure you take a calculator you know how to use.

An excellent way to jump-start your preparation for the tests is to take advantage of NSCA's "CATTS On-Line – the Prep Course for NICET Audio Certification™." CATTS On-Line™ is a multimedia Internet-based training program that provides a structured review of the most difficult and important work elements you will encounter on the NICET tests. Demos, registration information, and entry into CATTS On-Line™ can be found on the Internet at NSCA's Web site, http://www.nsca.org. Call NSCA at (800) 446-6722 or (319) 366-6722 for more information.

Start your study program by carefully reading the NICET *Program Detail Manual*. Get familiar with all of the work elements, especially those in levels I and II, since that's where your testing will begin. If you're like most technicians, you probably are stronger in some topic areas than others. In that case it would be overkill to study for each work element with equal fervor. Narrow the focus of your studies down by making a list of those work elements that concern you the most. Conversely, decide which work elements you feel reasonably confident about and leave your review of those for the end of your study effort. You may find that you've run out of time to prepare (The test is tomorrow!), and you'll be better off having spent time on the things you are the rustiest in rather than just going down the list more or less arbitrarily.

Do your homework. Once you've established which work elements you need to brush up on the most, decide what your study resources for that topic will be. Make a list of books, people you can ask, videos, or even chapters in this book that you will get information from. Do it methodically. Tests are methodical, and they are made by methodical people. So if you want to be successful you too have to think methodically.

After you've decided on the work elements you will target and figured out what you will use to study from for each, then figure out how much total time you have until the test. Decide how many days or weeks you are going to spend studying each topic. You don't necessarily want to divide up your time equally. It depends on what topics you need the most work on. This is the time to get out a calendar and *write it down*. This many weeks for this, this many weeks for that, etc. Set aside a fixed time of day or day of the week to study. Think of your study time as part of your job: if you miss you might be in trouble. Reduce the temptation to procrastinate or to be distracted by making sure others, such as family members and friends, understand that your study time cannot be put off.

As it was pointed out earlier, you won't have time at the test to pore through books looking for the answers to every question. For this reason, it is important to mark the books you will bring with highlighters, "sticky notes," or bookmarks. You'll have to decide what to mark, but things like formulas, reference tables, and other lists of things that you don't normally need to memorize are the most likely candidates. Get familiar with where things are in your books, and make it easy to go right to them.

Your final preparation the evening before, and the morning of the test should involve rest and sensible eating and drinking. Don't stay up all night "cramming" for the test and drinking five gallons of coffee—in most cases you'd be better off not studying at all and going to bed early.

Test-Taking Strategies

NICET's tests are multiple choice. However, don't be fooled into thinking that for each question there will always be one answer that is obviously correct while the rest are obviously incorrect. In many cases the differences between one possible answer and the next are very subtle. Also, since your total test time is based on the number of work elements and questions you signed up for, you should not spend too much time on each answer. A good strategy is to give yourself a minute or less to answer each question. If you still haven't answered the question after one minute, move on to the next question and plan to go back if you have time. You are more likely to get more answers correct overall this way. If you are running out of time, or if you just can't answer some questions no matter how hard you try, *do not leave any question blank.* You are better off guessing or putting down a random response than putting nothing at all. Statistically, even if you randomly answered all of the questions there is a good probability that you'd get approximately 20 percent or more correct. It's not so different than rolling dice. Now 20 percent won't allow you to pass, but if you intelligently answered most of the questions, then the 20 percent on the rest is better than zero, and it could make the difference between passing and not passing.

Moving Up: Strategies for the Subsequent Tests

If you plan to get certified at level II or III, then you should sign up for the maximum allowable work elements on your first test, which is 34. This should include at least 12 Level I work elements (the number needed for Level II certification) with the remaining 22 coming from the Level II work elements. This MUST include all of the core work elements. See page 3 of the NICET *Program Detail Manual* for the specifics on which work elements are required for each level of certification. Even if you only want a Level I, you should sign up for at least 12, if not all 14, of the Level I work elements, just in case you don't pass one or two. Nine must be passed to get a Level I certification.

If you are signing up for your second or third exam sitting, you should make sure and sign up to retest on any work elements you failed, then sign up for any core elements that are required, and finally, choose which noncore general and special work elements you feel the most comfortable with. Plan on going in for testing at least twice if you want a Level II certification, and at least three times for Level III. If you fail a work element you can take it again (though the questions will be slightly different) twice before you will be required to get remedial training.

Costs of Certification

As of this writing, the cost at application time to take a NICET test is $90. You will have to pay this amount each time you sign up to test. If for some reason you can't make the scheduled test time, and if you give at least 19 days advance notice, you can reschedule without reapplying and without paying an additional fee. If you give from five to 18 days advance notice, you can reschedule without reapplying, but you must pay an additional $45. See page v of the NICET *General Information Handbook* for more information on other fees for other circumstances.

Recertification

Once you are certified by NICET your certified status is good for three years. At the end of the three-year period you must get recertified. This is accomplished by providing to NICET evidence of efforts you have made to improve your skills and knowledge through continuing professional development. NICET awards Continuing Professional Development Points, or CPDs, based on work experience and training. Most of your points can be earned simply by continuing to work in the audio field. Other ways to earn points are by taking technical, management and other professional development courses at colleges, training seminars, technical schools, and the like. Earning CPD points is not difficult as long as the classes or training you take cover skills or knowledge that haven't already been counted toward your existing certification or previous CPD points. See policy #30 on pages 59-63 of the NICET *General Information Handbook* for the specific details about how CPD points are earned and applied to recertification.

Being Certified: Promote It!

Achieving certification is something to be proud of! It's also a tool for promoting yourself and your employer. After you get formal notice of certification, which includes a certificate and an official NICET reference number, take advantage of the status by attaching your new credential to your name on business cards, company letterhead, correspondence, and your resume. For example, if you are "John Doe" before you are certified, you'll be "John Doe, CET" once you get certified. The "CET" stands for "Certified Engineering Technician."

You might just think it's a few letters and that it doesn't do much for you, but the fact is that both employers and customers care about it. It shows to them that they are working with true professionals, and it suggests not only that you know what you are doing and that your work is reliable, but also that you have pride in yourself and the work that you do. Certifications exist in many different areas of today's commercial culture, from auto repair to customer service, from medical technology to public accounting. In many of these industries you wouldn't even consider working with someone who isn't certified. Your certification could be the catalyst for you receiving a pay raise, an advancement, or it could give you entry to a new and better position at a new employer. It can also be used by your employer to win contracts, which will make the likelihood of profits being passed on to you even greater.

There is another reason why getting certified may be important for you in the near future: it is predicted that by the year 2003 most contracts for audio installations will require that all work be done by certified technicians. If this is true, then without certification you may be out of a job! Getting certified *now* has many benefits and is relatively painless for most experienced audio technicians, while getting certified *later* may be—well, it may be too late.

Appendix D

Selected Resources for Further Study

Many of these books are available from the NSCA Book Catalog. If you or your firm is an NSCA member, the book may be cheaper.

Glen Ballou, *Handbook for Sound Engineers: The New Audio Cyclopedia*. 2nd edition (Butterworth-Heinemann). ISBN # 0672227525. $89.95. Expensive, but worth it. The second edition isn't a drastic change from the first edition, so you won't be at a loss when you find a secondhand copy of the first edition.

Motion Picture Sound Engineering, edited by the Academy of Motion Picture Arts and Sciences. (D. Van Nostrand, Inc. New York, 1938). The book is long since out of print, but if you find a copy, keep it. It's an excellent reference.

Philip Giddings, *Audio Systems Design and Installation*, (Howard W. Sams, Indianapolis, IN) ISBN: 0240802861. $39.95. Paperback. Sams has reprinted this book in paperback. This book is a continual reference, and well worth the money. Mr. Giddings has lots of practical references.

Carolyn and Don Davis, *Sound System Engineering*, (Howard W. Sams, Indianapolis, IN) ISBN: 0240803051. $54.95. Paperback. As with Mr. Giddings' book, Sams has reprinted this book in paperback. The Davises discuss acoustics as well. An excellent reference.

Harry Mileaf, Editor-in-Chief, *Electronics one-seven*, (Hayden Books, Carmel, IN) ISBN: 0810459612. The book is out of print, but will be found through book search services. An excellent reference and study guide for many aspects of electronics.

Gary Davis and Ralph Jones, *Sound Reinforcement Handbook*, (Hal Leonard Corp., Milwaukee, WI & Yamaha Corporation of America, Buena Park, CA) ISBN: 0-88188-900-8. $34.95. Paperback. The book could stand some updating, nevertheless an excellent reference handbook. Even though sponsored by Yamaha, the book does not tout Yamaha. A very readable book.

Mark W. Earley, John Caloggero, Joseph V. Sheehan, *National Electrical Code Handbook*, (National Fire Protection Association, Quincy, MA) ISBN: 0-87765-405-0. $89.50. An expensive book, contains not only the National Electrical Code, but excellent interpretations by three excellent individuals, who serve in various advisory capacities to NFPA. A good addition to your company's reference shelves.

Stephen H. Lampen, *Wire, Cable, and Fiber Optics for Video & Audio Engineers*, (McGraw-Hill Publishing, New York, NY), ISBN: 0-07-038134-8. Paperback. $34.95. Not very expensive, but contains a tremendous amount of information concerning wire, cable, and fiber optics not easily available anywhere else.

Principles of Electricity applied to Telephone and Telegraph Work, (American Telephone and Telegraph Co., New York, NY, 1953). This book was published by AT&T (yes, that's Ma Bell!) for its employees. Out of print for some years, but if you find a copy, keep it. The title is like an entrance to a gold mine, nothing on the face but wait until you get inside!

Ben Duncan, *High Performance Audio Power Amplifiers,* (Newnes/Butterworth-Heinemann Ltd., 1996) ISBN: 0-7506-2629-1. $63.00 from discount booksellers. A somewhat specialized book, but more on the subject of power amplifiers than many designers know. Lots of discussion on various manufacturers' circuit topologies. (And he does provide names.)

Henry W. Ott, *Noise Reduction Techniques in Electronic Systems*, John Wiley & Sons, New York, NY, 1988. ISBN: 0-471-85068-3. $84.95. Mr. Ott provides a readable book on a complex subject. The book has been enlarged for the 1988 edition.

Ralph Morrison, *Grounding and Shielding Techniques in Instrumentation*, John Wiley & Sons, New York, NY, 1986. ISBN: 0-471-83805-5. $79.95. Like Mr. Ott's book, Mr. Morrison discusses the subject on a practical level, even more so than Mr. Ott.

Bob Metzler, *Audio Measurement Handbook*, Audio Precision, Inc., Beaverton, OR, 1993. No ISBN number, privately published. Probably available upon request. Mr. Metzler, one of the founders of Audio Precision, discusses the wide-ranging subject of audio measurements, going from the basic of frequency-response to digital audio measurements.

Staff, *Altec-Lansing Sound System Manual,* Altec-Lansing, Anaheim, CA, 1981 and 1982. No ISBN number, privately published. Depending on the age of your company, and the extent of its library, one of these may be available. Although the data is directed towards their loudspeakers existing at that time, there is a good amount of information available.

Index

Symbols

1/3-octave analyzer 104, 182, 208, 212, 222, 241
1/3-octave display 213
1/3-octave equalizer 180, 211, 212

A

absorption coefficient 7, 9, 11, 16
AC 62
AC impedance 158
AC power system 97
AC resistance 62
acoustic modeling 203
acoustic power 3
acoustical frequency response 3
acoustical mapping 191
acoustician 15
active crossover 214
AF 76
AGC 220
AGC device 221
agreement device 90
AHJ 20, 203
alternating current 62
American National Standards Institute 208

amplifier output waveform 108, 112

amplifier power 3

AND gate 86

anechoic chamber 103

ANSI 208

Architect 229

architectural mapping 188

attenuate 119

audio frequency 76

audio oscillator 170, 171, 173, 176, 178

audio spectrum analyzer 210, 211

audio transformers 29

Audio voltmeter 108, 114

audio voltmeter 173, 176, 180

aural effects creation 221

Authority Having Jurisdiction 20, 203

Automatic Gain Control 220

Automatic Gain Control) device 220

autotransformer 130

autotransformers 29

AUX 119

AUX bus 120

B

balanced input 96

balanced load 96

bar graph 213

base 74, 84

block diagram 236

boundary microphone 105
branch circuit 116
branch circuit wiring system 34
bus bar 98

C

cable inductance 158
CAD 237
calibrated microphone 210
calibrated oscilloscope 217
Capacitive reactance 65
capacitive reactance 62
cardioid 102, 106
cardioid microphone 102
cathode ray tube 209
CATV 35, 39
central cluster 202
choke 64
Class 1 29
Class 2 29
Class 3 29
clipping 223
clipping level 172
closed loop 58
cluster support elements 202
coaxial cable 36, 39, 98
coaxial shield 37
collector 74, 84
comb effect 106, 143

comb filter effect 144

comb filtering 139

common collector circuit 85

community antenna television 35

compressor 221

computer-aided design 237

condenser microphone 107

Cone loudspeaker 142

console 117

conventional bolt 140

coverage angle 143

critical distance 10

crossover 176, 222

Crossover filter 176

crossover frequency 176, 214, 222

Crossover network 145

CRT 209, 217

D

damping factor 116

dB 6, 102, 110

dBu 6

DC 62

DC resistance 62, 158

Davis, Don and Carolyn 13, 103

decibel 5, 118

delay device 218

Deutsche Industrie Normal 208

diaphragm loudspeakers 142

digital voltmeter 163, 178
DIN 208
diode 79
dummy load 108, 109, 114
DVM 77, 163, 178
dynamic microphone 107

E

EC 228
echo 13, 15, 103, 119
EIA 76
electret 105
electret microphone 107
Electrical Contractor 228
electrolytic capacitor 74
electromagnetic interference 200
electronic crossover 222
Electronic Industries Alliance 76
EMI 200
emitter 74, 84
equalization 119
equalizer 118, 168
external hum field 105

F

fader 117
feedback 13, 211, 221
FET 74, 78

field-effect transistor 74

filter response 176

filter slope 176

Fine Print Note 23

Fitzroy, Daniel 12

fixed array 139

flat response 176

flutter 13, 15, 16

FPN 23, 25, 37

free-field situation 103

frequency counter 176

frequency response 171

function generator 108

G

gain 118

gain parameters 171

GC 203, 228, 230

General Contractor 203, 228

germanium 74

graded bolt 140

graphic equalizer 208, 210

graticule 217

grille cloth 136

ground isolator 95

ground loop 92

ground reference 96

ground-lifter 95

grounding conductor 37

grounding electrode 37, 38
group bus 123

H

Hääs Effect 16, 215, 218
Hääs, Helmut 218
harmonic distortion analyzer 182
haystack curve 118
high-frequency power amplifier 222
high-frequency voice content 222
high-resistance fault 160
hum bucking unit 105
hyper-cardioid 102, 106

I

IC 89, 117
IEC 208
impedance 62, 63, 116, 127, 141, 158
impedance bridge 158, 163
in-house documentation 236
inductance 64
inductive reactance 64
input channel 168
input fader 117
input trim 171, 173
inputs 117
integrated circuit 89, 117
International Electronics Committee 208

J

Japanese Industry Standard 76
JEDEC 75
JIS 76
Joint Electron Device Engineering Council 76

K

Kirchhoff, Gustav 58
Kirchhoff's law 58

L

lag 72
LCD 209
lead 72
Lead Installation Technician 21
Lead Technician 21
LED 116, 209
LED indicators 116
level control 222
light emitting diode 209
limiter 221
liquid crystal display 209
load impedance 116
lobing 139
logarithmic addition 6
logic gate 86
loudspeaker array 134, 139

low-frequency power amplifier 222
low-frequency voice content 222
low-pass filter 176
low-resistance fault 160
low-voltage jacketed cable 39

M

magnetic microphone 104
main mix bus 120
massive ground system 98
master antenna television 35
matching transformer 129
Material Safety Data Sheet 40
MATV 35, 39
maximum acoustic gain 13
mixer 117, 120, 168, 171, 223
mixing console 117
mixing desk 117
movable array 139
MSDS 40
multipole branch circuit cable connector 34

N

NAG 13, 103
NAND gate 87
narrow-band filters 2
NEC® 20
Needed Acoustical Gain 13, 103, 223

negative phase angle 71
newton 5
NICET 22
noise generator 211
NOM situation 103
NOR gate 87
notch filter 211
NPN 73
NSCA 22

O

Ohm's Law 181
omnidirectional 102
operator 71
OR gate 87
oscillator 109, 112
oscilloscope 108, 109, 112, 114
oscilloscope gain 109
oscilloscope graticule 217
oscilloscope trace 109, 115
OSHA 20, 40, 134
output bus 120, 173
output level 172
output resistance 85
output signal amplitude 84
outputs 117
Owner 203, 228

P

PAG 13, 103

pan pot 118

parametric equalization 118, 211

parasitic oscillation 179

pascal 5

passive crossover 142, 214

PCB 75

peak program meter 123

PFL 119

phantom power switch 107

phantom-powered 107

phase alignment 215

phase angle 71

phase distortion 145

picowatt 3

piezoelectric 105

pink noise 212, 213, 221, 241

pink noise generator 180, 182, 212, 213, 223

pinouts 75

planar unit 142

plenum use 40

PNP 73

polarity elements 145

positive phase angle 71

Potential Acoustic Gain 13, 103, 223

potentiometer 119

power amplifier 110, 112, 129, 142, 222

power amplifier output 114

PPM 123

Pre Fader Listen 119
pressure zone microphone 105
Pro-Electron 76
pseudo-random noise 211

Q

Q 118

R

random noise 211
random noise generator 211
real-time audio 208
real-time audio spectrum analyzer 208, 212, 214
reverb 119
reverberation 13, 15, 103, 188
reverberation effect 118
reverberation time 11, 15
rigging hardware 135
Right to Know Law 40
riser use 40
rms 62
root-mean-squared 62
rotary gain control 118

S

sabin 7
Sabine, Wallace 7, 11
screw eye 140
Senior Technician 20
shackle bolt 140
signal amplitude 84
signal delay 215, 217
signal phase 81
signal polarity 84
signal-to-noise ratio 223
silicon 74
sine wave 7, 109, 115
sine wave tone 7
Sine-wave generator 108, 114
SLM 213
solo switch 118
Sound Contractor 228
sound energy 5
sound intensity 4
sound power 3, 4
sound pressure level 6, 102, 128, 137, 210, 221
sound reinforcement field 136
sound reinforcement mixer 124
sound-level meter 213
source impedance 116
spatial visualization 191
SPL 6, 13, 102, 128, 137, 210, 213, 221
stage gain 84
steel eye 140

straight-line control 118

submaster control 168, 172, 174

supercardioid 102

surface-mounted device 75

sweep tones 212

sweepable 119

system diagram 236

system gain 223

Systems Layout Person 20

T

TDS system 144

TEF analyzer 140, 217, 219

terminating resistor 173

THD 170, 174

THD Analyzer 108

timbre 15

Time Delay Spectrometry system 144

Time/Energy/Frequency analyzer 217

Total Harmonic Distortion 170

transistor 79

trim control 171

trim pot 120

U

unbalanced source 96

unbalanced wiring 95

V

vector 67
vector force 135
voice coil gap 107
VU meter 180, 181, 213

W

wavelength 2
welded chain 140
wire chain 140
wire frame model 191
working load limit 135

X

XOR gate 87

Audio Systems Technology, Level I

Handbook for Installers and Engineers
NSCA

This book is a one-stop information source for today's audio technician. It can be used as a study guide to prepare for NICET audio technician certification exams, as well as a comprehensive reference for the installer of audio systems—both out in the field and at the bench.

Designed to correspond with Level I work elements on the NICET tests, this valuable handbook presents the basics of audio installation as it is practiced in the industry today. Topics include: Basic Electronic Circuits; Basic Math; Basics of Microphones & Loudspeakers; Basic Wiring; Switches and Connectors; Codes, Standards and Safety; and Reading Plans and Specifications.

Additionally, information about getting certified by NICET is included, with tips and strategies to help with your success on the NICET exams.

Audio
320 pages • paperback • 7 3/8 x 9¼"
ISBN: 0-7906-1162-7 • Sams 61162
$34.95

Audio Systems Technology, Level II

Handbook for Installers and Engineers
NSCA

Designed to correspond with Level II work elements on the NICET tests, this book presents intermediate level content on audio installation as it is practiced in the industry today. Some of the topics: Audio Calculations; Acoustical Measurements; Microphones, Loudspeakers and Mixers; Trigonometry and Geometry; Wiring and Cabling; Effective Business Communication; and Bench Test Equipment.

Information about getting certified by NICET is included, with tips and strategies for the test-taker.

Audio
432 pages • paperback • 7 3/8 x 9¼"
ISBN: 0-7906-1163-5 • Sams 61163
$39.95

To order your copy today or locate your nearest Prompt® distributor : 1-800-428-7267

Prices subject to change.

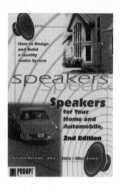